SUSTAINABLE HUMAN DEVELOPMENT ACROSS THE LIFE COURSE

Evidence from Longitudinal Research

Edited by
Prerna Banati

Foreword by
Richard M. Lerner

BRISTOL
UNIVERSITY
PRESS

First published in Great Britain in 2021 by

Bristol University Press
University of Bristol
1-9 Old Park Hill
Bristol
BS2 8BB
UK
t: +44 (0)117 954 5940
e: bup-info@bristol.ac.uk

Details of international sales and distribution partners are available at bristoluniversitypress.co.uk

British Library Cataloguing in Publication Data
A catalogue record for this book is available from the British Library

ISBN 978-1-5292-0482-7 hardcover
ISBN 978-1-5292-0484-1 paperback
ISBN 978-1-5292-0485-8 ePub
ISBN 978-1-5292-0483-4 ePdf

Cover design: Liam Roberts
Front cover image: iStock/MickyWiswedel
Bristol University Press uses environmentally responsible print partners.
Printed and bound in Great Britain by CMP, Poole

For uncounted children and adolescents everywhere.

Thank you to PLN for all the nudging and DBN who shared his mum with this project.

The views, thoughts and opinions expressed in this book belong solely to its contributors and do not necessarily reflect those of UNICEF.

Contents

List of Figures, Tables and Boxes

Figures

Tables

Boxes

Notes on Contributors

Bassam Abu Hamad has a PhD in Human Resource Management and is Associate Professor of Public Health at Al-Quds University, Israel, and currently, General Coordinator of the Public Health master's degree programmes in Gaza. Bassam is also Associate Director (Middle East and North Africa [MENA] region) of the longitudinal research programme Gender and Adolescence: Global Evidence (GAGE). Abu Hamad focuses on public health policies and programming, social determinants of health, vulnerabilities of refugees, women and children, psychosocial, disability and violence in conflict-affected settings.

Emily Agnew is Research Specialist at the University of California San Francisco, USA. Her research focuses on the development of mathematical modelling and statistical techniques, and their application in understanding the transmission of HIV and its interactions with interventions, to predict outcomes in disease incidence, cost-effectiveness and, ultimately, public health policy.

Jennifer Ahern is Associate Dean for Research and Professor of Epidemiology at University of California, Berkeley, School of Public Health, USA. She examines the effects of the social and physical environment, and programmes and policies that alter the social and physical environment, on many aspects of health (such as violence, substance use, mental health and gestational health). Dr Ahern has a methodological focus to her work, including application of causal inference methods and semi-parametric estimation approaches, aimed at improving the rigour of observational research, and optimizing public health intervention planning. Her research has been supported by a New Innovator Award from the National Institutes of Health (NIH), Office of the Director.

Suha M. Al-Hassan is Associate Professor at the Hashemite University, Jordan, and Emirates College for Advanced Education (ECAE), UAE.

Al-Hassan holds a BA in Psychology and MEd in Special Education from Jordan University and a PhD in Early Childhood Special Education and Applied Behaviour Analysis from The Ohio State University. While at ECAE Al-Hassan held the positions of Academic Dean and Chair of the graduate programmes and professional development. Prior to joining ECAE, Al-Hassan was Dean of Queen Rania Faculty for Childhood at the Hashemite University in Jordan. Al-Hassan has consulted for several national and international agencies, such as UNICEF, on matters pertaining to childhood and special education. Her research focus includes parenting and child development, parental involvement in education, school readiness and cross-cultural research.

Liane Peña Alampay is Professor of Psychology at the Ateneo de Manila University, Philippines. Her research focuses on parenting and child and adolescent development in cultural contexts and interventions for youth and families at risk. She is Principal Investigator of Parenting for Lifelong Health (Philippines), which aims to culturally adapt and test evidence-based parent support interventions to prevent child maltreatment among vulnerable Filipino families.

Dario Bacchini is Full Professor of Developmental Psychology and Education at the department of Humanistic Studies, University of Naples "Federico II", Italy, where he is also Coordinator of the Doctoral Programme in 'Mind, Gender and Language'. His research interests focus on antisocial behavior in adolescence, moral development, school bullying and parenting. He leads many interventions to prevent school bullying. He is a consultant to the local government for the school policy related to disruptive and bullying behaviours.

Sarah Baird is Associate Professor of Global Health and Economics at George Washington University, USA, where she focuses on the microeconomics of health and education in low- and middle-income countries with an emphasis on gender and youth. She is also Impact Evaluation Lead for the Gender and Adolescence: Global Evidence (GAGE) programme. Her current work investigates different policy approaches to improve outcomes for adolescents ranging from cash transfers, to group interpersonal psychotherapy, to social norms change.

Prerna Banati has over 20 years of experience advancing evidence and research for United Nations agencies and other international organizations. Currently she is a senior advisor at UNICEF where she has been supporting evidence generation and providing technical advice to rights-based country programmes of cooperation in collaboration with governments, civil society and the private sector. Over her career, she has led a number of high-profile action-research programmes, most recently a Department for International Development-funded gender-responsive, adolescent-sensitive social protection, and prior to that on the social and structural determinants of adolescent well-being. She also developed and led the Global Longitudinal Research Initiative (GLORI), a network of cohort studies following children and adolescents living across diverse contexts and countries. Before joining UNICEF, she was Takemi Fellow at Harvard University and has worked for the World Health Organization and the Global Fund to fight AIDS, TB and malaria, and also in academia, for NGOs and in the private sector. She sits on a number of advisory boards and has authored many publications in the field of adolescent health and well-being, reproductive health, mental health, HIV prevention and migration. She has a PhD from the University of Cambridge, UK.

Robert W. Blum is Professor at the Johns Hopkins Bloomberg School of Public Health, USA. He has edited two books and written over 325 journal articles, book chapters and special reports. He is a past-president of the Society for Adolescent Medicine and a past chair of the Guttmacher Institute Board of Directors. In 2006, he was elected to the US National Academy of Medicine. He is a consultant to the World Bank, UNICEF, UNFPA and the WHO. His honours include both the APHA Herbert Needleman Award 'for scientific achievement and courageous advocacy' and the Martha May Eliot Award honouring 'extraordinary service to mothers and children [and adolescents]'. He is Principal Investigator of the 11-country Global Early Adolescent Study and co-Principal Investigator on the National Adolescent Mental Health Surveys, a three-country adolescent mental health study in Kenya, Indonesia and Vietnam.

Marc H. Bornstein holds a BA from Columbia College, USA, MS and PhD degrees from Yale University, USA, honorary doctorates from the University of Padua and University of Trento, Italy, and an Honorary Professorship at the University of Heidelberg, Germany. Bornstein is President Emeritus of the Society for Research in Child Development, and he has held faculty positions at Princeton University and New York University, USA, as well as visiting academic appointments in Bamenda (Cameroon), Bristol, London, Munich, New York, Oxford, Paris, Santiago (Chile), Seoul, Tokyo, Trento and the Institute for Fiscal Studies (London). Bornstein is Editor Emeritus of *Child Development* and founding Editor of *Parenting: Science and Practice*. He has administered both Federal and Foundation grants, sits on the editorial boards of several professional journals, is a member of scholarly societies in a variety of disciplines, and consults for governments, foundations, universities, publishers, the media and UNICEF. Bornstein has published widely in experimental, methodological, comparative, developmental and cultural science as well as neuroscience, paediatrics and aesthetics.

Lei Chang was born in Tianjin, China, received his BA from Hebei University, Baoding, China, and his MS and PhD from the University of Southern California, Los Angeles. He is Chair Professor of Psychology and Head of Department of Psychology, University of Macau, Macau, and previously taught at University of Central Florida, USA, the Chinese University of Hong Kong – where he was also Department Head – and the Education University of Hong Kong, Hong Kong, where he was a chair professor. He conducts research in the areas of evolutionary psychology (including cultural evolution and social learning, life history and childhood environmental impact, and sociosexuality and human mating behaviour research), developmental science focusing on parenting and child and adolescent social and cognitive development, and statistics and psychometrics where he focuses on applications and textbooks.

Kirby Deater-Deckard is Professor in Psychological and Brain Sciences at the University of Massachusetts Amherst, USA, where he serves as area leader in developmental science, graduate programme director in neuroscience and behaviour and director of the Healthy Development Initiative in Springfield, MA. He received his BA from The Pennsylvania State University, and his MA and PhD from the University of Virginia. Deater-Deckard's research focuses on the transactions between biological, cognitive and environmental factors in the development and intergenerational transmission of self-regulation and related psychological and health outcomes. His collaborative research is supported by funding from the National Science Foundation and National Institutes of Health. His current research focuses specifically on the development and intergenerational transmission of individual differences in executive function and the role of parenting and broader contextual factors that can influence these developmental processes.

Laura Di Giunta is Associate Professor at Sapienza University of Rome, Italy. Her research focuses on continuity and change of individual differences in predicting youth (mal)adjustment, accounting for socialization and culture factors, especially in emotion regulation, adjustment and social competence. With the support of the Jacobs Foundation, her research is aimed at disentangling the emotion regulation-related mechanisms predictive of youth adjustment. Her work relies on mobile ecological momentary assessments of youth emotion regulation-related mechanisms with both normative and clinical adolescent samples, and a focus on physiological indicators of youth emotion regulation.

Kenneth A. Dodge is the Pritzker Professor of Public Policy and Professor of Psychology and Neuroscience at Duke University, USA. He studies the development and prevention of aggressive and violent behaviours. His work provides a model for understanding how some young children grow up to engage in aggression and violence and provides a framework for intervening early to prevent the costly consequences of violence for children and their communities.

Haridhan Goswami is Senior Lecturer in sociology at Manchester Metropolitan University, UK. He has expertise in research with children's and young people's subjective well-being, survey design, testing reliability and validity of data collection instruments and multivariate analysis of data. Goswami has provided expert advice on research with children and young people and their subjective well-being to two European Commission-funded projects: MYWEB and European Cohort Development Project. He has also led statistical analysis of large-scale survey data for a number of national and international projects, including MYPLACE (funded by European Commission), National Surveys (2008, 2010) on Child Well-being in England (funded by The Children's Society) and Safeguarding Young People: Professionals' Attitudes and Responses to Maltreated Children (funded by the National Lottery). Goswami is Principal Investigator of the Child Well-Being Survey in Bangladesh which is being conducted in collaboration with Children's Worlds: The International Survey of Children's Well-Being. He is Coordinator of the South Asian Research Network for Childhood and Youth Studies (SARNCYS: https://www2.mmu.ac.uk/mcys/south-asian-network/) at Manchester Metropolitan University, UK.

Sevtap Gurdal is a postdoctoral fellow at the Centre for Child and Youth Studies at University West, Sweden. She earned her PhD in Psychology from Gothenburg University, Sweden. Her research interests are parenting and children. Earlier research projects include parent attributions, parent attitudes and child agency in different contexts. Her ongoing research is about professionals' work and experiences about internet gaming disorder and children's agency. She also has a gender perspective on gaming disorder.

Kristina Jackson is Professor (Research) at the Centre for Alcohol and Addiction Studies in the Department of Behavioural and Social Sciences at Brown University, USA. Her research largely centres on the developmental course of substance use among adolescents and young adults. She has an extensive history of research funding from the National Institute on Alcohol Abuse and Alcoholism and the National Institute on Drug Abuse to examine individual- and contextual-level risk factors for substance use initiation and progression to increasingly severe use among adolescents. She has also conducted work on the remission of substance involvement in college students and across young adulthood, and employs fine-grained approaches to study co-use of alcohol, tobacco and marijuana. She is an expert in the application of quantitative methods to the study of substance use and has received several career awards to apply developmental methods to research in underage substance use.

Nicola Jones is Principal Research Fellow at the Overseas Development Institute in the UK. She is Director of the Gender and Adolescence: Global Evidence (GAGE) longitudinal research programme. Her research focuses on the experiences of young people in developmental and humanitarian contexts, and the ways in which policies and programmes can strengthen their capabilities and well-being. She is co-editor of *Empowering Adolescents in Developing Countries: Gender Justice and Norm Change* (2018) and *Social Policy in the Middle East and North Africa: The New Social Protection Paradigm and Universal Coverage* (2019).

Kathleen Kahn is Personal Professor in the School of Public Health, University of the Witwatersrand, South Africa, and executive scientist in the MRC/Wits Rural Public Health and Health Transitions Research Unit (Agincourt). A physician with a PhD in public health and epidemiology, Kahn has spent over 25 years working in rural South Africa and regionally. Since inception of the Agincourt health and socio-demographic surveillance system in 1992, she has led work on mortality and cause of death measurement, using verbal autopsy to track transitions over a period of dramatic socio-political change and the HIV epidemic. Her research focuses on adolescent and young adult health and development including HIV prevention, non-communicable disease risk and mental health, as well as a life course approach to health and ageing.

Leah R. Koenig is a doctoral student in the field of Epidemiology and Translational Sciences at the University of California San Francisco, USA. From 2017 to 2020 she served as Assistant Study Director of the Global Early Adolescent Study at the Johns Hopkins Bloomberg School of Public Health. Her research interests include life course, mixed methods and social epidemiology approaches to the areas of gender inequality and sexual and reproductive health research.

Jennifer E. Lansford is Research Professor at the Sanford School of Public Policy and Faculty Fellow of the Centre for Child and Family Policy at Duke University, USA. She earned her PhD in Developmental Psychology from the University of Michigan. Lansford leads the Parenting Across Cultures Project. Lansford has consulted for UNICEF on evaluations of parenting programmes and on the development of a set of international standards for parenting programmes. She serves in editorial roles on several academic journals and has served in a number of national and international leadership roles, including chairing the US National Institutes of Health Psychosocial Development, Risk and Prevention Study Section; chairing the U. National Committee for Psychological Science of the National Academies of Sciences, Engineering and Medicine; and chairing the Society for Research in Child Development International Affairs Committee.

Richard M. Lerner is the Bergstrom Chair in Applied Developmental Science and Director of the Institute for Applied Research in Youth Development at Tufts University, USA. Lerner has more than 700 scholarly publications, including more than 80 authored or edited books. He was Founding Editor of the *Journal of Research on Adolescence and of Applied Developmental Science*. He is a fellow of the American Association for the Advancement of Science, the American Psychological Association (APA) and the Association for Psychological Science (APS). Lerner is the 2013 recipient of the APA Division 7 Urie Bronfenbrenner Award for Lifetime Contribution to Developmental Psychology in the Service of Science and Society, the 2014 recipient of the APA Gold Medal for Life Achievement in the Application of Psychology and the 2015 recipient of the APA Ernest R. Hilgard Lifetime Achievement Award for Distinguished Career Contributions to General Psychology. He received the International Society for the Study of Behavioural Development Distinguished Scientific Award for the Applications of Behavioural Development in 2016, and the Society for Research in Child Development Distinguished Contributions to Public Policy and Practice in Child Development in 2017. He is also the recipient of the 2020 APS James McKeen Cattell Fellow Award, for lifetime outstanding contributions to applied psychological research.

Mengmeng Li is Research Associate at the Department of Population, Family and Reproductive Health at the Johns Hopkins Bloomberg School of Public Health, USA. Since 2017 she has worked as the senior data analyst for the Global Early Adolescent Study under the leadership of Robert W. Blum. Her research interests focus on maternal, fetal and perinatal health related to Assisted Reproductive Technology, and on adolescent health in the field of gender inequality and mental health. She is currently a doctoral student at the Johns Hopkins Bloomberg School of Public Health studying Maternal and Child Health with a concentration on Epidemiology Research Methods.

Sheri A. Lippman is an epidemiologist and Associate Professor of Medicine at the University of California, San Francisco, USA. Lippman's research focuses on the identification of the key social and structural factors that influence health behaviours and vulnerability to HIV/STI, and interventions to address social and structural barriers to HIV prevention, testing and treatment.

Qin Liu is Professor of Maternal and Child Health at the School of Public Health and Management at Chongqing Medical University, China. Her research interests and experiences focus on evidence-based synthesis, child growth and development, child mental health and behaviours, child nutrition, health education and interventions for children and families. She is particularly interested in initiation mechanisms and influencing factors of pubertal development.

Qian Long is Assistant Professor of Global Health in the Global Health Research Centre, Duke Kunshan University, China. She had medical and international health training in China and the Netherlands. She completed a doctoral degree at the University of Helsinki, Finland, and had postdoctoral training at the Duke Global Health Institute, Duke University, USA, and Duke Kunshan University. Her research interests and experiences focus on equity issues in relation to health systems development, including maternal and child health, tuberculosis control, and non-communicable disease management in poor areas and among vulnerable groups of China and other low- and middle-income countries. She is a youth member of the Global Health Committee, Chinese Preventive Medical Association. She was a technical officer in the Department of Reproductive Health and Research, the World Health Organization, working in the area of maternal and perinatal health.

Lilli Loveday is Research Manager for 'Real Choices, Real Lives' at Plan International UK. Her research, as well as her wider programmatic and advisory work, focuses on gender (including gender-based violence), gender equality and rights, as well as understanding processes of change (norms/behaviour). Alongside her research work, Lilli provides technical expertise on gender and social norms change to support NGO interventions in the global south. Previously, she worked in West Africa to support the implementation of a human rights programme (focusing on women's health and women's rights) to promote positive social change. She has also undertaken qualitative research on women's economic participation, female genital cutting (FGC) in The Gambia, the impacts of drought on children's long-term well-being and the impacts of cash transfers, including on social dynamics.

Susan E. Luczak is Professor (Research) in the Department of Psychology at the University of Southern California, USA, and Co-International Director of the Joint Child Health Project (JCHP). Her research focuses on the life course development of alcohol use and problems and its measurement under naturalistic conditions. She has been Principal Investigator of JCHP research projects funded by grants from the US National Institute on Alcohol Abuse and Alcoholism (K08 AA014265, R01 AA18179) and a Fulbright Scholar Award in the African Regional Research Programme from the US Department of State Bureau of Educational and Cultural Affairs (8465-MC). The research was conducted in collaboration with the University of Mauritius, the Mauritian Ministry of Health and Quality of Life and the Mauritian Ministry of Gender Equality, Child Development and Family Welfare. In addition to her research conducted in Mauritius, her two other major lines of research focus on genetic and environmental risk and protective factors for drinking in American university students, and real-time measurement of alcohol consumption including web app monitoring, wearable biosensors and the conversion of transdermal alcohol data into estimated levels of breath and blood alcohol concentration.

Tashneem Mahoomed is National Director of the Joint Child Health Project (JCHP), a research organization founded in 1972 with funding from the World Health Organization in collaboration with the Mauritian Ministry of Health, professors from the USA (Sarnoff Mednick), UK (Peter Venables), Europe (Fini Schulsinger) and Cyril Dalais in Mauritius as the first JCHP National Director. She has been Principal Investigator of the JCHP subcontracts for multiple US National Institutes of Health-funded research projects headed by Professor Susan Luczak from the University of Southern California and Professor Adrian Raine from the University of Pennsylvania, USA. She received her bachelor's degree from the University of South Africa (Pretoria) in Psychology and Information Technology in 2003 and has been with the JCHP since 2004. Her research focus is on psychophysiology, including brain function (electroencephalography, event-related potentials), skin conductance and cardiovascular function.

Patrick S. Malone is Senior Research Scientist with the Duke University Centre for Child and Family Policy, USA. His specialization is quantitative psychology, and his independent research programme focuses on developing statistical models of change over time, especially in health behaviours and developmental psychopathology. He is particularly interested in novel approaches to understanding ethnic and cultural differences in adolescent substance use and other health risk behaviours.

Torsten B. Neilands is a quantitative methodologist and Professor of Medicine at the University of California, San Francisco (UCSF). Neilands heads the Methods Core at the UCSF Centre for AIDS Prevention Studies and leads NIH-sponsored programmes to train the next generation of social and behavioural HIV/AIDS scientists conducting research in the minority communities most disproportionately affected by the HIV epidemic.

Paul Oburu is Associate Professor in Child Development at Maseno University, Kenya, where he also served as the Director of Quality Assurance and Performance Management. His research interests include parenting, caregiving stress, mental health and adjustment problems of grandmother caregivers and orphaned children. His other research interests include caregiving challenges experienced by adolescent children taking care of other equally vulnerable siblings. Previously, he was the founding director of a global network of education researchers called Education Quality and Learning for all based at New York University, USA.

Shameem Oomur is Research Coordinator at the Joint Child Health Project (JCHP). She has been with the JCHP since 2008 conducting research funded by both the US National Institute on Alcohol Abuse and Alcoholism and the National Institute on Child Health and Human Development. Her position as JCHP Research Coordinator includes supervising all clinical interviews and overseeing data management in addition to manuscript preparation. She received her bachelor's degree from the University of Mauritius in Social Science with Specialization in Psychology in 2003. Her research emphasis is on clinical diagnosis and naturalistic recovery from addiction.

Concetta Pastorelli earned her laurea degree in psychology and PhD in Cognitive Psychology from Sapienza University of Rome, Italy. She is a full professor at the Department of Psychology of Sapienza University of Rome, and Director of the Interuniversity Centre for the Research in the Genesis and Development of Prosocial and Antisocial Motivations. She has been Director of the PhD Programme in Psychology and Social Neuroscience and the Master Programme in Health and Community Psychology at Sapienza University of Rome. Pastorelli has consulted for the Italian Ministry of Education on evaluations of life skills programmes and on the development of prevention programmes in Italian high schools. Her research projects include interventions to promote prosocial behaviors and academic achievement in different cultural contexts. Her research focuses on the determinants of aggressive and prosocial behaviours and school achievement, parental personality and parenting and children's and adolescents' adjustment.

Audrey Pettifor is Professor of Epidemiology at the University of North Carolina at Chapel Hill, USA, and Honorary Professor of Public Health at the University of the Witwatersrand, South Africa. Her research focuses on sexual behaviour and determinants of HIV/STI infection in sub-Saharan Africa. Her goal is to identify modifiable risk factors and develop novel interventions to prevent new HIV infections – particularly among adolescents and young women. Pettifor has expertise in sexual behavior, HIV prevention, HIV testing and structural interventions among adolescents and young adults in sub-Saharan Africa, and has published extensively in the area of HIV and sexual behaviour among youth in sub-Saharan

Africa. Pettifor has worked in South Africa for over 20 years and has also conducted research in Malawi, Madagascar, Kenya, Zimbabwe and the Demographic Republic of Congo.

Ilze Plavgo is Research Associate and PhD candidate at the European University Institute (EUI) in Italy. She holds an MA in international relations (UK) and an MSc in public policy and human development (the Netherlands). Her main research areas include inequality, poverty, education and social policy. Prior to the EUI, she worked as a social and economic policy analyst at the UNICEF Office of Research (Italy) where her primary research focus was on multidimensional poverty and child well-being. She has consulted for over a dozen UNICEF country offices on the measurement of child poverty and social protection systems. Her work has been published/is forthcoming in leading journals in the field such as *Child Indicators Research* and the *Journal of European Social Policy*, as well as in numerous United Nations publications. In her current research, she studies developments of social investment policies and their effect on well-being, employment and poverty among families with children.

Gary Pollock is Professor of Sociology in the Policy Evaluation and Research Unit at Manchester Metropolitan University, UK. For over 25 years he has conducted research on young people, principally using questionnaire survey methods. Pollock is a specialist in both longitudinal and international comparative survey methodology having worked on the British Household Panels survey since its original release and on a range of EU-funded projects on the employment and family context of their life course. Most recently he is leading the development of an input-harmonized, Europe-wide, accelerated birth cohort survey which focuses on collecting policy-relevant data to enhance child and young people's well-being over their life (https://www.eurocohort.eu/).

Jenny Rivett is an independent research consultant providing research support to the Plan International UK 'Real Choices, Real Lives' study since 2018. Her research covers a range of thematic areas including gender and adolescence, human rights and social norm change, with a particular focus on violence against children (VAC) and child protection. Her recent work includes a rigorous review of the impact of parenting programmes on adolescent mental health and experiences of violence, a rapid evidence assessment of programmes to protect children on the move and analysis of the intersections between climate change, security and VAC. Her work on the 'Real Choices, Real Lives' study focuses on longitudinal, qualitative analysis of the process of gender socialization and adolescent girls' everyday acts of resistance.

W. Andrew Rothenberg is Research Scientist at the Centre for Child and Family Policy at Duke University, USA, and a Clinical Associate at the University of Miami Miller School of Medicine's Mailman Center for Child Development, USA. He holds a BA from North Carolina State University, USA, and an MA and PhD from the University of North Carolina at Chapel Hill, USA. A clinical psychologist by training, Rothenberg investigates the intergenerational transmission of parenting and family processes in cultures around the world, explores strategies to prevent the intergenerational transmission of maladaptive parenting and family processes and implements preventative interventions in medically underserved communities.

Ann T. Skinner is Research Project Manager at the Duke University Center for Child and Family Policy, USA. She earned her BA in Psychology and MEd in Special Education from the College of William and Mary, USA, and is a doctoral candidate in Developmental Psychology at Gothenburg University, Sweden, and University West, Sweden. Her research focuses on the ways in which stressful community, familial and interpersonal events impact parent-child relationships and the development of aggression in youth. She has extensive experience in data management of multisite projects and in supervising teams for school- and community-based data collection.

Emma Sorbring is Professor of Child and Youth Studies and research director for the Centre for Child and Youth Studies at University West, Sweden. She earned her PhD and became Associate Professor in Psychology at Gothenburg University, Sweden. Her research and teaching interests focus on children, adolescents and families. Her projects focus on parental behaviour and children's adjustment, young people's decision-making, teenagers' internet use and parental strategies and sexual development in traditional and new settings (the internet). She serves in editorial roles on several academic journals and books. She has published several Swedish books on parenting, youth studies and methods, as well as international book chapters in the same areas.

Laurence Steinberg is Professor of Psychology at Temple University, USA, and an affiliate of King Abdulaziz University, Saudi Arabia.

His research focuses on psychological and brain development in adolescence.

Maheen Sultan is Senior Fellow of Practice and a founder of the Centre for Gender and Social Transformation at the BRAC Development Institute, BRAC University, Bangladesh. She is a development practitioner with over 25 years' experience in social development, poverty, civil society and community participation and gender equality. Sultan is also a women's rights activist and a member of Naripokkho, a Bangladeshi women's rights organization. She is co-editor of *Voicing Demands: Feminist Activism in Transitional Contexts* (2014).

Aleksandra Szymczyk is Research Associate at the Policy Evaluation and Research Unit at Manchester Metropolitan University, UK. She has been working on the Horizon 2020 European Cohort Development Project (ECDP), which has created the specification and business case for a European Research Infrastructure providing comparative cross-European longitudinal data on child and youth well-being. Currently, she is conducting research activities for the Horizon 2020 Migrant Children and Communities in a Transforming Europe Project (MiCREATE), which strives to stimulate inclusion of diverse groups of migrant children by adopting a child-centered approach to migrant children integration on an educational and policy level.

Sombat Tapanya is a clinical psychologist and an independent researcher at the Peace Culture Foundation, Thailand. His research and clinical practice focus on psychological trauma resulting from harsh parenting and abuse and the treatment and prevention of such trauma. He works with Save the Children International and UNICEF in Thailand and the Association of Southeast Asian Nations region.

Liliana Maria Uribe Tirado is Full Professor at Universidad de San Buenaventura, Colombia. She is actively involved in the implementation of a school-based intervention called CEPIDEA (Promoting Prosocial and Emotional Skills to Counteract Externalizing Problems in Adolescence in Colombia), aimed at promoting prosocial behavior in middle schools. She has also collaborated in the implementation of a research project that examines the promotive nature of identity development for adolescents in Colombia, Chile and the United States.

Stephen Tollman is Founding Director of the MRC/Wits Rural Public Health and Health Transitions Research Unit, South Africa.

Trained in African and US/UK institutions, his professional life is based in South Africa with extensive efforts building advanced research capability in African settings. In the early 1990s, he led establishment of the Agincourt Field Research Centre which, based on long-term health and socio-demographic surveillance, provides a platform for the SA Medical Research Council's only group addressing rural health and the rapid health and social transitions underway. Extensive observational work is complemented by interventions and evaluations addressing critical periods along the life course. The empirically derived mortality and cause-of-death series informs work on chronic conditions and is among the richest on the continent. This mortality series and related surveillance data, linked to health service registers, offer new insights into the complex demographic, epidemiological and social transitions underway. Tollman served as first Board Chair of the INDEPTH Network 2002-2006, leads INDEPTH multicenter efforts addressing Adult Health and Aging in Africa and Asia and recently played an instrumental role setting up the SA Population Research Infrastructure Network (SAPRIN).

Workneh Yadete has a master's degree in History from Addis Ababa University. He has more than 15 years of experiencing working with children, adolescents and young people in Ethiopia. Among his key research experiences, he has worked as a qualitative researcher for 10 years for Young Lives, a longitudinal 15-year and multi-country research project led by the University of Oxford, UK. Since 2017, Workneh has been working for the Gender and Adolescence: Global Evidence (GAGE) programme as Country Research Uptake and Impact Coordinator and Qualitative Research Lead. He is also Managing Director of the Quest Research training and consultancy firm which conducts social research in Ethiopia. His areas of interest include education and learning, gender norms and adolescents' transition, child labour, health and sexual and reproductive health, migration and internal displacement.

Saengduean Yotanyamaneewong is a clinical psychologist and Lecturer in the Psychology Department, Chiang Mai University, Thailand. Her research and teaching interests focus on children, adolescents and families. Her projects focus on parenting, parental burnout and emotional and social development in children and adolescents.

Foreword: Understanding and Enhancing Human Development Among Global Youth – On the Unique Value of Developmentally Oriented Longitudinal Research

Richard M. Lerner
Institute for Applied Research in Youth Development
Tufts University, USA

The goal of developmental science is to describe, explain and optimize within-person change and between-people differences in within-person change across the life span (ontogeny) (Lerner, 2018). As such, repeated assessments of individuals across x-axis (temporal) divisions is the *sine qua non* of the essential features of developmental science research. In other words, to fulfil the goal of developmental science, longitudinal designs are required to obtain evidence contributing to understanding or to enhancing ontogenetic change (Collins, 2006). However, measuring one or more individuals at two or more successive ontogenetic points is a necessary but insufficient basis for developmental longitudinal research.

As is documented by the chapters across this volume, repeated measures must be taken at points of ontogeny for which there is a theoretical basis for expecting these measures (1) to assess changing features of (that is, variational or, ideally, transformational tipping points in) the process of development and/or (2) to constitute optimal ontogenetic points in which to enact interventions to enhance the course of developmental change. As is now understood by increasing numbers of developmental scientists, the development process involves relations between attributes of the individual and features of their tiered social, institutional, physical and cultural ecology, an ecology that changes integratively across history (for example, Bronfenbrenner and Morris, 2006; Elder et al, 2015; Overton, 2015).

Moreover, the developmental relations between an individual and the context are not independent. Contemporary theories of human development which emphasize that individual–context relations are mutually influential, represented most often in the literature as individual↔context relations, are at the cutting-edge of developmental science (Dick and Müller, 2017; Lerner, 2015, 2018). The individual–context relations depicted in these models involve dynamic and systematic relations across time and place (Elder et al, 2015). Dynamic models of human development processes require developmentally oriented longitudinal research to be tested.

The chapters in this volume both reflect and expand the theoretical, methodological and empirical foundations of this relational, dynamic developmental systems approach to using longitudinal methods to describe, explain and optimize the ontogenetic development of diverse global youth. Indeed, the chapters portray the ways in which developmentally oriented longitudinal research is uniquely suited to illuminate the features of both individuals and contexts that must be integratively studied to actualize the health and sustainable development of young people.

Banati (2020, p 1), noting that 'At its heart, sustainable development is about families and communities living in peace and prosperity, their children growing up safe and healthy, and transitioning to productive adulthood', presents a compelling vision of the way in which the levels of the ecology of human development must be aligned across a child's lifespan to enable the child to thrive. Banati's vision is richly illuminated by the chapters in this book: together, they demonstrate that when a child is embedded in families, communities and the broader ecology of human development that are marked by personal and contextual safety, when resources needed for physical and mental health and economic well-being are equitably distributed and accessible to the diverse youth and their families within a nation, then each child – across all instances of their specific individuality – will thrive across the life course; each child will have a pathway to an adulthood involving positive contributions to self, family, community and civil society.

The chapters in this book illuminate the manner in which the use of longitudinal methods enables integrative understanding of the specific dynamics of individual–context relations across time and place. The chapters document the singular contributions of developmentally predicated longitudinal methodology in depicting mutually influential relations between youth and context, point to the challenges involved in conducting high-quality developmentally oriented longitudinal research, and present important ideas for productively addressing these challenges.

Among the key assets of developmentally oriented longitudinal research documented across the chapters are the ways in which this approach to studying sustainable human development can identify not only variational (quantitative) change but also transformational (qualitative) change. In addition, the findings presented throughout the book illustrate the ways in which changing individual–context relations across the life course moderate sustainable human development. Moreover, the chapters also illustrate the fundamental importance of how time, and the coaction of its different instantiations (Elder, 1998) – ontogenetic, family and generational (historical) time – moderate the developmental process.

At the same time, this book illustrates the challenges of conducting theoretically predicated and methodologically rigorous, developmentally oriented longitudinal research. The study of developmental processes obviously involves the assessment of systematic and successive change and, within dynamic conceptions of this process, such assessment must involve the study of the individual, the context and the coaction of individual and context – that is, individual–context relations, including individual–individual relationships (see Overton, 2015, for a discussion of the three moments of developmental analysis involved in programmatic research framed by dynamic, relational developmental systems-based models). Accordingly, the approach to longitudinal methodology illustrated by the research in this book points to the need to integrate change-sensitive measures, research designs and data analysis procedures.

For example, measures must not only possess reliability and validity; they must also have at least strong measurement invariance across (obviously) ontogenetic (for example, age) time points, and across family and historical time points. In addition, measures must be invariant across other instances of individual specificity, for instance, gender, race, area of residence (such as rural or urban), socioeconomic status and culture. Clearly, then, using measures designed to index traits, which are attributes *claimed* to be invariant across time and place (for example, Costa and McCrea, 1980; McCrae et al, 2000), are of no use in a developmentally appropriate approach to measurement.

In addition, the designs of research must include repeated use of these measures at x-axis points selected on the basis of, ideally, theoretical understanding of key ontogenetic transition points in the developmental process under investigation or, at least, on the basis of empirical evidence that the selected x-axis points are potentially instances of such ontogenetic variation (Lerner, 2018). Moreover, the data-analytic procedures used to assess whether there is variation in the scores derived from change-sensitive measures employed to index individual, context and individual–context relations must be able to depict systematic within-individual change across successive x-axis points if, in fact, such systematic change occurs.

Here, however, lies a major challenge for extant developmentally oriented longitudinal research. Most approaches to data analysis in past longitudinal research have been variable-centred or, more recently, person-centred. Clearly, in a field defined as having its fundamental focus on within-person change, assessing how variables co-vary across ontogenetic time, or even how groups of individuals differ in how variables co-vary across ontogenetic time, respectively, are insufficient for depicting how variables co-vary within a specific individual across time and place (Rose, 2016; Molenaar and Nesselroade, 2015). Variable-centred and person-centred data analysis methods are associated with mathematical ideas found in the ergodic theorems, which involve assumptions of homogeneity across individuals and stationarity of the dynamic model of each member of a sample (Molenaar and Nesselroade, 2015). However, Bornstein (2017, 2019) has presented theoretical ideas (associated with dynamic models) and empirical evidence, in particular about the development of global youth, documenting the presence of a specificity principle for developmental analysis.

This principle underscores that, in addition to any nomothetic or group-differential attributes of a person, each individual has specific, idiographic attributes. Idiographic features of development exist because each child possesses specific physical/physiological attributes (including genetic and epigenetic characteristics; Molenaar, 2014; Slavich and Cole, 2013) and, as well, specific psychological, behavioural and social relationship attributes. Idiographic attributes of a person co-act dynamically with specific contextual attributes at specific times and places across specific periods of life, and this coaction increases the depth and breadth of a person's specificity and, as well, constitute across time and place their specific pathway of ontogenetic development. Such specificity means that human development is not ergodic, that is, no two individuals (including monozygotic [MZ] twins; Richardson, 2017; Slavich and Cole, 2013) have the same characteristics of individuality within or across ontogenetic time points (Rose, 2016).

Of course, developmentally oriented longitudinal research about global youth should not abandon either variable or person-specific data-analytic foci. Such analytic foci should be used when they are predicated on the specific questions addressed in a specific investigation. Nevertheless, the importance of the specificity principle, coupled with the non-ergodic nature of human development, means that questions about person-specific change across ontogenetic points should be included in a complete programme of developmental science research and, as such, methods of idiographic data analysis, for instance, such as dynamic factor analysis (Molenaar and Nesselroade, 2015; Ram and Grimm, 2015), should be included in such scholarship.

Although such analyses provide information about the pathways of a specific person, data from a specific individual can be linked to idiographic data from one or more other individuals through integrative latent-variable data analysis procedures such as the idiographic filter (Molenaar and Nesselroade, 2012, 2015). The use of statistical procedures that enable latent-variable integrative data analysis (IDA) across multiple individuals is only one instance of such methods (Curran and Hussong, 2009). Indeed, IDA methods have also been used to integrate different variable-centred longitudinal data sets (for example, Callina et al, 2017) and, as such, they represent an instance of the future innovations in longitudinal methodology pointed to by Banati and by the authors of the chapters in this book for future advances in developmentally oriented longitudinal research about sustainable human development. Banati (2020), summarizing the significance of IDA methods, points to the value of linking information across longitudinal data sets. She notes that such links can elucidate both the generality and the specificity of development across variables, times and places. Contributing to such cross-study linkages thus increases the contribution of any single longitudinal investigation.

Of course, using IDA across studies will require more access by different investigators to the data sets collected by other researchers. Such collaboration may set the stage for another instance of contribution by different teams of developmentally oriented longitudinal researchers. As envisioned by Banati (2020), and as illustrated by different longitudinal projects she has assembled to contribute to this book, a more precise understanding of the course of sustainable human development can be realized if developmental scientists create cross-national, comparative – and what she terms harmonized – developmentally oriented longitudinal studies. There is already evidence that such harmonization is illuminating what is general and what is specific about individual–context relational pathways of sustainable life-course change among youth developing in different nations (for example, Lerner et al, 2018; Tirrell et al, 2019).

In sum, the set of longitudinal studies within this book portrays the value of developmentally oriented longitudinal research for providing theoretically and methodologically invaluable insight about the nature of the individual and context coactions involved in sustainable development across the life course. In addition, this book documents the unrivalled potential of such developmental science for evidence-based applications that will enable future developmental researchers to contribute increasing more useful information about how to equitably promote individual health and well-being and positive engagement with civil society. Promoting such development through enhancing the positive outcome of individual–context coactions will contribute to a more socially just life for all global youth.

More than any other existing volume, this book illuminates our present developmental–longitudinal knowledge base about sustainable youth development. In addition, this book is a beacon for future progress. It stands as an invaluable marker of where developmental science is and where it needs to go to create thriving for present cohorts of global youth and for cohorts to be born across the rest of this century.

Acknowledgements

The preparation of this foreword was supported in part by grants from the Chan Zuckerberg Initiative, Compassion International, the Templeton Religion Trust and the Templeton World Charity Foundation.

References

Banati, P. (2020) Introduction: measuring sustainable human development across the life course. In P. Banati (Ed) *Sustainable Development Across the Life Course: Evidence from Longitudinal Research* (pp 1–30). Bristol: Policy Press/Bristol University Press.

Bornstein, M.H. (2017) The specificity principle in acculturation science. *Perspectives in Psychological Science* 12(1): 3–45.

Bornstein, M.H. (2019) Fostering optimal development and averting detrimental development: prescriptions, proscriptions, and specificity. *Applied Developmental Science* 23(4): 340–45.

Bronfenbrenner, U. and Morris, P.A. (2006). The bioecological model of human development. In W. Damon and R.M. Lerner (Eds) *Handbook of Child Psychology: Vol 1: Theoretical Models of Human Development* (6th edn, pp 793–828). Hoboken, NJ: Wiley.

Callina, K.S., Johnson, S.K., Tirrell, J.M., Batanova, M., Weiner, M. and Lerner, R.M. (2017) Modeling pathways of character development across the first three decades of life: an application of integrative data analysis techniques. *Journal of Youth and Adolescence* 46(6): 1216–37.

Collins, L.M. (2006) Analysis of longitudinal data: the integration of theoretical model, temporal design, and statistical model. *Annual Review of Psychology* 57: 505–28.

Costa Jr, P.T. and McCrae, R.R. (1980) Still stable after all these years: personality as a key to some issues in adulthood and old age. In P.B. Baltes and O.G. Brim Jr (Eds) *Life Span Development and Behavior: Vol 3* (pp 65–102). New York: Academic Press.

Curran, P.J. and Hussong, A.M. (2009) Integrative data analysis: the simultaneous analysis of multiple data sets. *Psychological Methods* 14: 81–100.

Dick, A.S. and Müller, U. (Eds) (2017) *Advancing Developmental Science: Philosophy, Theory, and Method*. New York: Routledge.

Elder Jr, G.H. (1998) The life course and human development. In W. Damon and R.M. Lerner (Eds) *Handbook of Child Psychology: Vol 1: Theoretical Models of Human Development* (5th edn, pp 939–91). New York: Wiley.

Elder, G.H., Shanahan, M.J. and Jennings, J.A. (2015) Human development in time and place. In M.H. Bornstein and T. Leventhal (Eds) *Handbook of Child Psychology and Developmental Science: Vol 4: Ecological Settings and Processes in Developmental Systems* (7th edn, pp 6–54). Hoboken, NJ: Wiley.

Lerner, R.M. (2015) Preface. In R.M. Lerner (Editor-in-Chief) *Handbook of Child Psychology and Developmental Science* (7th edn, pp xv–xxi). Hoboken, NJ: Wiley.

Lerner, R.M. (2018) *Concepts and Theories of Human Development* (4th edn). New York: Routledge.

Lerner, R.M., Tirrell, J.M., Dowling, E.M., Geldhof, J., Gestsdóttir, S., Lerner, J.V. et al (2018) The end of the beginning: evidence and absences studying PYD in a global context. *Adolescent Research Review* 4(1): 1–14. doi.org/10.1007/s40894-018-0093-4

McCrae, R.R., Costa Jr, P.T., Ostendorf, F., Angleitner, A., Hrebícková, M., Avia, M.D. et al (2000) Nature over nurture: temperament, personality, and life span development. *Journal of Personality and Social Psychology* 78: 173–86.

Molenaar, P.C.M. (2014) Dynamic models of biological pattern formation have surprising implications for understanding the epigenetics of development. *Research in Human Development* 11: 50–62.

Molenaar, P.C.M. and Nesselroade, J.R. (2012) Merging the idiographic filter with dynamic factor analysis to model process. *Applied Developmental Science* 16: 210–19.

Molenaar, P.C.M. and Nesselroade, J.R. (2015) Systems methods for developmental research. In W.F. Overton and P.C.M. Molenaar (Eds) *Handbook of Child Psychology and Developmental Science: Vol 1: Theory and Method* (7th edn, pp 652–82). Hoboken, NJ: Wiley.

Overton, W.F. (2015) Process and relational developmental systems. In W.F. Overton and P.C.M. Molenaar (Eds) *Handbook of Child Psychology and Developmental Science: Vol 1: Theory and Method* (7th edn, pp 9–62). Hoboken, NJ: Wiley.

Ram, N. and Grimm, K.J. (2015) Growth curve modeling and longitudinal factor analysis. In W.F. Overton and P.C.M. Molenaar (Eds) *Handbook of Child Psychology and Developmental Science: Vol 1: Theory and Method* (7th edn, pp 758–88). Hoboken, NJ: Wiley.

Richardson, K. (2017) *Genes, Brains, and Human Potential: The Science and Ideology of Human Intelligence*. New York: Columbia University Press.

Rose, T. (2016) *The End of Average: How We Succeed in a World That Values Sameness*. New York: HarperCollins.

Slavich, G.M. and Cole, S.W. (2013) The emerging field of human social genomics. *Clinical Psychological Science* 1: 331–48.

Tirrell, J.M., Dowling, E.M., Gansert, P., Buckingham, M., Wong, C.A., Suzuki, S. et al (2019) Toward a measure for assessing features of effective youth development programs: contextual safety and the "Big Three" components of positive youth development programs in Rwanda. *Child & Youth Care Forum* 49(2): 201–22. https://doi.org/10.1007/s10566-019-09524-6

Introduction: Measuring Sustainable Human Development Across the Life Course

Prerna Banati

The sustainable development challenge

In 2015, electrifying optimism surrounded the adoption of the Sustainable Development Goals (SDGs) as world leaders agreed to a 15-year deal to advance economic, social and environmental development globally, with a focus on those most left behind. The successor to the Millennium Development Goals (MDGs), the SDGs laid out in 'The Road to Dignity by 2030: Ending Poverty, Transforming All Lives and Protecting the Planet' (United Nations, 2015a) describes 17 ambitious goals, seen in Figure 0.1, that include: ending poverty and ensuring well-being for all ages, inclusive and equitable education, gender equality and empowerment, decent work and reducing inequality within and among countries (United Nations, 2015b). The global indicator framework, developed by the Inter-Agency and Expert Group on SDG Indicators (IAEG-SDGs), was agreed to at the 47th session of the UN Statistical Commission held in March 2016 and contains 230 indicators and 169 targets (United Nations, 2016).

At its heart, sustainable development is about families and communities living in peace and prosperity, their children growing up safe and healthy, and transitioning to productive adulthood. Chambers and Conway (1991, p 6) were perhaps the first to define sustainable livelihoods 'which can cope with and recover from stress and shocks, maintain or enhance its capabilities and assets, and provide sustainable livelihood opportunities for the next generation; and which contributes

Figure 0.1: The UN's Sustainable Development Goal framework

Source: United Nations, 2015a

net benefits to their livelihoods at the local and global levels and in the short and long term'.

Global goals such as the SDGs and the MDGs have undoubtedly driven sustainable development progress. Global averages have improved: children born today are less poor, and experience generally rising living standards, with many families living in better homes, and having access to consumer goods, and services such as electricity, water and sanitation and roads. Major improvements in health and education have been documented, with children born today less likely to be stunted and more likely to complete primary school than their counterparts born in 2000 (United Nations, 2015b).

Keeping in mind the lessons learned from the historical application of global goals (United Nations, 2015b), when looking forward, three key challenges beset the realization of the Sustainable Development agenda.

The first challenge is that progress has not been equitable – and inequalities are not adequately monitored and detected. Throughout the MDG period, advancements were uneven across regions, genders and age groups (Verma and Petersen, 2018). Disadvantage is increasingly concentrated in the most vulnerable and marginalized, and, arguably, inequalities are becoming further entrenched (Edwards, 2015). Gaps are growing between rich and poor; between rural and urban areas; between ethnic majority and ethnic minority children (OECD, 2015). Families that were left furthest behind now face the greatest risks, such as impact from health shocks or repeated illness leading to lost income.

The second challenge is the complexity of multiple influences – in particular, how sectoral inputs converge to create development success. As with its predecessor the Millennium Development Goals, the SDGs are organized in sectoral silos. However, successful human development relies on multiple, interacting and compounding influences sourced from different levels of the social ecology (individual, family, community, state). Understanding how inputs are interconnected (complementary or antagonistic), and in particular the interactions of social norms with development services, is crucial for effective and efficient prioritization of development actions. There is abundant evidence that achieving learning outcomes among children relies on inputs that extend beyond the education sector, such as how parents and communities value a child's education (UNGEI, 2019). Good health, physical safety and adequate nutrition are implicated in learning success. The health sector has arguably gone the furthest in recognizing the social determinants of health, including the critical roles of poverty and inequality in shaping good health outcomes (Marmot and Wilkinson, 2005).

The third challenge relates to timing – in particular, when to intervene and how to sequence interventions. With the exception of the target of 2030, the SDGs do not provide insight into temporal sequencing, and the importance of timing to human development. The timing of interventions is crucial to success and, unsurprisingly, benefits seen in one age group can be derived from interventions in an earlier age group with sustainable improvement sometimes requiring multiple interventions (Banati and Lansford, 2018; Banati et al, 2015). The reference to timing can be seen in two ways (Elder, 1994). The first relates to age – both the biological meanings but also the social meanings which are vested in culture and norms. The timing of social roles (such as parenthood) and events (such as marriage) play a role in shaping development trajectories. The second relates to historical time, which is seen, for example, by contrasting the experiences of older and younger generations of the same history. By contrasting how the SDGs play out for these two different cohorts we can gather insight into the role of historical timing and therefore social change in improving human well-being.

About this book

The approaching mid-point of the Sustainable Development Goal era provides an opportune moment to review these challenges and take stock of progress. Determining where acceleration is needed, or if course correction is more appropriate, will rely on sound measurement of where we are relative to the global commitments. The current efforts to measure the SDGs have been helpful in telling us that we are missing the mark as defined by agreed targets. These measures have drawn our attention to the existence of problems, but have been unable to measure the dynamic, complex and intergenerational nature of human development.

This book brings attention to the value to be gained from applying the powerful analytic potential of longitudinal data to understand and measure global development challenges such as the SDGs. This is the first effort to curate findings from a collection of longitudinal studies operating in over 50 different countries and working across a number of development sectors. These studies were selected to showcase the complexity, as well as the diversity, of development challenges ranging across non-communicable diseases, gender equality, Human Immunodeficiency Virus (HIV) prevention, education trajectories, social protection, child marriage, disability, urbanization, psychosocial health and parenting. Studies that lent themselves to multisectorality were prioritized. The selection criteria for studies include those currently collecting data (active studies) with findings demonstrating some direct relevance for the sustainable development agenda. In addition, the selection sought to highlight innovation in multisectorality, or cross-sectoral issues, or address specific methodological challenges associated with the longitudinal design to evaluate policy impacts. Taken together, the studies illustrate the strength of the longitudinal design to capture the situation of inequalities, the time-sensitivity of multiple convergences that impact lifetime outcomes, including the complex dynamics and interplay of human agency and the constraints of social norms and institutions; and how these influences shape intra- and intergenerational trajectories of individuals and ultimately societies.

Given the centrality of children to the SDG transformational agenda, this collection focuses on child and adolescent development. The younger population have most to gain from the success of the SDGs, and young people have played a key role in determining the priorities of the sustainable development agenda (Verma and Petersen, 2018). In some ways, the success of the SDGs hinge on how well they do for children. As the global goals are operationalized in this coming decade of action, improvements in the lives of today's children as they grow will determine the success of global investments in the sustainable development agenda.

The unique value of the longitudinal design to understand development challenges

Longitudinal studies have had enormous value, contributing to the construction of effective public policy and design of effective public programmes. Many governments have invested in multiple waves of longitudinal data as well as new studies. The UK has funded four national longitudinal studies, two of which (the National Survey of Health and Development, established in 1946; and the National Child Development Study, established in 1958) have continued for over 50 years. Ireland (Growing up in Ireland), Denmark (the Danish National Birth Cohort) and the US (the National Longitudinal Study of Youth) have invested in nationally representative cohort studies.

With growing interest in learning about 'what works' in developing settings, donors and countries are investing in longitudinal study designs, and these are now widespread throughout the globe, including in poor-country settings with weak infrastructure. Yet many pressing development questions remain and, despite these investments, there are few fora for presentation and discussion of policy and programme-relevant research.

A longitudinal study begins by identifying key research questions relevant for the focus group under investigation. A cursory review of existing longitudinal studies shows that data collection can happen as often as every few months, or every few years. In some cases, there may be decade-long gaps between questionnaires (such as seen in the Instituto de Nutrición de Centroamérica y Panamá [INCAP] study in Guatemala). Data collected in each wave appreciates the value of the study significantly. Subsequent waves of data collection often depend on funding. The diversity of longitudinal studies includes birth cohorts, impact evaluations, observational studies, panel studies or censuses (UNICEF, 2014).

The unique added value of longitudinal research has been previously documented (Banati, 2018; Banati et al, 2015) and is summarized in Table 0.1.

A core strength of the longitudinal design is that it can capture the dynamic nature of development. By tracking households, families or individuals in changing contexts over time, such data can track movements into and out of situations, for example how households move into and out of poverty. Crucially, longitudinal studies can provide an understanding of the drivers underpinning SDG indicators; provide an assessment of the timing of development windows; quality check cross-sectional estimates; and help determine 'what works' in programme and policy interventions.

Longitudinal research helps us to understand *trajectories* and can aid our efforts to understand human development by describing pathways or long-term patterns of change (Elder, 1985, p 31; Elder et al, 2003; Liefbroer and Dykstra, 2000). The individual life course is made up of many interconnected trajectories including career, family and educational pathways (Settersten Jr and Mayer, 1997). These trajectories are 'punctuated by a sequence of successive life events and transitions, which are brief in scope, and refer to changes in state' (Settersten Jr and Mayer, 1997). Each transition influences the probability of the next occurring. An event is usually conceptualized as a relatively abrupt change, while a transition is usually conceptualized as a more gradual evolving change.

Transitions and events are typically placed within, and help describe, a larger trajectory, and the trajectory gives them a clear meaning (Settersten Jr and Mayer, 1997; Elder, 1985). Turning points denote a substantial change in the direction of one's life and can be determined either subjectively or objectively (Hareven, 2000, pp 153, 329; Settersten Jr and Mayer, 1997). Critical periods are a phase within the life span during which there is a heightened sensitivity to exogenous stimuli.

Table 0.1: Unique added value of longitudinal research

Longitudinal studies can help to...	Example	Implications for development programming
1. Understand enduring change and equitable progress by analysing the dynamics of risk in a given cohort.	Evidence suggests there is significant movement into and out of poverty (known as churning). Some studies show the poor are poor some of the time only. But some families stay poor. Analysis of households that experience repeated or persistent poverty can help understand who stays poor, and what strategies can be employed to prevent families from falling below the poverty line.	In the UK, the 2006 Action Plan on Social Exclusion drew on evidence from the British Household Panel Survey. This survey revealed that 'a small group of people experience particularly persistent and severe deprivation and exclusion throughout their lifetime'. The resulting Action Plan argued that tackling such marginalization requires highly localized and tailored responses that cut across government departments. In Indonesia, such analysis using longitudinal data from Indonesia Family Life Survey (IFLS) improved the targeting of programmes and made the case for the expansion of social safety nets.
2. Unpack drivers and determinants of well-being outcomes, and reveal hidden problems and opportunities.	Analysis of data from the British Cohort Study of children born in 1970 showed that by the time they entered school, higher-ability children from disadvantaged backgrounds were overtaken by less able children from privileged backgrounds. In Jamaica, longitudinal research linked premature and early deliveries to undiagnosed hypertension in pregnant mothers (Samms-Vaughn, 2014).	In the UK, free pre-school was introduced in disadvantaged areas. In response to the longitudinal evidence generated in Jamaica, an information card added to expectant mothers' maternity record books advised them of the signs and risks of hypertension. This led to a 60% decline in hypertension and related complications in pregnancies and deliveries (Samms-Vaughn, 2014).

(continued)

Table 0.1: Unique added value of longitudinal research (continued)

Longitudinal studies can help to…	Example	Implications for development programming
3. Illuminate trends, trajectories and movements in people's lives, including reflecting on how patterns evolve over time and along the life cycle.	Young Lives longitudinal research in Vietnam has shown a high share of children in the bottom quintile in mathematics scores at age 12 had left school by age 15, further limiting their life chances. A core strength of longitudinal research is the ability to look beyond statistical means to reflect on how patterns evolve over time and along the life cycle.	This analysis suggests that investment in education and learning for primary- and secondary-age children is crucial to ensure long-term well-being, with impacts on future annual earnings and increased labour market participation.
4. Aid interpretation of the unforeseen by providing a platform for identifying and following the unexpected.	A longitudinal study operating during the time of the 1984 famine in Ethiopia (Dercon and Porter, 2014) was instrumental in identifying the long-term impacts on adults who experienced the famine as infants. The authors find that by adulthood, affected infants were significantly shorter by at least 5 cm.	The analysis in Ethiopia pointed to the need to provide additional support to the children of this cohort, whose height loss could lead to income losses of around 5% per year over their lifetime. The evidence also suggests that the relief operations at the time made little difference to those who survived.
5. Contribute to the evidence of the effectiveness of development interventions by identifying what works in which contexts, and to improve the targeting of interventions.	Impact evaluations including randomized control trials and quasi-experimental studies are now commonly seen. These are designed to evaluate the impact of an intervention. The Transfer Project is a multi-country effort to look at the impacts of unconditional cash transfers on a diverse set of development outcomes.	Results of the Zambia impact evaluation of the social case transfer were widely disseminated and helped convince the government to scale-up the programme nationally. The government increased its budget allocation, with an initial investment in evaluations of US$5 million leveraging US$150 million for children over five years The programme currently reaches 12% of the population (Transfer Project, 2020).

Table 0.1: Unique added value of longitudinal research (continued)

Longitudinal studies can help to...	Example	Implications for development programming
6. Highlight questions that may need to be addressed in future.	By observing changes to context or behaviours over time, such as internet use, longitudinal studies can highlight research questions for future study. The ALSPAC study of children of the 1990s living in Bristol explored the role of online connectivity in reducing suicide. Evidence demonstrated the preventative influence of the internet; while some participants used online peer support groups, formal online help was unsatisfactory (ALSPAC, 2020).	The study advocated for improving clinicians' understanding of the online world and supported a review of web-based suicide-prevention services for vulnerable people.

Source: Adapted from UNICEF, 2014

These periods are particularly conducive to programmatic interventions and growing evidence indicates that critical periods exist beyond prenatal development into early childhood and even older children (see Banati and Lansford, 2018).

Insights to SDG challenges from longitudinal research

In this section, a deeper review of the three key challenges to advancing the SDG agenda is presented, using longitudinal examples that exploit three of the six value-added contributions of longitudinal research presented in Table 0.1.

Challenge 1: Addressing inequalities through longitudinal analysis of risk dynamics

Increasing inequalities are undermining development progress, and contributing to social and political instability (Houle, 2018). In particular, as income inequalities and the difference between rich and poor widens, progress towards meeting the poverty eradication goal is in jeopardy. While efforts to disaggregate data (by sex, income and geography) to measure inequalities is part of the current SDG measurement frame, this doesn't permit the detection of movements into and out of extreme conditions such as poverty. Indeed, a number of studies presented in the volume demonstrate the effectiveness of a design that represents more dominantly the most marginalized groups that the SDGs are purposely targeting.

One way in which longitudinal research can inform the SDG challenge is to assess the lasting effect of experiencing a given 'state of being' such as poverty, and the ways in which exiting this 'state of being' can be achieved. Differences, by country, in the persistence of poor outcomes for some groups (such as child poverty, malnutrition in childhood, bullying in school, inactivity in youth, and so on), how populations move into and out of such experiences, and their lasting effect, can inform priority setting in country responses to the SDGs, as well as the design of policy interventions to address them. What is evident is that a simple indication of the level – as most goals will be operationalized in the SDGs – provides insufficient information on the dynamics of risk to help policy makers design the most appropriate response.

Literature on poverty dynamics provides some of the best illustrations of how longitudinal findings augment cross-sectional data. Analysis of poverty dynamics captures the mobility of households or individuals by measuring their well-being over time (rather than static measures of poverty, which cannot detect the dynamics of poverty). In most developing country settings, where homes are subject to major economic fluctuations due to seasonal agriculture, or a sick adult requiring medical care, the dynamics of poverty are essential to measure, and central to our aspiration of improving upward economic mobility. Indeed, countries with identical poverty and inequality levels may have different levels of mobility across the poverty line, changing the identities of who is poor and not to different extents. Indeed, the only cases where cross-sectional or static assessments of poverty are adequate are when there is complete immobility in experiences of poverty (Yacub, 2000).

For example, longitudinal data can demonstrate how individuals who are vulnerable but not considered poor by cross-sectional estimates can also fall below the poverty line. Three rounds of panel data collected for Indonesia between 2008 and 2010 showed that while approximately 25% of all Indonesians were living under the poverty line in at least one round, 43% fell below the official line at least once (World Bank, 2012). These findings reinforced the case for the expansion of social assistance coverage to both poor and 'vulnerable non-poor people' (World Bank, 2012). ODI analysis of Tanzania, Uganda and Vietnam shows that although these three countries have comparable poverty rates around 20%, the proportion of the poor living in poverty for at least two out of four consecutive years has been higher in Vietnam and lower in Tanzania (about 10–12% of total population in the former and 5–6% in the latter; ODI, 2014). Of interest, although Uganda and Vietnam have relatively higher rates of persistent poverty than Tanzania, more people demonstrated upward financial mobility in Uganda and Vietnam over the period of study. In this case of Tanzania, Uganda and Vietnam, in the absence of longitudinal data, the result would be that all countries would assume they had similar poverty challenges, requiring similar policy responses, when in reality they do not.

Longitudinal surveys that map changes to well-being across the life course also have the advantage of being able to identify sociodemographic groups in society with a higher or lesser vulnerability to risk. For instance, single-parent families or large families may be likely to experience higher risks of persistent poverty, as might people with lower levels of education. Policy makers with information on which groups are at the highest risk of poor outcomes can focus their interventions and resources on those in need of additional support. A good example of such analysis is presented in work by Plavgo

(Chapter 2 in this volume). Using 15 years of data from the Young Lives study, the author unpacks the unequal educational trajectories observed among children in Ethiopia by investigating the relationship between children's early cognitive abilities and later parental decisions regarding investments in higher levels of education. The findings identify two sources of inequality in educational opportunities. Firstly, poorer children on average develop lower cognitive abilities during childhood which negatively affect their later school transitions. Secondly, poorer children are considerably less likely to move on to secondary and higher education, including when their initial endowments are high. Policy implications from this study – exploiting social protection interventions that level household living conditions and access to pre-schools, as well as provision of financial support and improvements in secondary school accessibility to reduce barriers for poorer children to transition to higher education – have relevance to SDG 4 on advancing inclusive and equitable quality education and promoting lifelong learning.

Challenge 2: Addressing multiple influences by unpacking drivers of well-being

Bronfenbrenner's (1986, p 725) seminal work explored the nature of contextual influences affecting families, including what he called the 'genetic–environment' interaction. In exploring families, he notes the role of three 'exosystems' that also affect the development of the child through family processes, namely parental employment and work; family support networks; and the wider community. In subsequent work, the social–ecological model developed by Bronfenbrenner (2005) extends to include structural forces, including the policy environment in which children grow up. Well-being at a particular life stage is the result of many interacting influences operating across the social ecology.

Bell and colleagues (2013) define a framework for advancing equity in child health, applying Marmot's social determinants approach to children, a progressive model that promotes a wider vision of what influences health outcomes. Within the framework, emphasis is placed on the macro-level context, including 'wider national and transnational influences, including aspects of the political, economic, social, environmental and historical context, cultural norms and values, governance and human rights and the experience of violence and armed conflict' (Bell et al, 2013, p 7). The importance of descriptive cross-sectional statistics to support the prioritization of issues is noted. At the same time, the authors note that the evidence base on the impact of determinants and drivers requires strengthening longitudinal studies. They articulate the gaps that longitudinal data could fill, including

> what factors are associated with children doing better than might be expected (protective factors), and worse than expected (risk factors). Cohort analysis could be utilised to determine if selected children's outcomes change over time and the drivers of that change; and whether inequalities in well-being within cohorts are stable or change over time. (Bell et al, 2013, p 35)

In an extensive review of over 100 longitudinal studies that was designed to explore links between educational outcomes and other well-being outcomes (health, material well-being, risk behaviours and so on), Richardson (2018) undertook a meta-analysis controlling for study factors (for example, country of test, sample sizes, significances, subsampling). The authors' preliminary findings suggest some clear priorities for interventions. In particular, health factors and experiences of neglect and abuse in childhood are significantly more likely to explain a greater variation in educational outcomes in later childhood than material resources, and educational outcomes in childhood are more closely linked to adult material well-being, risk-taking and family functioning than to health outcomes.

A number of longstanding observational longitudinal studies over the last decades (such as Add Health, the British Birth cohorts, National Longitudinal Survey of Youth [NLSY] or Growing up in Ireland) present a wealth of information on the multidimensional nature of children's lives. By unpacking influences on child well-being across the life course, they continue to clear the fog by empirically developing the evidence base of what drives healthy and happy child outcomes. Work by Lansford and colleagues (Chapter 4 in this volume) illustrates this using longitudinal data from 10 years of the Parenting across Cultures project in nine countries (China, Colombia, Italy, Jordan, Kenya, Philippines, Sweden, Thailand and the United States). The team have used longitudinal data to understand processes operating at different levels, including biological, social and cultural, in the development of self-regulation and risk-taking, with a focus on SDG Target 3.4 to promote well-being and mental health. The study finds that positive social relationships are among the best predictors of well-being and mental health, and harsh treatment by parents, peers and others predicts poorer mental health and behavioural adjustment among children. The authors implicate both individual- and culture-level predictors in the development of externalizing behavioural problems, such as aggression and delinquency, from ages 7 to 14. For example, not only did individual mothers' and children's endorsement of aggression and authoritarian attitudes predict higher initial levels of externalizing behavioural problems and growth in externalizing behaviours over time, but cultural norms endorsing aggression and authoritarian attitudes exacerbated these effects. This finding emphasizes the need to address cultural norms that increase the risk of children's behavioural problems as a necessary part of promoting children's well-being to achieve the SDGs.

Similarly, presenting findings from analysis of 13 years of data from Plan International's qualitative longitudinal study 'Real Choices, Real Lives', Rivett and Loveday (Chapter 1 in this volume) explore the potential for gender norm change among adolescent girls in Benin, Togo and Uganda. The authors use longitudinal data to unpack the dynamics of complex gender socialization processes taking place through a girl's life by mapping and investigating influences operating at micro, meso and macro levels. Findings identify both the reproduction and rejection of gendered social norms taking place through daily activities and behaviours over time. Family, peers and community were found to be significant in facilitating instances where girls challenge norms. Wider structural factors were also found to play a role in shifting gendered household dynamics and attitudes. Using longitudinal analysis, the study demonstrates the non-linear and complex process of disrupting gender socialization with implications for the delivery model and duration of the programmatic response to SDG 5 which calls for gender equality and the empowerment of all women and girls.

Challenge 3: Identifying effective timing and sequencing by illuminating trends and trajectories

The SDGs aim to be action-oriented and universally applicable to all countries, taking into account different national realities. It is also evident that there are many possible pathways to development, consistent with the many variations globally in contexts and cultures for children and youth to develop well and thrive. Yet robust evidence is limited on the effective timing and sequencing of development actions and understanding how inputs are interconnected (complementary or antagonistic) and sequenced is crucial for effective and efficient prioritization, reducing costs while increasing returns.

Globally, the science of early childhood brain development has demonstrated the lifetime value to be gained from early investment. In experimental work by Heckman and colleagues (2012), three- to four-year-old African American children attending a flagship pre-school programme focused on providing early childhood development activities were followed until they were 40 years old. The programme improved aggressive, antisocial and rule-breaking behaviours, which in turn improved a number of labour market outcomes, health behaviours and criminal activities. The programme also enhanced academic motivation among girls. Understanding the mechanisms through which programmes can have a positive lifelong effect can help improve the programme response and make the case for expanded intervention.

The first 1,000 days are a well-acknowledged critical period for development (Britto, 2013), where an absence of adequate inputs can have lifetime consequences. More than 200 million children in developing countries are at risk of not meeting their developmental potential in the first years of life as a result of poverty, inadequate stimulation and malnutrition (Grantham-McGregor et al, 2007). This early disadvantage is likely to result in lower educational achievement and subsequently lower earnings in later life, therefore perpetuating social inequities and contributing to the intergenerational transmission of poverty, poor health and development (Baker-Henningham and Lopez Boo, 2010). Interventions in early childhood which promote the formation of cognitive-language, social and emotional skills can reduce inequalities between advantaged and disadvantaged children, and also improve the productivity of the society as a whole (Heckman, 2006).

Evidence is growing to suggest the adolescent period may also be a unique critical window. Exploiting longitudinal data, research by Lundeen and colleagues (2014) using Young Lives data has uncovered a catch-up window during adolescence that may provide an opportunity to redress gaps in exposures and vulnerabilities experienced in early childhood. Evidence published indicates that some stunting might be reversible and catch-up growth possible. In the study, around 50% of children stunted at year 1 were no longer stunted at year 8 in the absence of intervention, suggesting accelerated growth after the first 1,000 days can occur. Unsurprisingly, catch-up growth depends on the degree of stunting experienced during infancy. This has significant implications for nutritional programming for adolescents. Height for age and height for weight indicators have long been recognized as being associated with outcomes across the board, and indicative of outcomes in a number of other well-being domains, such as diminished mental ability and learning capacity.

Longitudinal research is well suited to exploring linkages between life stages, such as early childhood and adolescence. Portrait and colleagues (2011) analysed data from the Amsterdam Longitudinal Aging Study to understand the effects of early life exposure to the Dutch famine (during the winter of 1944–45) on the prevalence of heart disease, peripheral arterial disease and diabetes mellitus at ages 60–76. The authors found that across four age classes (0–1 years; 2–5 years; 6–10 years; and 11–14 years) the exposure to severe undernutrition at ages 11–14 was the most significantly associated with a higher probability of developing diabetes mellitus and/or peripheral arterial diseases among women aged 60–76. Evidence from Falconi and colleagues (2014), using cohort mortality data in France (1816–1919), England and Wales (1841–1919) and Sweden (1861–1919), also demonstrates that early adolescence is a sensitive developmental period for males, with findings suggesting that stressors experienced during the ages of 10–14 are related to shorter life spans.

Life course theory supports these findings. Elder (1998, p 3) notes that 'the developmental impact of a succession of life transitions or events is contingent on when they occur in a person's life'. The timing of life transitions has long-term consequences through effects on subsequent transitions. The ability of public policy to shape life transitions and their impacts can be exemplified in global efforts to reduce child marriage rates, for example. Marriage is a momentous life transition, and in many parts of the world marks the beginning of 'adulthood'. Early marriage tends to perpetuate the cycle of poverty by cutting short girls' education, pushing them into early and repeated pregnancies, and limiting their opportunities for employment.

Cumulative advantage and disadvantage work in patterns of changing cohort trajectories (DiPrete and Eirich, 2006). The impact of stressors on an individual are cumulative, making it difficult for individuals to catch up once they fall behind. For example, Costello and colleagues (2007), using longitudinal data, have shown that low birth weight baby girls show increased risk for depression during adolescence. Studies of divergent trajectories have contributed to analysis of population inequality, particularly in health (Ross and Wu, 1996), with significant implications for development planning.

In this volume, Pettifor and colleagues demonstrate the value of programme intervention in early adolescence using longitudinal data from the Agincourt Health and Demographic Surveillance site, which has been collecting data for 28 years in rural South Africa. Through latent class growth analysis, the authors explore the impact of early life transitions and key life events on HIV incidence among adolescent girls in the cohort, identifying that for each of the life events analysed, experiencing the event earlier in adolescence compared to later in adolescence was associated with an increased risk of HIV infection. The authors conclude that while HIV incidence in sub-Saharan Africa peaks in young women after the age of 18, life events that happen before the age of 15, in particular pregnancy, leaving school, parental death and coital debut, place adolescent girls at increased risk for HIV infection throughout adolescence and into early adulthood. This provides important evidence to inform the timing of interventions to reduce HIV risk, by encouraging a look beyond age descriptors to understand adolescent experiences and the potential sequencing of risk behaviours that lead to ultimate infection. This clearly points to the need for a life course look at HIV prevention by focusing on age and stage, even for very young adolescents (SDG 3).

Final remarks and chapter summaries

This introductory chapter has demonstrated how longitudinal analysis can enable the global community to address the achievement of the SDGs through a convergent approach. The foundations of most longitudinal research presented in this volume rest on the life course developmental science model, which has been previously shown to have value for the SDGs (Banati, 2018). A diverse set of contributors were invited to critically present their longitudinal research. All studies are currently operational and exist at different stages. The Joint Child Health Project from Mauritius is 48 years old, while the European Cohort Development Project is a mere few months along. The studies present findings, but also innovations in their design and data collection efforts.

Chapter 1 presents findings from analysis of 13 years of data from Plan International's qualitative longitudinal study 'Real Choices, Real Lives'. In the chapter, Rivett and Loveday explore the potential for gender norm change among adolescent girls in Benin, Togo and Uganda. The authors observe the gender socialization process across the course of an individual girl's life, by mapping and investigating influences operating at micro, meso and macro levels which facilitate both the reproduction and rejection of gendered social norms. Social influences of family, peers and community were found to be significant in facilitating instances where girls challenge norms. Wider structural factors were also found to play a role in shifting gendered household dynamics and attitudes. Using longitudinal analysis, the study demonstrates the non-linear and complex process of disrupting gender socialization, and the limitations of quantitative SDG indicators in capturing the nuance when measuring gender inequalities to ensure that any achievements reflect the lived experiences of adolescent girls (SDG 5).

In Chapter 2 Plavgo uses 15 years of data from the Young Lives study to unpack the unequal educational trajectories observed among children in Ethiopia by investigating the relationship between children's early cognitive abilities and later parental decisions regarding investments in higher levels of education. The findings identify two sources of inequality in educational opportunities. Firstly, poorer children on average develop lower cognitive abilities during childhood which negatively affect their later school transitions. Secondly, poorer children are considerably less likely to move on to secondary and higher education, also when their initial endowments are high. Resulting policy implications include those such as social protection interventions that level household living conditions and access to pre-schools. In addition, the author notes potential value in financial support and improvements in secondary school accessibility to reduce barriers for poorer children to transition to higher education (SDG 4).

In Chapter 3 Pettifor and colleagues exploit data from the Agincourt Health and Demographic Surveillance site, which has been collecting data for 28 years in rural South Africa. Through latent class growth analysis, the authors explore the impact of early life transitions and key life events on HIV incidence among adolescent girls in the cohort. Results show that for each of the life events, experiencing the event earlier in adolescence compared to later in adolescence was associated with an increased risk of HIV infection. The authors conclude that while HIV incidence in sub-Saharan Africa peaks in young women after the age of 18, life events that happen before the age of 15, in particular pregnancy, leaving school, parental death and coital debut, place adolescent girls at increased risk for HIV infection throughout adolescence and into early adulthood. Implications identified for programmes include the need for a long-term view of prevention by focusing on younger adolescents with the goal of prevention over the life course (SDG 3).

Chapter 4 uses longitudinal data from 10 years of the Parenting across Cultures project. Lansford and colleagues describe cultural differences across nine countries (China, Colombia, Italy, Jordan, Kenya, Philippines, Sweden, Thailand and the United States), using longitudinal data to understand biological, familial and cultural processes in the development of self-regulation and risk-taking. The Parenting across Cultures project recruited eight-year-old children, their mothers and fathers, and continues with annual interviews through early adulthood. In particular, the project aims to understand how risk-taking develops across adolescence as a function of biological maturation (puberty and age) and socialization (parenting and culture), exploring topics such as child discipline and its impacts on children's aggression and anxiety, the development of risk-taking behaviour, and youth competence and maladaptation. It demonstrates wide-ranging implications for policy actions to meet the Sustainable Development Goals (SDG 1, 3, 4, 5, 11, 16).

In Chapter 5 Koenig, Li and Blum share lessons from the Global Early Adolescent Study, a multinational longitudinal study operating in 10 longitudinal sites operating in Democratic Republic of Congo, Malawi, South Africa, China, Indonesia, Ecuador, Chile, Brazil, the USA and Belgium that aims to understand how gender shapes vulnerable young people's lives beginning in early adolescence. Highlighting the value of longitudinal research in tracking the dynamic nature of gender norms, the study has contributed to the development of new measurement tools to assess perceptions of gender norms and empowerment at entry into puberty (10–14 years of age), and findings that describe gendered perceptions, empowerment and health indicators throughout the course of early adolescence. Their research has demonstrated the influence of gender norms not only in adolescence but also into adulthood, noting that policies need to address the continuum of gender equality predictors and barriers, including at community and local levels. The authors note the importance of innovation in the measurement of age-specific gender norms, and the need to capture contextual, social, behavioural and health aspects of adolescents' lives. They detail the lessons learned, and challenges experienced, in undertaking multinational longitudinal research with vulnerable young adolescents, including ethical issues and research implementation issues (SDG 3, 5).

In Chapter 6 Baird and colleagues present findings from the innovative Gender and Adolescence: Global Evidence (GAGE) research programme operating in six countries (Bangladesh, Ethiopia, Jordan, Lebanon, Nepal and Rwanda), which follows 18,000 adolescents (10–19 years) in East Africa, the Middle East and North Africa (MENA) and South Asia over nine years (2015–24) using a mixed-methods longitudinal research design. The findings of the study are organized in a framework focusing on six capability domains closely linked to the SDGs: education and learning; bodily integrity and freedom from violence; health and nutrition; psychosocial well-being; voice and agency; and economic empowerment. The study couples findings from observational longitudinal research with nested experimental and quasi-experimental evaluations of adolescent programming to explore the impact of different support packages on adolescent development and well-being. To capture the dynamism of this life stage, the study follows two cohorts, girls and boys, and undertakes complementary research with female caregivers to understand intergenerational dynamics. By purposely sampling disadvantaged adolescents (those who married early, have a disability, or are internally displaced or refugees), the study contributes to understanding approaches aiming to 'leave no one behind' (SDG 3, 4, 5, 10, 16).

In Chapter 7 Pollack and colleagues describe the value proposition for an input-harmonized, integrated and comparative multi-country birth cohort to advancing child well-being in Europe. Birth cohort surveys across the world have been central to our understanding of the factors which contribute to enhancing child holistic well-being. The European Cohort Development Project has been developing the design and business case for such a survey since 2018. This survey comprises a common questionnaire, common sampling and fieldwork procedures and will thus allow a direct comparison of the well-being of children as they grow up across Europe in different national contexts. The authors describe the central role of the longitudinal design in advancing the life-course approach to policy making in childhood, with important links to developmental science and evolving capacities of children as they age. The introduction of participatory approaches to measurement as children are followed longitudinally provides an innovative methodology to ensure findings are child-led (SDG 1–11).

Chapter 8 uses the rich data available from the Joint Child Health Project, a longitudinal study that has followed a birth cohort on the tropical island nation of Mauritius for 48 years. Luczak and colleagues have synthesized the key findings from research conducted over the study period with a focus on drinking risk behaviours. Data are now available on the children of the original cohort, as well as their family units (siblings, partners). Highlighting the results, the chapter demonstrates the value of long-term longitudinal family studies for identifying how multiple familial factors combine to influence diverse behaviours of younger generations during developmental periods when risk-taking behaviours typically emerge. The study investigates parental factors in offspring alcohol involvement, focusing on norms, attitudes and beliefs. Results highlight the value of longitudinal, multi-informant family studies for elucidating how familial factors combine to influence drinking behaviours of younger generations during developmental periods when drinking and high-risk drinking typically emerge (SDG 3).

In the conclusion, the limitations to the effective use of longitudinal research findings are presented, some challenges to the implementation of these studies are discussed, and a policy evaluation model for longitudinal research is proposed.

References

ALSPAC (2020) Suicidal people need better online support. Available at www.bris.ac.uk/alspac/news/2016/suicide-and-the-internet.html

Baker-Henningham, H. and Lopez Boo, F. (2010) Early childhood stimulation interventions in developing countries: a comprehensive literature review. IDB working paper series: 213.

Banati, P. (2018) Bringing lifecourse theory to the sustainable development goals. In S. Verma and A. Peterson (Eds) *Developmental Science and Sustainable Development Goals for Children and Youth* (pp 313–328). New York, NY: Springer.

Banati, P. and Lansford, J.E. (2018) Introduction: adolescence in global context. In J.E. Lansford and P. Banati (Eds) *Handbook of Adolescent Development Research and Its Impact on Global Policy* (pp 1–26). Oxford: Oxford University Press.

Banati, P., Dornan, P. and Knowles, C. (2015) Tracking the children of the millennium: insights from a longitudinal cohort study. UNICEF Innocenti Research Brief (IRB_2015-3).

Bell, R., Donkin, A. and Marmot, M. (2013) Tackling structural and social issues to reduce inequities in children's outcomes in low-to middle-income countries. UNICEF Office of Research Discussion Paper No.2013-02. UNICEF Office of Research, Florence.

Bhutta, Z.A., Das, J.K., Rizvi, A., Gaffey, M.F., Walker, N., Horton, S. et al (2013) Lancet Nutrition Interventions Review Group; Maternal and Child Nutrition Study Group. Evidence-based interventions for improvement of maternal and child nutrition: what can be done and at what cost? *The Lancet* 382: 452–77.

Britto, P.R., Engle, P.L. and Super, C.M. (2013) *Handbook of Early Childhood Development Research and Its Impact on Global Policy*. Oxford: Oxford University Press.

Bronfenbrenner, U. (1986) Ecology of the family as a context for human-development – research perspectives. *Developmental Psychology* 22(6): 723–42.

Bronfenbrenner, U. (2005) *Making Human Beings Human: Bioecological Perspectives on Human Development*. Thousand Oaks, CA: Sage.

Chambers, R. and Conway, G.R. (1991) Sustainable rural livelihoods: practical concepts for the 21st century. Institute of Development Studies Discussion Paper 296. Available at https://opendocs.ids.ac.uk/opendocs/bitstream/handle/20.500.12413/775/Dp296.pdf

Costello, E.J., Worthman, C., Erkanli, A. and Angold, A. (2007) Prediction from low birth weight to female adolescent depression a test of competing hypotheses. *Archives of General Psychiatry* 64(3): 338–44.

Dercon, S. and Porter, C. (2014) Live Aid revisited: long-term impacts of the 1984 Ethiopian famine on children. *Journal of the European Economic Association* 12(4): 927–48.

DiPrete, T.A. and Eirich, G.M. (2006) Cumulative advantage as a mechanism for inequality: a review of theoretical and empirical developments. *Annual Review of Sociology* 32(1): 271–97.

Edwards, M. (2015) *Global Childhoods: Critical Approaches to the Early Years*. St Albans: Critical Publishing.

Elder, G.H. (1985) *Life Course Dynamics: Trajectories and Transitions 1968–1980*. Ithaca, NY: Cornell University Press.

Elder, G.H. (1994) Time, human agency, and social change: perspectives on the life course. *Social Psychology Quarterly* 3(1): 4–15.

Elder, G.H. (1998) The life course as development theory. *Child Development* 69(1): 1–12.

Elder, G.H., Johnson, M.K. and Crosnoe, R. (2003) The emergence and development of life course theory. In J.T. Mortimer and M.J. Shanahan (Eds) *Handbook of the Life Course: Handbooks of Sociology and Social Research* (pp 3–19). Boston, MA: Springer.

Falconi, A., Gemmill, A., Dahl, R.E. and Catalano, R. (2014) Adolescent experience predicts longevity: evidence from historical epidemiology. *Journal of Developmental Origins of Health and Disease* 5(3): 171–7.

Grantham-McGregor, S., Cheung, Y.B., Cueto, S., Glewwe, P., Richter, L. and Strupp, B. (2007) International Child Development Steering Group: developmental potential in the first 5 years for children in developing countries. *The Lancet* 369: 60–70.

Hareven, T.K. (2000) *Families, History, and Social Change: Life Course and Cross-Cultural Perspectives*. Boulder, CO: Westview Press.

Heckman, J. (2006) Skill formation and the economics of investing in disadvantaged children. *Science* 312: 1900–2.

Heckman, J.J., Pinto, R. and Savelyev, P.A. (2012) Understanding the mechanisms through which an influential early childhood program boosted adult outcomes. NBER Working Paper No. 18581, November.

Houle, C. (2018) Does economic inequality breed political inequality? *Democratization* 25(8): 1500–18.

Liefbroer, A.C. and Dykstra, P.A. (2000) Levenslopen in verandering: een studie naar ontwikkelingen in de levenslopen van Nederlanders geboren tussen 1900 en 1970. WRR serie Voorstudies en achtergronden V 107. Den Haag: Sdu Uitgevers.

Lundeen, E., Behrman, J.R., Crookston, B.T., Dearden, K.A., Engle, P., Georgiadis, A. et al (2014) Growth faltering and recovery in children aged 1–8 years in four low- and middle-income countries: young lives. *Public Health and Nutrition* 17(9): 2131–7.

Marmot, M. and Wilkinson, R. (2005) *Social Determinants of Health*. Oxford: Oxford University Press.

Oversea Development Institute (ODI) (2014) A place for panel data in the data revolution. ODI Briefing paper, 42.

Organization for Economic Cooperation and Development (OECD) (2015) In it together: why less inequality benefits all. Available at www.oecd.org/social/in-it-together-why-less-inequality-benefits-all-9789264235120-en.htm

Portrait, F., Teeuwiszen, E. and Deeg, D. (2011) Early life undernutrition and chronic diseases at older ages: the effects of the Dutch famine on cardiovascular diseases and diabetes. *Social Science & Medicine* 73: 711–18.

Ross, C.E. and Wu, C.-L. (1996) Education, age, and the cumulative advantage in health. *Journal of Health and Social Behaviour* 37: 104–20.

Richardson, D. (2018) Inclusive education for children from vulnerable families. Remarks prepared for the UN EGM, New York, 15/16 May 2018, 'Family policies for inclusive societies'.

Transfer Project (2020) Beyond internal validity: towards a broader understanding of credibility in development policy research. *World Development* 127(104802): 1–3.

Samms-Vaughn, M. (2014) Translating research from cohort studies into policy: the case of Jamaica. Paper presented at the UNICEF Office of Research.

Settersten Jr, R.A. and Mayer, K.U. (1997) The measurement of age, age structuring, and the life course. *Annual Review of Sociology* 23: 233–61.

United Nations Children's Fund (UNICEF) (2014) Strength in numbers: how longitudinal research can support child development. UNICEF Office of Research Innocenti report. Report authored by Kate Dunn and Prerna Banati. Available at www.unicef-irc.org/article/1176-strength-in-numbers-how-longitudinal-research-can-support-child-development.html

United Nations Girls Education Initiative (UNGEI) (2019) Global education monitoring gender report 2019: building bridges for gender equality. Available at www.ungei.org/resources/index_6549.html

United Nations (2015a) The future we want: outcome document for the Sustainable Development Agenda. Available at https://sustainabledevelopment.un.org/content/documents/733FutureWeWant.pdf

United Nations (2015b) The millennium development goals report 2015. Available at www.un.org/millenniumgoals/2015_MDG_Report/pdf/MDG%202015%20rev%20(July%201).pdf

United Nations (2016) Resolution adopted by the General Assembly on 6 July 2017 71/313. Work of the Statistical Commission pertaining to the 2030 Agenda for Sustainable Development. Available at https://undocs.org/A/RES/71/313

Verma, S. and Petersen, A. (2018) *Developmental Science and Sustainable Development Goals for Children and Youth*. New York, NY: Springer.

World Bank (2012) *Protecting Poor and Vulnerable Households in Indonesia*. Jakarta: The World Bank.

Yacub, S. (2000) Poverty dynamics in developing countries. Development Bibliography 16. Brighton, Sussex: Institute for Development Studies.

1

Exploring the Potential for Gender Norm Change in Adolescent Girls: Evidence from 'Real Choices, Real Lives' Longitudinal, Qualitative Study Data

Jenny Rivett and Lilli Loveday

Introduction

The targets outlined by Sustainable Development Goal 5 – to achieve social, economic and political gender equality, eliminate all forms of violence against women and girls, and ensure universal access to sexual and reproductive healthcare and rights – underscore the persistence of gender-based discrimination in almost all public and private spheres, and, despite progress, the scale of the work still needed to realize an equal and equitable society (United Nations, 2015). As global goals, the SDG targets and indicators inevitably lack nuance in terms of implementation, leaving governments and stakeholders space to adapt and implement according to context. However, the notion of gender equality in particular can remain superficial when measured according to female–male ratios and quotas, legal frameworks and quantitative data – making the SDG 5 indicators relatively limited in terms of reflecting the lived experience of individuals in society.

The negative outcomes of gender inequality which SGD 5 seeks to redress, and which disproportionately affect women and girls, are increasingly well-documented and understood. However, while there is a growing emphasis in the international development community on gender transformative interventions, understandings of the often deep-seated social norms at the core of persistent gender inequalities, and importantly how norms can change, remains limited, hindering progress on the SDG 5 objectives.

Gendered social norms are reproduced during the process of gender socialization which begins from birth as an individual interacts with various social- and structural-level concepts of gender. These are the norms which hold in place the socially constructed set of 'acceptable' behaviours for males and females, transgression of which can bring social – and sometimes violent – consequences. Conceptualizations of gender vary between contexts and are often rooted in historical, religious and socioeconomic factors, but in all cases where what is 'acceptable' for males and females differs, gendered norms impact individuals' equal opportunities, treatment and rights in society, reinforcing and perpetuating inequalities. Norms dictating what it means to be 'masculine', for example, are increasingly regarded as a core driver of sexual and gender-based violence (Abebe et al, 2018), hence better understanding of the gender socialization process is highly valuable in achieving SGD target 5.2 – to eliminate all forms of violence against women and girls.

Understanding gender socialization and facilitating gendered social norm change is therefore crucial to realizing the objectives of SDG 5; however, measuring norm change via quantitative indicators fails to reflect the nuance of attitudes and experiences. The ability of longitudinal, qualitative data to capture shifts in norms over time instead makes it a significantly more effective method of measuring social change and informing gender transformative interventions.

The 'Real Choices, Real Lives' cohort study

Since 2007, the children's rights charity Plan International UK has been tracking the lives of over 120[1] girls across nine countries, in three regions: sub-Saharan Africa (Benin, Togo and Uganda), South-East Asia (Cambodia, the Philippines and Vietnam) and Latin America and the Caribbean (Brazil, the Dominican Republic and El Salvador). The longitudinal, qualitative cohort study, 'Real Choices, Real Lives', intends to follow the girls from their birth in 2006 until 2024 when they turn 18, providing a unique insight into the interaction between gender, age and poverty over a girl's life course.

Unlike SDG 5's large-scale, quantitative indicators of gender equality, the cohort study's qualitative data enables in-depth exploration into the gendered attitudes and behaviours of individual girls and their families and the gender socialization process, while its longitudinal nature is able to capture shifts in social norms. In this way, existing and future evidence from the study is especially valuable in informing programming, policy and research which seeks to facilitate gender norm change and achieve the goals of SDG 5.

Research methodology

Using longitudinal, qualitative data

The 'Real Choices, Real Lives' cohort study data is collected through annual in-depth qualitative interviews undertaken with a key caregiver for each girl and, from 2013 onwards, with the girl herself. Additional research methods have been used over the course of the study, including story-telling exercises, attitudes assessment, community and social network mapping and creative drawing activities. The design of each annual qualitative research instrument draws from a combination of grounded theory, intersectional feminist theory and the capabilities approach to development. By conducting annual data analysis for every girl in the cohort, the study is able to capture the constants in a girl's life, as well as the important events, changes and shifting relationships during the life course.

The longitudinal design is central to the study's unique value in understanding the complexity of dynamic influences in an individual girl's life, and in tracking disruption of the gender socialization process over time. Importantly, for translating these observations into practical recommendations informing policy and programming, longitudinal research enables an investigation into the causes, determinants or drivers of disruption to the gender socialization process. By mapping the varying levels of influences both of the reproduction of gendered norms and where there is evidence of the gender socialization process across a girl's life course, this research can inform gender transformative interventions in terms of when, through whom and in which spaces girls are already showing the potential for norm change.

Qualitative data presents a particularly effective means to capture the realities of gendered norms, through articulations of attitudes and descriptions of behaviours which reflect, reiterate or challenge norms. Social norms are difficult to measure in a quantitative sense and attempts to do so overlook the nuance of concepts which can be deeply ingrained. In this way, the 'Real Choices, Real Lives' study is able to probe gendered attitudes and behaviours and observe their complexities and frequent contradictions.

Exploring the gender socialization process

Gender socialization – the process of the reproduction, or transferral, of socially 'acceptable' behaviours allocated for males and females (gender norms) in any given context – occurs via interaction with various individual, social and structural influences, wherein the individual adapts attitudes and behaviours which adhere to their allocated gender. Judith Butler (1993, 1999, 2009), among others, argues however that there can be 'slippage' in the reproduction of gendered social norms, wherein these 'acceptable' behaviours are exposed as social constructions – subject to change – rather than being biological truths.

It is on this understanding that the gender socialization process not only *can* be disrupted but *must* be disrupted in order to achieve social norm change, that the 'Real Choices, Real Lives' longitudinal data has been analysed to identify where there is the potential for this disruption to occur. The markers of where there is the potential for disruption of the gender socialization process are referred to in this analysis as 'glitches'[2] (Plan International UK, 2019a, 2019b, 2019c), that is, not a direct indication of a shift in gender norms, but where there appears to be a window of opportunity where gendered social norms have not been perfectly reproduced, and gender norm change could be facilitated.

The analysis of the longitudinal, qualitative data of both the girls and their main caregivers sought to identify *when* in the girls' life – until 2018/19 – she demonstrates 'glitches' in the gender socialization process; *where* – in which areas of her life – she demonstrates 'glitches'; *how* these 'glitches' present – either as a verbal comment, critique, attitude, or described behaviour; and, most significantly, to explore *why* this 'glitch' may have occurred. All four strands of investigation are valuable for informing gender transformative interventions, and all four depend on both the longitudinal and qualitative nature of this research study.

To investigate the *when* and *where*, longitudinal analysis was conducted for all of the cohort girls still involved in the study in 2017–19, creating a map of 'glitches' for each girl. In this way, commonalities could be observed in each cohort girl, country, region and between regions, as well as evidence of particular circumstances where certain girls demonstrated more or stronger challenges to gendered norms. In categorizing the *how*, social science literature surrounding 'resistance' identifies verbal and behavioural, individual, collective and institutional acts of resistance against any given dominant discourse, norm or system (Hollander and Einwohner, 2004; Scott, 1989). This qualitative study data allows for verbal and described behavioural 'glitches' to be observed in the individual girls and their family members. Though verbal-only observations of 'glitches' represent a limitation in terms of observing the wider impact of attitudes which challenge gendered norms on individual and group behaviours, they are indications of the vital first steps towards social transformation.

The exploration of *why* girls challenge, rather than reiterating gendered norms, is both the most interesting and difficult factor to observe. This analysis was carried out by adapting the theory of gender socialization (UNICEF, 2017), which identifies the individual-, social- and structural-level influences which communicate gendered social norms to an individual, and to investigate instead the influencing factors which appear to help disrupt the process.

Main findings

- Early adolescence is a key point in the life course for identity formation and heightened awareness of gendered norms, making it a critical point for interventions to disrupt – rather that ingrain – gender-inequitable attitudes and practices.
- The process of challenging gendered norms and disrupting gender socialization is not linear – it varies and fluctuates across time as well as across different aspects of girls' lives, creating limited but powerful windows of opportunity for norm change.
- Social-level influences – household dynamics and the wider community – are the most significant for an individual in reproducing or challenging gendered social norms. Understanding a girl's full, and unique, social context allows for the identification of key people and spaces where there is the potential for disruption.
- Structural-level laws, discourse related to gender equality and socioeconomic factors show evidence of influencing gender roles in households and gender-equitable attitudes and should be taken into account in policy and programming. This is particularly the case for attitudes concerning child and early marriage, girls'

education, gender equality and rights; however, laws prohibiting corporal punishment appear to have limited effect in most of these nine contexts.

- A number of obstacles persist in preventing the translation of attitudes which challenge gendered social norms into changed behaviours – principally the real and perceived risks of gender based violence (GBV), which limit girls' freedoms; the use of corporal punishment, which limits girls' agency; and harmful norms, which associate violence and aggression with 'masculinity'.

Longitudinal case studies

Three case studies will be used to present these findings: Margaret in Benin, Juliana in Brazil and Ly in Vietnam. Further detail can be found in Plan International UK's series of regional reports 'Real Choices, Real Lives: Girls Challenging the Gender Rules' (2019a, 2019b, 2019c). To construct and analyse longitudinal case studies through the lens of gender socialization, the qualitative data held for each girl was mapped to present the girl's own attitudes and described behaviours in relation to the presence/absence, attitudes and behaviours of key people in her life, her socioeconomic status, education and academic progress, physical and cognitive development, and evidence of her interactions with social- and structural-level institutions and concepts concerning gender norms. Looking at where an individual appears to 'accept' gendered expectations and reiterate gendered social norms, as well as where they appear to challenge said expectations and norms, enabled a greater understanding of the factor(s) – often a combination of more than one – which contributed to a shift. Along with a case study, a timeline of the 'glitches' to the gender socialization process demonstrated by a girl was used to track constants and changes in her attitudes and behaviours regarding gendered norms.

Box 1.1: Margaret, Benin

Margaret is 11 years old and the second eldest child in a family of six: she has an older sister, aged 16, two younger brothers, 9 and 6, and a younger sister, aged 2. Margaret was living with her mother, father and four siblings in a village in the south-western Couffo department of Benin until 2017 when she was sent to live with her paternal aunt, uncle and 13-year-old female cousin because "she was not obeying her parents" (Interviewer observation,

2017). Both of Margaret's parents work – her mother as a farmer and seller of cornmeal, and her father as a seasonal farmer and carpenter – but the household income is not always stable. In Margaret's aunt's home, both her aunt and uncle work: her aunt as a seller and her uncle as a primary school teacher. All of Margaret's siblings and cousins of school age are attending school. However, both Margaret and her older sister (16) have repeated primary school grades – Margaret repeated Grade 2 and then Grade 3 twice, which means she is three years behind for her age. Margaret's family hope that she will succeed in finishing her BAC[3] and discuss the importance of girls' education primarily in relation to their daughters' capacity to look after their parents in the future. Margaret would like to go to university and thinks that her parents want her to be a midwife or policewoman. She herself would like to be rich, a nun and unmarried with no children. In both the parental and the aunt's home, the division of labour is strict and according to gendered expectations of roles, with women performing all household chores apart from in exceptional circumstances such as illness or pregnancy. Margaret and her older sister are allocated household chores while her brothers are not. Her father regards older females teaching girls to do household tasks as preparation for their future, as he commented in 2016, "they train them and then they marry". Margaret is closer to her father than her mother, she confides in him and says she admires him "the most" because he gives her things "straight away" when she asks.

Summary of 'glitches' timeline:

- *2014, notices a difference:* "No my junior brothers are too young for domestic chores, but other boys of my age do domestic chores too. No, it's not in all the homes. In many homes they don't do anything, they just play."
- *2014, attitude and described behaviour:* [How does she feel about the type/quantity of chores she is allocated?] "Sometimes I cry when I don't want to do it. No, I always do it in the end. I realize that it's not too much for me, but sometimes I wish I could have more time to play."
- *2014, father's description of behaviour:* "When I observe my daughter Margaret, I think of moving her to Cotonou, to stay with my [older] sister. Because when I speak to her, she doesn't listen, she's not obedient and she does not fear me."
- *2015, notices a difference:* "Our mother gives us our jobs, but the boys refuse to do any domestic chores so it's me and my sister who have to do it."
- *2016, describes behaviour:* "I don't do anything in the house. I don't do the tasks my mother gives me, I do what I want."
- *2016, father's description of behaviour:* "Margaret is not a very well-behaved girl, she doesn't obey us, she is headstrong and afraid of no-one."

- *2017, notices a difference:* "Yes, I think there is a difference; men cultivate the land while women do all the domestic chores, fetch water, go to the mill and sell products. Girls also do these things, but boys do nothing."
- *2017, acceptance of norm:* "I think it's fair because it's the duty of women and girls to be responsible for domestic chores."
- *2017, acceptance of norm:* "I would make the effort to do [what my parents ask of me] because I wouldn't want my parents to think of me as disobedient."

Early adolescence and the non-linear process of disruption

In 2018, the average age of girls participating in Plan UK's 'Real Choices, Real Lives' cohort study was 12, falling into the category of early adolescence, which, though different for each individual girl, has been found to be a critical period of identity development. The cohort data shows that while stronger for some girls than others, the physical and emotional changes that come with the first stages of puberty often represent a catalyst for family and wider society to increasingly view girls as young adults rather than children and enforce gendered expectations of behaviour more strictly. In some cases this can be due to understandings that upon beginning menstruating girls are at higher risk of gender-based violence including rape, of early pregnancy, as well as of early marriage, and the gendered norms enforced are often intended to protect girls; however, they also perpetuate gender-inequitable attitudes and practices.

The cohort data demonstrates that for some girls, the increasing emphasis from family members and the wider community on what is 'acceptable' for them to do as girls, where it is 'acceptable' for them to go as girls, and what they are expected to contribute to their households and communities as girls, ingrains and solidifies a girl's gendered attitudes and sees her reproducing said gendered norms. However, for other girls this heightened awareness of gendered expectations, and how they have a disproportionate impact on girls' rather than boys' freedoms and ability to choose how they spend their time, can instead spark a push-back against gendered norms and provide a potential window of opportunity to create alternative outcomes to the gender socialization process. The longitudinal nature of the cohort data enables us to observe how and where the girls can 'switch' from expressing relative acceptance of the gendered expectations of them to expressing a challenge to them, and vice versa.

This longitudinal analysis also highlights an important point, however: that the process of challenging or 'disrupting' gender socialization is not always linear – that is, while some girls first notice gendered differences in expectations of behaviour for themselves and their male peers, and then move on to questioning, critiquing and eventually challenging those gender norms, for other girls this process is somewhat more complex. The data shows that for some cohort girls in early adolescence the period of time where they begin to question gender norms can be cut short or reversed due to a shift in the influencing factors in their lives.

Looking at Margaret's case in Benin (see Box 1.1), we can see where critique of gender norms related to an inequitable division of labour in the household – where females bear the burden of domestic responsibilities – appears to be 'stamped out' by an apparent intervention from extended family. Margaret demonstrates a number of varying 'types' of glitches to the gender socialization process, from identifying gendered differences for herself and her brothers in 2014 and 2015, to describing behaviour which challenges these expectations in 2016 – which is also reflected in her father's complaints about her disobedient behaviour in 2014 and 2016. The potential to disrupt these norms within Margaret's household, however small, appeared to disappear in 2017 when Margaret expressed attitudes which support a gendered division of labour and traditional gender roles.

Using the longitudinal and qualitative data collected from Margaret and her family, we can see that in 2017 Margaret was sent to live with her extended family – namely her paternal aunt, uncle and female cousin. Her father indicated that this was his plan for Margaret as early as 2014, specifically due to Margaret's behaviour which did not reproduce the gendered expectations that as his daughter she should obey and 'fear' him, and the role he felt his sister would play in 'correcting' Margaret's behaviour. In 2017, Margaret also vocalized attitudes which conformed to her father's expectations that she obey him. In response to being asked if she felt she could say no to her parents when they ask her to do something she doesn't want to do, she stated that she unequivocally would, so as not to challenge the expectation that she be obedient to them.

Margaret's case enables us to investigate not only one of the most common areas where the cohort girls show glitches in gender socialization – the unequal and gendered division of labour – but how shifting dynamics in a girl's social and familial sphere can reverse or 'stunt' her challenges to gender norms. This case also underlines the importance of context-specific and sensitive analysis to inform social norm change interventions, as in Benin the practice of 'child fostering' – where girls like Margaret, are sent to live with extended family members, often specifically to be cared for by female family members – is common in many parts of the country.

Box 1.2: Juliana, Brazil

Juliana is 13 years old, and lives with her maternal grandparents and younger sister (11) in an urban area in the north-eastern state of Maranhão in Brazil. Until 2018, Juliana had frequent contact with her mother (28), step-father (33) and two half-brothers (8 and 4) who lived nearby until they moved out of the area. Juliana's grandmother is her main carer and she appeared to have no contact with her father – who was imprisoned for some time for gang-related activities – until 2018 when she describes having some communication with him. The household has seen a number of shifts in dynamics due to the 2014 economic crisis in Brazil, which led to Juliana's grandfather being unemployed for much of the period 2014–18 and Juliana's grandmother becoming the family's breadwinner as a domestic worker, having never previously worked. In 2018, Juliana's grandfather became employed as a janitor, shifting the family dynamics once again. Education is a priority for Juliana's grandmother, and the low quality of post-primary schooling in the area is a major concern, impacting Juliana's academic progress. Juliana is in the correct school grade for her age and would like to attend university and work with computers. Prior to becoming employed, Juliana's grandmother carried out the majority of domestic tasks in the home, with some help from Juliana and her sister, however this changed when her husband became unemployed and she began working, and Juliana's grandfather began to take part in household work for the first time. Juliana has a close and positive relationship with her grandmother, who has expressed highly gendered attitudes with regard to traditional roles, apart from during the period of time she was the family breadwinner where she demonstrated some shifts in her attitude.

Summary of 'glitches' timeline

- *2015, acceptance of norm:* "I make my bed, tidy my dressing table and sweep the floor. I have to sweep the house too, because my uncle tells me to do it … I like washing the dishes … [I don't like] sweeping the house, because my arm hurts."
- *2016, notices a difference and attitude shift:* "There are men who wash the dishes, sweep the house, and there are men who don't, so the women have to do it every day. [Do you think this is right, this is fair?] No, I don't think so."

- *2017, describes a shift in dynamics:* "[Males and females] do the same things ... [for example] when we finish lunch, everyone washes their own plate."
- *2018, describes another shift in dynamics:* "I take care of the whole house, because they [my grandparents] can't be here all the time ... because they're working, both of them, and I stay at home alone, together with my sister."

Further areas showing 'glitches' in 2018

- *2016, reiterates norm:* "[It is important for girls to be beautiful] because if they were ugly the boys would not like them."
- *2018, attitude shift:* "For me, appearance doesn't matter."
- *2017, awareness of expectations:* "My grandfather, he likes me to behave well in places and he likes me to play girls' games, because I like playing ball, so he lets me play sometimes, but he likes me to play with girls' things, to do girls' things."
- *2018, challenges norm:* "They [my school friends] make fun of me, they say I'm a tomboy, that I'm always playing ball, all the time, with the boys ... then I tell them that this is sexist, because a girl can play ball just like a boy."

Social- and structural-level influences of disruption

The theory of gender socialization which outlines the varying levels of influence in an individual's life contributing to the reproduction of gender norms – individual-level, social-level and structural-level influences – was inverted in this analysis to investigate which of these influences could instead be facilitating girls to *challenge* the gender socialization process. The interaction of the three levels is often complex and specific to a particular girl's context, including her personal development on the individual level, however, the cohort data broadly suggests that social-level influences in the family, household, peer group and community represent the most significant influencing factors during early adolescence. It is evident from the data that the attitudes and behaviours of a girl's main carers and male peers regarding gender norms and roles play a central role in her expression of challenges to these norms.

The longitudinal data shows that a number of the cohort girls are exposed to non-normative gender roles in their households – in some cases for an extended period of time, such as in single-parent families or polygamous families, and in others due to short-term circumstances, such as illness, pregnancy or shifts in the employment of household members. In the latter case, there is evidence that structural-level factors such as economics and national labour legislation can impact traditional gender roles on the social level and provide an opportunity for individuals to be exposed to alternative household structures.

Looking at the case of Juliana in Brazil (Box 1.2), the shifts in her grandparents' behaviour in the household from traditional gender roles – male breadwinner and female home maker – to female breadwinner and indications of a more equitable division of labour in the home, can be seen to impact not only the division of labour in the home, but the gendered attitudes of Juliana's grandmother, and the attitudes and behaviours of Juliana herself. Though born out of necessity – due to the 2014 economic crisis in Brazil leading to Juliana's grandfather becoming unemployed – rather than an active attempt to redress gender-inequitable practices in the home, the impact on Juliana's household is significant, as earlier in the study both of her grandparents expressed particularly strong gendered attitudes. Juliana's grandmother also explained how her informal employment as a domestic worker was impacted by labour law reforms in Brazil requiring all employees to have a formal contract, the details of which, including minimum wage, holiday pay and back payment for previous years' work, she successfully negotiated with her employer. This enabled the precarious nature of her employment as a domestic worker to offer more financial stability to the household, as well as appearing to give her further confidence to manage the family's finances and request her husband share the load of household work. Juliana shows awareness of an inequitable division of labour in 2016 and criticizes it, then in 2017 describes a shift in her household dynamics. However, once again highlighting the often limited windows of opportunity presented by such circumstances, by 2018 her grandfather had found a job, and the practicalities of both carers being in employment then required Juliana to carry the burden of looking after the home.

While investigating the extent of the impact these shifts have had on Juliana's attitudes towards gender is difficult, in 2017 and 2018 the qualitative data shows her to be significantly more vocal and critical of gendered norms such as those dictating that football is an unacceptable sport for girls; not only does she dismiss this idea and continue to play the sport, but challenges her peers who bully her for it. The interaction between structural-, social- and individual-level factors is clearly complex, and Juliana's case provides an example of why looking at all influencing factors in a girls' life is necessary to identify where, when and with whom valuable points of intervention may present themselves.

Box 1.3: Ly, Vietnam

Ly is 13 years old and lives along with her mother in a village in the Quang Ngai Province on the south-central coast of Vietnam. Ly's father died before she was born, and her maternal grandmother lived in the home until her death in 2018. Ly's mother's most stable source of income comes from farming, but she takes on secondary activities such as bricklaying and bundling wool. Ly is in Grade 7, the correct school year for her age and, having previously been described as "lazy" in studying, Ly aspires to go to university, something her mother thinks is out of reach. Ly is described by her mother and the researchers as cognitively mature and has started menstruating, however she reports knowing little about sexual and reproductive health and her mother's advice is for her to keep her distance from boys and she prohibits her from going out in the evening. Despite living in an all-female house, Ly is very aware of a gendered division of labour in the community, which she criticizes. Ly and her mother both describe having a strained relationship, in particular because Ly rarely obeys her mother and from 2015 has requested payment for helping her mother with household tasks. Ly's mother describes her daughter as "stubborn" and "not docile", among aspects of Ly's behaviour which diverge from expectations of girls in the community.

Summary of 'glitches' timeline

- *2016, reiterates norm:* "Yes [it is important for girls to be beautiful] because there are many people who love beautiful girls."
- *2016, describes behaviour:* "I make friends with everyone. I hang out with them but if they tease me, I will hit them."
- *2016, mother's description of behaviour:* "She doesn't like wearing skirts, [she] likes boys' clothes, she often wears a cap instead of a wide-brimmed hat … she wears men's clothes."
- *2017, mother's description of behaviour:* "She has not been docile, still stubborn."
- *2018, describes behaviour:* "Everyone in my class is scared of me because I am aggressive."
- *2018, describes behaviour:* "I look like a boy … yes [my style has changed] I am more manly [Did you choose your clothes or did your mother?] I did [it] for myself."

Further areas showing 'glitches' in 2018

- *2016, reiterates norm:* "I would like to marry a doctor. Have one boy and one girl. [The girl next door says if there are two girls, there will be no one to take care of their parents after they get married]."
- *2018, attitude shift:* "No [I don't want to get married or have children] because I don't like it."
- *2014, notices a difference:* "Boys do not have to do housework. They just go to play. They play skipping, football."
- *2018, describes behaviour:* "[At school I am a] team leader ... [I should] clean up, but I never do. I asked some boys to clean up for me ... I request them to and they must follow."

Harmful norms of 'masculinity' and persistent obstacles to social norm change

The analysis of the longitudinal cohort data to investigate where, when, how and why the girls challenge gendered norms also underlines the obstacles to gendered social norm change that persist in preventing the realization of alternative outcomes for girls and boys. The most evident and common barrier experienced by the girls is the risk and prevalence of violence in their lives. Violence takes various forms and is of varying severity across the cohort; however, in all cases it represents either an obstruction to the girls' ability to challenge gendered norms, or a factor which perpetuates and ingrains harmful concepts of 'masculinity' and 'femininity'. The use of corporal punishment at home and in school, the real and perceived risks of gender-based violence from males in the wider community, and in the Latin America and Caribbean countries in particular, community and gang violence are consistently reported by cohort girls and their families. Risks of GBV are cited by many parents and carers as the basis for placing increasing limitations on the girls' movement and access to spaces, and while there are girls who identify a disparity between their own freedoms and those of their male peers and criticize this, there is little evidence of active challenges to these restrictions, as evidently to do so would likely require the girls putting themselves in danger. While such expectations of behaviour intend to maintain the safety of girls, rather than addressing the root causes of these risks of violence, the onus is placed on girls and women to protect themselves from males, reiterating gendered norms which associate males with violence and females with vulnerability.

The use of corporal punishment – though illegal at school in all nine cohort countries – is prevalent in the study data both at home and at school, and can be seen not only to limit girls' abilities to use their voices and exert agency, but also to play a role in the normalization of violence and its association with 'masculinity'. Across the cohort, but in the South-East Asia countries in particular, the cohort girls report witnessing their male peers being subjected to more frequent and severe physical punishment and violent discipline. The impact of this, from the perspective of the girls, on understandings of gender and violence are important to highlight.

Looking at the case of Ly in Vietnam (see Box 1.3), we see how exposure on the social level to harmful associations between violence and males can interact with an individual's development of concepts of gender and identity during early adolescence. Until 2016, Ly reiterated a number of gendered norms which dictate 'acceptable' appearances and behaviours for girls. After this point, Ly expressed attitudes and behaviours which strongly challenged these norms, reflected in her mother's descriptions of Ly's behaviour and appearance. In order to challenge the gendered labels widely iterated in the South-East Asia cohort which categorize males as 'strong' and females as 'weak', Ly describes how she takes on characteristics traditionally associated with males. Descriptions of her aggressive behaviour, how her peers fear her, indicating that she has, or would, physically hit a peer are expressed by Ly alongside statements identifying herself as "more manly"; and her mother outlines Ly's changing preferences for traditionally men's, rather than women's, clothes. Ly is one of a number of cohort girls who describe themselves as violent or aggressive, as partaking in traditionally 'male' sports, wearing traditionally 'male' clothes, and making this association with being more like a boy and less like a girl. In this way, the cohort girls explicitly demonstrate the binary nature of gendered norms and how often the only way to realize a desire to challenge restrictive social expectations of 'femininity' for girls appears to be to embody concepts of 'masculinity'. As boys and men are depicted by those around the cohort girls as a threat and a source of violence, perpetuated by the normalization of their public subjection to corporal punishment, these harmful gendered norms are not only reproduced, but reinforced by the girls' attempts to embody 'masculinity' in their rejection of acceptable 'feminine' behaviours.

Conclusions

Analysis of the 'Real Choices, Real Lives' cohort study data underlines the unique value that longitudinal, qualitative data brings to research of the complex concepts of gender and social norms. Observing the gender socialization process of an individual requires an in-depth and long-term engagement with the varying influencing factors and shifting dynamics in their life in order to fully understand the dynamic nature of socialization and identify markers of where norms do not perfectly reproduce. While analysis of qualitative data can present difficulties in terms translation into 'generalizable' findings, arguably qualitative longitudinal data is more able to capture nuances of change, and hence detect 'glitches', than quantitative data. At the same time, observing the direct voice of girls over time allows us to see the change through the girls' eyes, which facilitates the ability to capture shifts. In this way, longitudinal and qualitative data can also enable a better understanding of progress on the objectives of SDG 5 by presenting substantive indicators of social change rather than quantified measures of equality.

To advance the empowerment of women and girls and achieve equality between the sexes it is necessary to look to the roots of gender-inequitable attitudes and behaviours, which lie in the critical process of gender socialization where the gender 'rules' are formed. While understandings of young children's development have benefited from focused research, the significance of gender in forming identities in early adolescence has been largely overlooked until relatively recently. As a period where girls are increasingly required to embody social expectations of 'femininity' and the role of a woman in family, community and wider society – often in stark contrast to the relative freedoms they experienced in childhood – early adolescence represents a moment of heightened awareness of gendered expectations, which can either reinforce the reproduction of gendered norms or in fact incite a pushback against them.

The 'Real Choices, Real Lives' data demonstrates that social-level influences are highly significant in facilitating moments of disruption to the gender socialization process, as well as of course in ingraining gendered norms. However, the data also shows that the social level is unique to each girl, and understanding how her relationships with the people, institutions and social structures around her develop and change over time is essential when considering potential points of intervention. The fluctuating nature of gender socialization and the 'when', 'where' and 'how' of its disruption is evident in the cohort data, which, while highlighting the complex and sometimes narrow windows of opportunity for norm change, also indicate circumstances which may not have previously been considered as significant for intervention, such as the impact of the economic crisis in Brazil on

Juliana's household dynamics, and of the practice of child fostering on Margaret's attitudes and behaviours in Benin.

The wider longitudinal analysis of the nine countries involved in the 'Real Choices, Real Lives' cohort study found that all participating girls had shown at least one instance of a 'glitch' in the reproduction of gendered norms by 2018, by identifying differences in expectations between themselves and their male peers, questioning this disparity, or directly challenging these norms. These findings evidence the potential power within each girl to reject inequitable norms and realize alternative outcomes for their futures; however, the persistence of major obstacles to norm change, such as the continued prevalence of violence in girls' lives, means that without the alignment of wider social and political factors, social transformation remains limited.

Notes

[1] The original sample in 2006 included 146 girls; however, there were a number of deaths in the first year and there have been dropouts. Over the years, some girls and/or their families have been unavailable (for example through migration).

[2] The term 'glitch' was developed during this data analysis by researchers at Plan International UK to indicate where an individual shows some level of disruption to the gender socialization.

[3] The baccalauréat is a French qualification that students are required to take to graduate from high school.

References

Abebe, K.Z., Jones, K.A., Culyba, A.J., Feliz, N.B., Anderson, H., Torres, J. et al (2018) Engendering healthy masculinities to prevent sexual violence: rationale for and design of the Manhood 2.0 trial. *Contemporary Clinical Trials* 71: 18–32.

Butler, J. (1993) *Bodies that Matter*. New York: Routledge.

Butler, J. (1999) *Gender Trouble: Feminism and the Subversion of Identity*. New York: Routledge.

Butler, J. (2009) Imitation and gender insubordination. In L. Storey (Ed) *Cultural Theory and Popular Culture: A Reader* (4th edn, pp 373–87). Harlow: Pearson Education.

Hollander, J.A. & Einwohner, R.L. (2004) Conceptualizing resistance. *Sociological Forum* 19(4): 533–54.

Plan International UK (2019a) Real choices, real lives: girls challenging the gender rules (Benin, Togo, and Uganda). March 2019. London: Plan International UK. Available at https://plan-uk.org/file/plan-uk-real-choices-real-lives-report-2019pdf/download?token=1XZdZ07F

Plan International UK (2019b) Real choices, real lives: girls challenging the gender rules (Cambodia, the Philippines, and Vietnam). August 2019. London: Plan International UK. Available at https://plan-uk.org/file/rcrl-girls-challenging-the-gender-rules-cambodia-the-philippines-and-vietnam-full-reportpdf/download?token=5h8Q8s4Q

Plan International UK (2019c) Real choices, real lives: girls challenging the gender rules (Brazil, the Dominican Republic, and El Salvador). September 2019. London: Plan International UK. Available at https://plan-uk.org/file/girls-challenging-the-gender-rules-lac-full-reportpdf/download?token=gIFoumI9

Scott, J. (1989) Everyday forms of resistance. *Copenhagen Papers in East and Southeast Asian Studies* 4: 33–62.

United Nations (2015) The future we want: outcome document for the Sustainable Development Agenda. Available at https://sustainabledevelopment.un.org/content/documents/733FutureWeWant.pdf

United Nations Children's Fund (UNICEF) (2017) What is gender socialisation and why does it matter? 18 August. Available at https://blogs.unicef.org/evidence-for-action/what-is-gender-socialization-and-why-does-it-matter/

2

Unequal Educational Trajectories: The Case of Ethiopia

Ilze Plavgo

Introduction

Obtaining education is widely acknowledged to constitute one of the main starting conditions for later opportunities over the life course, regarded as a quintessential means to improve productivity, promote a healthy lifestyle, empower and increase civic participation, raise individual capabilities, and reduce intergenerational transmission of poverty (Buchmann and Hannum, 2001; Hanushek and Woessmann, 2008; Sen, 1999). Considerable progress has been made in terms of increasing enrolment rates at a primary and secondary school level all over the world, especially after the World Education Forum in Dakar in 2000 in which the international community committed to achieving Education for All by 2015 (UNESCO, 2017a), and the Millennium Development Summit of 2000 in which the world's leaders committed to meeting the Millennium Development Goals (MDGs), among which was universalization of primary school enrolments and gender parity (UN, 2015). The steepest progress in pupil's enrolments has taken place in sub-Saharan Africa, where primary school enrolment rates between 1990 and 2015 on average increased from 52% to 80% (UN, 2015). One of the most notable increases was observed in Ethiopia, the case study of this chapter, where net primary school enrolments grew from 19% in 1994 to 85% in 2015, and net secondary school enrolments increased from 11% in 1999 to 31% in 2015 (World Bank, 2019).

Despite this progress, recent evidence shows that getting children into school has not translated into knowledge acquisition. According to UNESCO, the latest estimated share of children not achieving minimum proficiency levels in reading and mathematics by the time of primary school completion age in sub-Saharan Africa was about 85% on average (UNESCO UIS, 2017: 7; UNESCO, 2017a). It is becoming more and more evident that children's learning outcomes depend not only on school availability but also on school quality and home environments where learning and decision making about children's educational trajectories take place. Educational outcomes can be highly stratified by family background due to differences in living conditions in early childhood and parental resources during school age. This type of stratification – conventionally called inequality of educational opportunity – can be either equalized or further exacerbated depending on the educational systems and policies in place.

The most recent step towards stronger international commitment to address the issues of quality and inequality in education was the agreement of the Sustainable Development Goal 4 (SDG 4) in 2015. The main contribution of SDG 4 which sets it apart from all previous international commitments is its emphasis on learning quality and equity at all levels of education (United Nations Sustainable Development, 2015). To identify appropriate interventions for reducing inequalities in learning opportunities, it is important to identify the sources and timing of disparities in educational trajectories. This chapter studies inequality of educational opportunities in low-income contexts, analysing to what extent and at what transition points children's educational opportunities become socially stratified. Firstly, it looks at the extent to which children's cognitive development and educational trajectories differ by the family's socioeconomic status (SES) and whether disparities vary across the different educational levels. Secondly, it studies whether transition to higher levels of education is sensitive to children's initial cognitive endowments, and whether this varies by parental SES. The case of Ethiopia was selected since it has witnessed one of the highest levels of educational expansion in the world after extensive school reforms in 1994, while inequalities in primary and secondary school progression persist. Ethiopia's child population is the second largest in Africa after Nigeria, and the ninth largest in the world (World Bank, 2019). Enabling equal educational opportunities in this part of the world will be a prerequisite to achieving the global SDG 4.

This chapter contributes to existing literature in two substantive ways. First, it uses a direct assessment of cognitive abilities measured early in childhood prior to the time when educational decisions were made, allowing study of the relationship between initial endowments and later educational transitions. The longitudinal design of this study minimizes the risk of endogeneity and reverse causality since it is possible to control for the order of events. Second, it tests whether differences in initial cognitive abilities are reinforced or compensated by families' educational investment decisions across three transition points of the educational cycle: transition to upper primary, secondary and higher education. Unlike cross-sectional data, the longitudinal design of this survey allows us to observe the same individuals' living conditions, cognitive development and school progression from early childhood to late adolescence, enabling educational trajectories to be studied without imposing any assumptions about the sequence of events.

The data used come from the Young Lives long-term longitudinal study, which followed the lives of two birth cohorts born around 1994 and 2001 in four countries, including 3,000 children in Ethiopia. Household and child-level surveys were carried out in five rounds every three to four years between 2002 and 2016. Findings point at two main sources of inequality of educational opportunity. Firstly, children from disadvantaged socioeconomic backgrounds tend to develop lower cognitive abilities early in childhood, already before formal schooling begins. Evidence also suggests that parents and schools reinforce this initial inequality since children with lower cognitive abilities are less likely to transit to higher levels of education. Secondly, also when comparing children with the same levels of initial cognitive abilities, poorer children tend to have lower chances to make transitions to higher levels of education compared to their more privileged peers, with increasing gaps at each educational transition.

The chapter proceeds with a section reviewing key theories and existing empirical findings on how disparities in educational outcomes develop in childhood. It then proceeds with a section outlining the context of Ethiopia, a description of the data and the research strategy, a findings section and a conclusion discussing the findings and their policy implications.

Theories and evidence on the mechanisms behind inequality of educational opportunity

Social stratification researchers have put forth several explanations as to why educational trajectories tend to differ by parental socioeconomic status. Following Boudon (1974), family conditions determine children's educational outcomes through two main pathways: indirectly by having an effect on children's cognitive abilities and scholastic performance, and directly by the decisions and choices made about educational transitions net of children's cognitive endowments and grades. These two pathways are called the primary and secondary effects of social origin, respectively. Primary effects indicate the extent to which a family's SES affects individuals' educational transitions through cognitive abilities or acquired performance. They operate through the transmission of genetic traits and through family influences and daily interactions, with parents transmitting sociocultural and educational resources that are crucial for cognitive and non-cognitive development (Blossfeld and von Maurice, 2011; Hackman et al, 2010). Disparities by SES in cognitive abilities are developed in early childhood due to differences in living conditions and cognitive stimulus, and tend to accumulate and reinforce with age (Carneiro and Heckman, 2005; Heckman, 2006; Rose et al, 2016: 17–19).

Secondary effects or choice effects are the SES gaps in educational outcomes that persist after holding cognitive abilities and previous performance constant. These effects stem from the assumption that parental SES affects the level of sensitivity to costs associated with educational investments (Ress and Azzolini, 2014). Disparities in educational choices are especially prominent at each of the educational transition points when families need to make decisions about their children's continuation to higher levels of education and about the school tracks and school types. Disparities in choices are driven by differences in economic and social resources as well as the motivation to avoid downward social mobility under the assumption that parents want their children to reach at least the same level of socioeconomic status as their own (Breen and Goldthorpe, 1997; Erikson and Jonsson, 1996). Figure 2.1 presents a simplified causal mechanism describing these pathways.

Figure 2.1: Causal mechanism describing primary and secondary effects of social origin

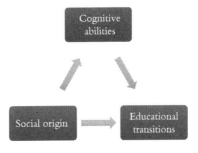

Source: Author's adaptation from Erikson et al (2005: Fig 2a, p 9732)

A growing base of evidence investigating parental investment behaviour in human capital concludes that parents tend to reinforce initial educational differences by investing more educational human capital in the more able children, thus intensifying inequality in educational opportunities (Ayalew, 2005; Behrman et al, 1994). As an example, Bacolod and Ranjan (2008) study how household wealth and child endowments jointly affect family decisions regarding children's schooling and work in Philippines, and find that high-ability children are more likely to be in school relative to low-ability children. Similarly, Dendir (2014) studies the relationship between children's cognitive abilities and parental decisions regarding school enrolment and work in Ethiopia and finds evidence of reinforcing parental investment as higher-ability children are more likely to be enrolled in school. These studies, however, do not assess if this relationship varies at different educational transition points, and do not study inequalities by parental socioeconomic status.

The secondary effects of social origin suggest that the observed reinforcing association does not apply to the same extent to families of all socioeconomic backgrounds. While less advantaged families are likely to condition educational investment decisions on their assessment of a child's cognitive and scholastic abilities, educational trajectories of children from more advantaged families are less dependent on prior endowments (Boudon, 1998; Breen and Goldthorpe, 1997; Goldthorpe, 1996). Previous research in a number of industrialized countries shows that lower grades are less consequential for students from more advantaged socioeconomic origins as they disproportionately move to higher levels of education also in the case of lower grades and other negative prior conditions (Bernardi, 2014; Blossfeld et al, 2016; Torche, 2016). This concept is referred to as the compensatory advantage of social origin. Not much is known, however, about whether this mechanism is generalizable to other regions in the world where educational systems are currently expanding and where variation in school quality is greater.

Based on the described theories and previous empirical findings, the following hypotheses are put forth for the case study of Ethiopia: H1 The level of early cognitive endowments varies by parental SES and is associated with later educational transition decisions; H2 Disparities in educational transitions by level of cognitive abilities accumulate and reinforce with age; and H3 For higher-SES families, decisions regarding educational transitions are less dependent on children's initial cognitive abilities compared to low-SES families.

Context of Ethiopia

In the 1990s, the government of Ethiopia placed education at the centre of its development policy, and has had a good record in expanding access to formal education ever since. The current education system is based on the 1994 Education and Training Policy and follows a format of eight years of primary school, two years of general secondary education, and two years of preparatory secondary education. Primary school officially starts at age seven, and is divided into two cycles of primary education lasting for four years each. The focus of the first cycle of primary school (Grades 1–4) is on basic literacy and numeracy and automatic promotion is common, while the second cycle (Grades 5–8) provides general education and access to it depends on a pupil's grades during the first cycle. The medium of instruction at the primary school level is generally a local language (20 in total) up until Grade 4 or 6 depending on the region. In parallel, Amharic and English are taught as subjects since Amharic is the language of communication at a country level, while English is a medium of instruction for secondary and tertiary education. Since 1994, primary and secondary public schools have no tuition fees, while higher levels of education are based on cost-sharing of lodging and fees. The government also invests in expanding tertiary education, increasing the number of public universities from 8 in 2008 to 31 in 2013. Public investment in education is relatively high compared to other countries in the region, amounting to about 20% of total government spending in the 2000s and nearly 4% as a share of GDP (Woldehanna and Araya, 2016).

The central objective of the government's educational reform efforts that started in 1994 was to increase access to schooling, especially at a lower primary school level. This objective is largely achieved since most primary school age children attend the first cycle of primary education. School fee abolition was one of the main reforms aiming at increasing enrolment. Transition to upper primary and secondary school level, by contrast, is lower and is socially and regionally stratified despite school fee abolition. Disparities in school attendance and completion persist, especially by location, parental education, household wealth, family composition and birth order, among other factors (Mani et al, 2013; Woldehanna et al, 2008). A growing base of evidence shows that educational expansion was not accompanied with a sufficient increase of investments in school infrastructure and teachers, thus leading to deteriorating teaching quality due to increasingly overcrowded classrooms, lack of teachers and school resources, and in some cases a shift from full-time to part-time schooling (Bhalotra et al, 2015;

Riddell, 2003; Tomasevski, 2006; World Bank and UNICEF, 2009). In 2008, the government started implementing the General Education Quality Improvement Programme, designed to improve teaching quality at all public primary and secondary schools, and to support transition to tertiary education (Woldehanna and Araya, 2016). The government of Ethiopia has also ratified the Sustainable Development Goals, among which SDG 4 aims to eliminate gender disparities and to ensure more equitable access to all levels of education and vocational training (UNESCO, 2017b; United Nations Sustainable Development, 2015). It is therefore timely to assess what guides family decision making regarding educational investments, and to what extent children's chances to transit from lower to higher levels of education are socially stratified.

Data, variables and research strategy

This study uses data from the Young Lives longitudinal survey obtained from the UK Data Archive (Boyden, 2018). The Young Lives study followed the lives of two birth cohorts in five survey rounds between 2002 and 2016 in four low- and middle-income countries including Ethiopia. The average age of the older birth cohort (1,000 children) during the five survey rounds was 7, 12, 15, 19 and 22 years, respectively, while the average age of the younger cohort (1,999 children) was 1, 5, 8, 12 and 15. Extensive child-, household- and community-level questionnaires were performed to gather data on children's living conditions, family composition, cognitive development, mathematics skills, reading skills and school history, allowing children's educational trajectories to be tracked from early childhood to late adolescence. The Young Lives Ethiopia sampling was based on sentinel site surveillance, purposefully selecting 20 sites to meet the study objectives. Households were randomly selected in each site. The selected sites are located in five administrative regions: Addis Ababa, Amhara, Oromia, Southern Nations, Nationalities and Peoples' Region (SNNP) and Tigray, and provide a balanced representation of Ethiopia's geographical and cultural diversity (Young Lives, 2018).

Sample

The analysis is based on two birth cohort samples. The younger cohort sample – children born around 2001 and followed from age 1 until age 15 – is used to study educational trajectories during primary school. The older cohort sample – children born around 1994 and followed from age 8 until age 22 – is used to study transitions to secondary and tertiary education.

The younger cohort children were followed for five rounds from around age 1 until age 15 between 2002 (Round 1) and 2016 (Round 5). Out of a total of 1,999 observations surveyed in Round 1, most of the children were followed up until Round 5. The attrition rate of this longitudinal survey for the younger cohort is low (9.4% between Rounds 1 and 5), so the risk of a bias in the results due to attrition is unlikely. The final sample of the younger cohort children with non-missing data on all the variables of interest is 1,744 observations, which is 87.4% of the initial younger cohort sample.[1]

The older cohort children were followed from around age 8 (Round 1) until age 22 (Round 5). To study the transition to secondary education, information collected in the first four rounds is used since attrition up until the fourth round is relatively low (9%). The final sample with non-missing data on all the variables of interest is 870 observations, which is 91% of the initial sample of the older cohort. To study transition to tertiary education, information collected in Round 5 is used to capture the sampled individuals in early adulthood. Attrition for the older cohort in Round 5 is considerably higher as only 86% of the older cohort individuals surveyed in Round 4 were followed in Round 5 when they reached around age 22. As a result, the final sample with non-missing data for the analysis of transition to tertiary education is 752, which is 75% of the original older cohort sample. Attrition of 25% is high and can lead to a bias in the results. Further analyses showed that the adolescents who were more likely not to be followed in the last round on average had higher household wealth.[2] Thus, the findings of the third outcome variable measuring disparities in transition to vocational and tertiary education are conservative and should be interpreted with caution since they are based on a sub-sample of adolescents that excludes the more advantaged groups.

Variables

School transitions

The outcome variables of interest are school transitions throughout the educational cycle in Ethiopia. The first outcome variable is transition to the secondary cycle of primary education, which starts at Grade 5. A total of 81% of all children of the younger cohort had reached this level of education or higher by age 15. The second outcome analysed is transition to secondary education, which starts at Grade 9. A total of 59% of all children of the older cohort had reached this level of education or higher by age 19. The third outcome variable is transition to higher education (post-secondary, vocational or university). A total of 30% of all children of the more restricted older cohort surveyed in Round 5 had achieved this level by age 22.

Socioeconomic status

The socioeconomic status of a child's family is measured by household wealth at a time when the child was of primary school age. The wealth index is a composite measure of the household's economic status comprising housing quality, service quality and asset ownership. For the purposes of this study, the sample is divided into three equal groups by household wealth representing three levels of family's SES: lowest, middle and highest.

As a robustness check, SES is also measured in absolute terms by parental educational attainment representing the educational capital of the child's family. It is measured by the highest level of education achieved by parents or caretakers, selecting the highest educational level of the two. Children are divided into three categories by the highest level of parental education achieved: no formal education, incomplete primary and complete primary education or higher. The share of children with parents with no education, incomplete primary and complete primary education or higher is 45%, 26% and 28% respectively for the older cohort and 44%, 25% and 31% for the younger cohort.[3]

Cognitive abilities

The main mediating variable is the level of a child's cognitive ability in early childhood measured by the Peabody Picture Vocabulary Test (PPVT). The PPVT is a measure of receptive vocabulary achievement which was first carried out at around age 5 for the younger cohort and at age 12 for the older cohort. The task of the test was to select the picture that best represents the meaning of a word presented orally by the examiner. Tests were untimed, did not require reading on the part of the respondents, were performed individually at home and generally took about 25 minutes. Scores were computed by subtracting the number of errors from the ceiling item. Previous reliability and validity tests of the PPVT of the Young Lives surveys in Ethiopia show that tests perform well in capturing the variation in ability among children in the study sample (Cueto et al, 2009; Cueto and León, 2012). The PPVT z-score distribution by socioeconomic status is provided in Figure 2.2.

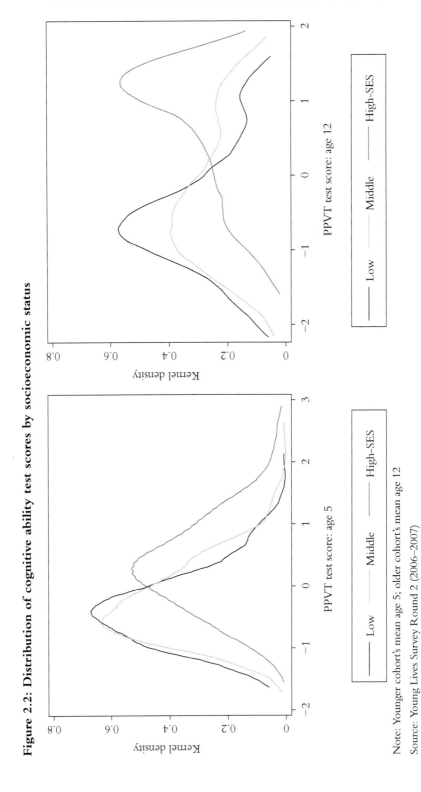

Figure 2.2: Distribution of cognitive ability test scores by socioeconomic status

Note: Younger cohort's mean age 5; older cohort's mean age 12

Source: Young Lives Survey Round 2 (2006–2007)

Table 2.1 lists descriptive statistics of individual and household variables in their original metrics for three samples which are used to study three educational outcomes measured at age 15, 19 and 22, respectively. Time-varying child and household characteristics are measured with a lag of seven years to capture children's and their families' circumstances when children were of school age. Children's cognitive abilities are measured with a lag of seven to ten years to capture their abilities in early childhood before educational decisions were made. In each of the three samples, about a half were female, the majority resided in rural areas and had parents with no or incomplete primary school.

Research strategy

A multivariate logistic regression model is used to estimate the effect of initial cognitive abilities and parental socioeconomic status on school transitions. To estimate whether families with a different socioeconomic status compensate or reinforce early disadvantage, an interaction term is introduced in the model to see if the effect of initial cognitive abilities on subsequent educational outcomes varies by family's SES. The model takes the following form:

$$E_{it} = \beta_0 + \beta_1 Ability_{i,t-2} + \beta_2 SES_{ij,t-1} + \beta_3 Ability_{i,t-2} \times SES_{ij,t-1} + \gamma X'_{ij,t-1} + \varepsilon_{ij} \tag{1}$$

where E_{it} is the educational status of individual i, expressed as a binary variable equal to 1 if the child made a transition to a given level of education by time t and 0 otherwise; $Ability_{i,t-2}$ is the child's cognitive ability in early childhood measured by a PPVT test score with a time lag of seven to ten years corresponding to the time before the educational level analysed; $SES_{i,t-1}$ indicates the socioeconomic status of the child's family measured with a time lag of seven years corresponding to school age one level below the educational level analysed; X'i,t–1 is a vector containing a set of child- and household-level covariates during school age to cancel out compositional differences that potentially affect children's educational status (age in months, gender, number of children in household by age group, region, ethnicity, area of residence, child's health status relative to peers and caretaker's age). Parameters β_1 and β_2 measure whether children's transition to higher levels of education is statistically directly associated with their cognitive abilities in early childhood and their family's

Table 2.1: Summary statistics: educational outcomes and individual variables

	Younger cohort		Older cohort		Older cohort	
	Age 15 (Round 1–5)		Age 19 (Round 1–4)		Age 22 (Round 1–5)	
	Mean	(sd)	Mean	(sd)	Mean	(sd)
Educational transition:						
Upper primary	0.81					
Secondary			0.59			
Vocational and tertiary					0.30	
Socioeconomic status (SES):						
Wealth index [a]	0.35	(0.19)	0.32	(0.19)	0.37	(0.18)
Parental education						
None	0.44		0.45		0.45	
Incomplete primary	0.25		0.26		0.28	
Complete primary/ higher	0.31		0.28		0.28	
Ability:						
PPVT score at around age 5	21.0	(11.5)				
PPVT score at around age 12			75.7	(26.3)	74.9	(26.1)
Other characteristics:						
Gender: female	0.47		0.47		0.47	
Age in months	181.0	(3.7)	228.7	(3.9)	264.3	(3.8)
Caretaker's age [a]	36.2	(9.0)	39.4	(9.7)	42.2	(9.5)
Number of children in household [a]						
Age 0–5	0.95	(0.83)	0.64	(0.76)	0.57	(0.71)
Age 6–12	0.81	(0.75)	1.07	(0.84)	1.19	(1.00)
Age 13–17	0.86	(0.88)	0.94	(0.83)	0.58	(0.67)
Child's health relative to peers [a,b]						
Same	0.39		0.49		0.49	
Better	0.49		0.44		0.43	
Worse	0.12		0.08		0.08	

Table 2.1: Summary statistics: educational outcomes and individual variables (continued)

	Younger cohort	Older cohort	Older cohort
Area of residence: rural [a]	0.65	0.64	0.65
Region [a]			
Tigray	0.21	0.21	0.20
Amhara	0.20	0.20	0.21
Oromiya	0.20	0.21	0.22
SNNP	0.25	0.23	0.23
Addis Ababa	0.14	0.14	0.14
Child's ethnic group:			
Amhara	0.29	0.29	0.30
Gurage	0.08	0.07	0.07
Oromo	0.21	0.21	0.20
Tigrian	0.23	0.23	0.22
Other	0.20	0.20	0.21
Observations	1,744	870	752

Note: Variables in their original metrics. [a] Observed with a seven-year lag. [b] Child's assessment of own health relative to other children of the same age.

socioeconomic status during school age, respectively; Parameter β_3 is the coefficient of interest estimating whether the effect of initial cognitive abilities on later educational transitions varies by family's SES. Parameter β_1 is expected to be positive (that is, a positive effect of higher initial cognitive abilities on later educational transitions). Parameter β_3 is expected to be negative in the case of a compensatory advantage (that is, low initial cognitive abilities are less consequential for higher-SES families), zero if the association between initial abilities and later school transitions does not differ by SES, and positive in case of a reinforcing effect of SES (that is, high cognitive abilities are more consequential for higher-SES families). Variables measuring the child's age in months and caretaker's age in years are centred, and the PPVT test score is standardized to have a mean of 0 and a standard deviation of 1 for easier interpretation of the regression results. All standard errors are clustered at sentinel site level, amounting to 21 clusters. The estimated coefficients are expressed as marginal probabilities to transit to a given level of education by time t.

Findings

The key questions that this section seeks to answer relate to the SDG 4 target of equal access to all levels of education and vocational training for all people irrespective of their gender, social origin and other characteristics. As educational systems become more meritocratic, it is generally expected that educational outcomes become less dependent on families' socioeconomic status and more dependent on children's cognitive endowments. To separate between the two, a longitudinal survey design is needed to distinguish between diverging educational trajectories due to initial endowments and due to family resources and choices net of initial endowments. The longitudinal design of the Young Lives survey allows educational trajectories of the same children to be observed over a period of 15 years and provides measures of early circumstances with a sufficient time lag before decisions regarding educational transitions are made. This design makes it possible to study the timing of divergence of children's educational trajectories and to analyse the pathways through which inequality in educational opportunities occurs. First, we look at the extent to which initial cognitive endowments vary by a family's SES. Second, we study the extent to which abilities determine transition to higher levels of education. Third, we analyse whether children with the same initial cognitive endowments have diverging educational transitions depending on their family's SES.[4] In correspondence with the SDG 4 target of equal access to all levels of education (UNESCO, 2017b), the educational trajectories studied in this section are transitions to upper primary, secondary and tertiary education.

The role of socioeconomic status in determining cognitive abilities

The second target of SDG 4 emphasizes the importance of equitable early childhood development so that all girls and boys are equally ready for primary education. This target requires early interventions since cognitive development is socially stratified early in childhood, a long time before children enter primary school. Figure 2.2 shows the distribution of cognitive ability test scores by socioeconomic status for a selected sample of children in Ethiopia. Findings are in line with previous research and show that children from families with a higher SES on average already score substantially better in cognitive ability tests before entering primary school, and that these disparities tend to accumulate and intensify with age. Previous research shows that unequal access to pre-school facilities explains some but not all the

Figure 2.3: Transition rates to higher levels of education by level of initial cognitive abilities

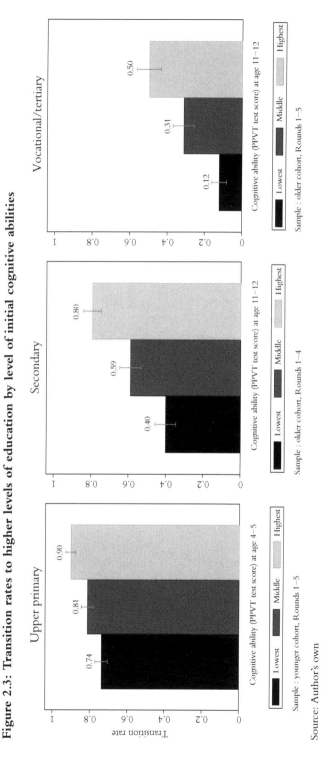

Source: Author's own

differences in cognitive development by socioeconomic status. As an example, Woldehanna (2016) examines the effect of pre-school access on children's cognitive performance in Ethiopia using the Young Lives data and finds that pre-school mediates about one third of the direct effect of a family's socioeconomic background and geographic location. These findings point to a need for more public investments not only in formal pre-school education but also in levelling of household living conditions to meet the target of reaching equitable cognitive performance and levelling of school readiness before children enter the classrooms.

The role of cognitive abilities in determining educational trajectories

The findings presented in Figure 2.3 confirm the crucial role played by cognitive abilities in determining children's educational trajectories. Low cognitive development during childhood is negatively associated with later educational transitions. On average, only 74% of children who scored poorly in the receptive vocabulary test measured before school age progressed to upper primary school, while as many as 90% of all children who scored highly made this transition. The gap in transition rates between lower- and higher-ability children increases progressively for secondary and higher levels of education. On average, only 40% of children who were among the bottom third of the distribution in the receptive vocabulary test measured at around age 12 made the transition to secondary school, while as many as 80% of high-ability children made this transition. Similarly, the proportion of adolescents and young adults who moved on to vocational or tertiary education was only 12% for low scorers versus 50% for high scorers based on cognitive tests measured at around age 12. Together, these findings underline that inequality in educational opportunities starts early with inequitable cognitive development in early childhood, and that the negative effect of low cognitive performance exacerbates at higher levels of educational transition points. Thus, the SDG 4 targets of equitable access to primary, secondary, vocational and tertiary education are unlikely to be reached before addressing the SDG target 4.2 of equitable access to quality early development, care and pre-primary education so that all children are equally ready for primary school.

The role of socioeconomic status in determining educational trajectories for children with the same initial cognitive abilities

The findings presented in this section show that inequitable early cognitive development is only one part of the explanation of the observed disparities in educational opportunities. Inequality in educational trajectories between children from lower- and higher-SES families persists also when children have the same level of initial cognitive abilities. In line with the compensatory advantage hypothesis, the more socioeconomically advantaged families are not sensitive to the level of children's cognitive abilities when deciding about their transition to upper primary school. As can be seen from Figure 2.4, most children from high-SES families transit from lower to upper primary school regardless of children's cognitive performance at age 5. For children from lower-SES families, by contrast, chances to reach upper primary school are substantially lower for those with low early cognitive abilities and increase progressively with higher cognitive performance levels. The estimates presented in Figure 2.4 are based on a sample of children born around 2001 in five regions in Ethiopia surveyed between 2002 at age 1 until 2016 when children were around age 15. The estimates are net of a wide range of individual and

Figure 2.4: Probability to transit to upper primary school

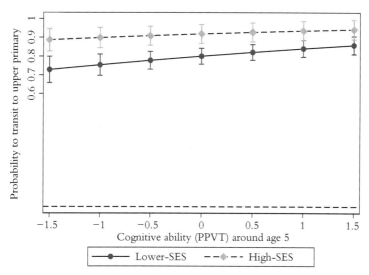

Note: N = 1744; SES = wealth. Logistic regression model with controls. Standard errors clustered by sentinel site.

Source: Young Lives Survey Rounds 1–5, younger cohort

Figure 2.5: Probability to transit to secondary school

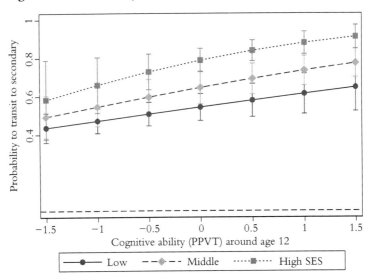

Note: N = 770; SES = wealth. Logistic regression model with controls. Standard errors clustered by sentinel site.

Source: Young Lives Survey Rounds 1–4, older cohort

household characteristics measured at school entry age (for details see the methods and variables section).

Figure 2.5 shows the relationship between cognitive ability test scores at around age 12 and later transition to general secondary education for a selected sample in Ethiopia. The estimates presented in Figure 2.5 are based on a sample of children born around 1994 and surveyed between 2002 and 2013 up until age 19. Contrary to upper primary education, no compensatory advantage mechanism can be observed for high-SES children in case of low cognitive performance at the end of primary school age. Children's probability to move up to secondary school increases with their level of cognitive abilities for both low- and high-SES families. Nevertheless, the SES gap in the probability to transit to secondary school is substantive and increases with the level of initial cognitive abilities. Among children who scored low on the cognitive ability test at around age 12, the probability to transit to secondary school for children from high-SES families is about 17 percentage points higher compared to children from low-SES families, but this difference is not statistically significant. For children with average and high cognitive ability test scores at around age 12, the gap in the probability to transit to secondary school between low- and high-SES families increases to 23 and 25 percentage points, respectively, and this

Figure 2.6: Probability to transit to vocational/tertiary education

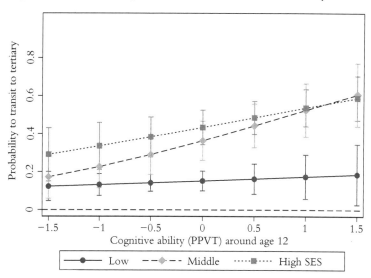

Note: N = 659; SES = wealth. Logistic regression model with controls. Standard errors clustered by sentinel site.

Source: Young Lives Survey Rounds 1–5, older cohort

difference is statistically significant. Among children with average and high PPVT test scores, on average only 55% to 65% of those from low-SES families move on to secondary education, compared to 80% to 90% of children from high-SES families with the same cognitive performance at primary school age.

The third educational transition of interest is that of vocational and tertiary education measured for a sample of children born around 1994 surveyed between 2002 and 2016 up until the mean age of the surveyed individuals was 22. Cognitive abilities were measured at around age 12 while the latest educational status was measured at age 22. As mentioned in the methodology section, this sampled cohort experienced a relatively high attrition rate between survey years 2013 and 2016, with a higher proportion of young adults from high-SES families dropping out of the survey in the final round. Thus, the estimates for the higher-SES group for this educational transition may be downward biased considering that some of the individuals from high-SES families were not captured in the last survey round.

As can be seen from Figure 2.6, parental socioeconomic status and cognitive performance together reinforce inequality in accessing post-secondary education. Higher cognitive performance during primary school age is associated with a higher probability to move on to tertiary education, but only for children from middle- and higher-SES families. Children from low-SES families, by contrast, have a substantially lower probability to transit to tertiary education, and their chances to make this transition remain low regardless of their cognitive endowments.[5] These findings reveal not only substantial inequalities by parental socioeconomic status net of cognitive abilities, but also a loss of potential talent. Children from low-SES families, even those with the highest cognitive ability levels, have considerably lower chances to access vocational training and university compared to high-SES students. To put it in perspective, high-ability low-SES children have lower chances to transit to vocational and tertiary education than low-ability high-SES children. Therefore, equalizing early childhood development and improving the quality of primary and secondary education can be regarded as necessary but insufficient preconditions to reach the SDG target 4.3 of equal access to technical, vocational and tertiary education. As pointed out by UNESCO (2017b), the provision of tertiary education ought to be made progressively free to eliminate existing financial barriers. Besides financial barriers, social stratification research points at additional mechanisms behind inequality in accessing tertiary education, such as differences in perceived returns to education and differences in parents' knowledge to navigate through the educational system (Boudon, 1998; Breen and Goldthorpe, 1997; Jackson, 2013), which also ought to be considered.

Conclusions

The SDG 4 aims to ensure equitable access to all levels of education starting from pre-school to vocational training and tertiary education (UNESCO, 2017b). In order to reach these goals, it is important to understand the mechanisms behind inequality in educational opportunities and the timing when children's educational trajectories begin to diverge. In this chapter, the Young Lives Ethiopia longitudinal survey data were used to understand the timing and sources of divergence in children's educational trajectories in low-income contexts. Following Boudon (1998), it was hypothesized that inequitable educational transitions by parental socioeconomic status are produced through two main pathways: disparities in cognitive performance developed during childhood, and differences in parental educational decisions net of children's cognitive abilities. Due to the longitudinal design of the data, it was possible to distinguish between the effect of children's early endowments measured in childhood and later parental educational investments.

In line with previous findings, the analysis showed that the SES gap in cognitive performance develops early in life when children are still in their home environment. Children from low-SES families on average score lower in cognitive ability tests compared to high-SES families, and this disparity increases with age. The findings also support the SDG 4.2 and confirm that early cognitive development is crucial for future chances to transit to higher levels of education. As an example, as many as 80% of the children scoring highly in cognitive tests at primary school age move on to secondary school, compared to only 40% from the bottom third of the ability distribution.

Initial educational inequalities tend to be reinforced by parental educational investments in children with higher abilities. The findings show one notable exception: that of transition to upper primary school for high-SES families. While low-SES families are sensitive to their children's cognitive performance, children from more advantaged families have a persistently high probability to transit to upper primary school regardless of their level of cognitive ability. The implication of this finding is that more advantaged families compensate their offspring's early disadvantage in case of low cognitive ability prior to school age.

Children from higher-SES families have considerably greater chances to move on to secondary education. Contrary to the primary school level, all types of families are sensitive to their children's cognitive performance at this level. These findings imply that in Ethiopia, families with relatively higher socioeconomic resources also evaluate their children's success probabilities before investing in secondary and post-secondary education. Early (dis)advantage also determines later educational transitions for more advantaged families as they do not compensate for low cognitive performance at later transition points. It should however be noted that children from high-SES families tend to score significantly higher on early cognitive ability tests and very few of them show low cognitive performance by the end of primary school. Thus, inequity in educational opportunities is reproduced early in childhood and reinforced with each educational transition. These findings show that the SDG 4 targets of equitable access to all levels of education are unlikely to be reached before addressing the SDG target 4.2 of reaching equitable cognitive performance through quality early development, care and pre-primary education so that all children are equally ready for primary school.

Inequality of educational opportunities is most striking at the post-secondary level. Children from low socioeconomic backgrounds face significant barriers to accessing post-secondary education. Children from low-SES families have equally low chances to access vocational education and university regardless of their initial cognitive ability level. This points at a loss of talent since those children who initially score highly in cognitive tests are substantially less likely to move on to higher education. This finding has direct policy implications as it shows that high-ability poorer children can keep up with their more advantaged peers and progress through primary school, but they are blocked at higher transition points. Thus, any policy aiming to equalize children's educational opportunities should aim not only at improving early childhood development and cognitive abilities through investments in children's living conditions, health and nutrition prior to school age, but also reduce the barriers faced by low-SES families in accessing post-secondary education.

For the purposes of this study, it was important that cognitive abilities are measured as early as possible to avoid the estimates being confounded by prior parental investments and school effects. In the longitudinal survey used, the first time the PPVT receptive vocabulary test was performed was in Round 2 when the younger cohort was age 5, thus fulfilling the study requirements for the analysis of transition to upper primary school level. The older cohort, by contrast, was around 12 years old when the PPVT test was performed. Thus, one of the main limitations of this longitudinal design is that for the analysis of transition to secondary and tertiary education, the PPVT test was measured only at the end of primary school age. The estimates concerning transition to secondary and tertiary education may therefore be confounded with prior family decisions based on children's early endowments not captured in this survey, and may incorporate both family and school effects. For future research seeking to analyse the timing and sources of inequality in educational trajectories from early childhood through all levels of education, it is important to capture individual endowments as early as possible before the school starting age.

Notes

[1] Two-sample t-tests were carried out to compare the initial and the excluded sample. Results show that differences in means are not statistically significant in most variables of interest, with a few exceptions. Among children who dropped out due to attrition or missing information, there were proportionally slightly more girls and more children living in households with a female household head.

[2] Two-sample t-tests were performed to identify differences between adolescents of the older cohort who were surveyed until Round 4 (age 19) but not followed in

Round 5 (age 22), totalling 13.5% of the older cohort sample. Those not followed in Round 5 on average came from households with a higher wealth index, scored higher on cognitive ability tests, and had higher transition rates to upper primary and secondary education. There were no statistically significant differences on other characteristics such as gender and parental education.

[3] Findings are largely similar regardless of the SES variable used and are available from the author upon request.

[4] The same analysis was performed by gender. The estimates show no statistically significant differences between boys and girls regarding the association between initial cognitive endowments and later educational transitions. Results can be obtained from the author upon request.

[5] Only children who attended upper primary school or higher are considered here so the estimates are not affected by children who never attended school.

References

Ayalew, T. (2005) Parental preference, heterogeneity, and human capital inequality. *Economic Development and Cultural Change* 53(2): 381–407.

Bacolod, M.P. and Ranjan, P. (2008) Why children work, attend school, or stay idle: the roles of ability and household wealth. *Economic Development and Cultural Change* 56(4): 791–828.

Behrman, J.R., Rosenzweig, M.R. and Taubman, P. (1994) Endowments and the allocation of schooling in the family and in the marriage market: the twins experiment. *Journal of Political Economy* 102(6): 1131–74.

Bernardi, F. (2014) Compensatory advantage as a mechanism of educational inequality: a regression discontinuity based on month of birth. *Sociology of Education* 87(2): 74–88.

Bhalotra, S., Harttgen, K. and Klasen, S. (2015) The impact of school fees on schooling outcomes and the intergenerational transmission of education. Background paper commissioned for the Education for All Global Monitoring Report 2013/14, Teaching and Learning: Achieving Quality for All.

Blossfeld, H.-P. and von Maurice, J. (2011) Education as a lifelong process. *Zeitschrift für Erziehungswissenschaft* 14(2): 19–34.

Blossfeld, H.-P., Buchholz, S., Skopek, J. and Triventi, M. (Eds) (2016) *Models of Secondary Education and Social Inequality: An International Comparison*. Cheltenham: Edward Elgar.

Boudon, R. (1974) *Education, Opportunity, and Social Inequality: Changing Prospects in Western Society*. New York: Wiley.

Boudon, R. (1998) Social mechanisms without black boxes. In P. Hedström and R. Swedberg (Eds) *Social Mechanisms: An Analytical Approach to Social Theory* (pp 172–203). Cambridge: Cambridge University Press.

Boyden, J. (2018) Young Lives: An International Study of Childhood Poverty: Rounds 1–5 Constructed Files, 2002–2016. 3rd edn, data collection. UK Data Service. http://doi.org/10.5255/UKDA-SN-7483-3

Breen, R. and Goldthorpe, J.H. (1997) Explaining educational differentials: TOWARDS a formal rational action theory. *Rationality and Society* 9(3): 275–305.

Buchmann, C. and Hannum, E. (2001) Education and stratification in developing countries: a review of theories and research. *Annual Review of Sociology* 27(1): 77–102.

Carneiro, P. and Heckman, J.J. (2005) Human capital. In J.J. Heckman, A.B. Krueger and B.M. Friedman (Eds) *Inequality in America: What Role for Human Capital Policies?* (pp 77–239). Cambridge, MA: The MIT Press.

Cueto, S. and León, J. (2012) Psychometric Characteristics of Cognitive Development and Achievement Instruments in Round 3 of Young Lives. Young Lives Technical Note 25. Oxford: Young Lives, Oxford Department of International Development.

Cueto, S., León, J., Guerrero, G.C. and Munoz, I. (2009) Psychometric Characteristics of Cognitive Development and Achievement Instruments in Round 2 of Young Lives. Young Lives Technical Note 15. Oxford: Young Lives, Oxford Department of International Development.

Dendir, S. (2014) Children's cognitive ability, schooling and work: evidence from Ethiopia. *International Journal of Educational Development* 38: 22–36.

Erikson, R. and Jonsson, J.O. (1996) *Can Education Be Equalized?: The Swedish Case in Comparative Perspective.* Boulder, CO: Westview Press.

Erikson, R., Goldthorpe, J.H., Jackson, M., Yaish, M. and Cox, D.R. (2005) On class differentials in educational attainment. *Proceedings of the National Academy of Sciences* 102(27): 9730–3.

Goldthorpe, J.H. (1996) Class analysis and the reorientation of class theory: the case of persisting differentials in educational attainment. *British Journal of Sociology* 47(3): 481–505.

Hackman, D.A., Farah, M.J. and Meaney, M.J. (2010) Socioeconomic status and the brain: mechanistic insights from human and animal research. *Nature Reviews Neuroscience* 11(9): 651–9.

Hanushek, E.A. and Woessmann, L. (2008) The role of cognitive skills in economic development. *Journal of Economic Literature* 46(3): 607–68.

Heckman, J.J. (2006) Skill formation and the economics of investing in disadvantaged children. *Science* 312(5782): 1900–2.

Jackson, M. (2013) How is inequality of educational opportunity generated? The case for primary and secondary effects. In M. Jackson (Ed) *Determined to Succeed? Performance versus Choice in Educational Attainment* (pp 1–55). Stanford, CA: Stanford University Press.

Mani, S., Hoddinott, J. and Strauss, J. (2013) Determinants of schooling: empirical evidence from rural Ethiopia. *Journal of African Economies* 22(5): 693–731.

Ress, A. and Azzolini, D. (2014) Primary and secondary effects of social background on educational attainment in Italy: evidence from an administrative dataset. *Italian Journal of Sociology of Education* 6(1): 53–80.

Riddell, A. (2003) The introduction of free primary education in Sub-Saharan Africa. Background paper prepared for the Education for All Global Monitoring Report 2003/2004: Gender and Education for All: The Leap to Equality 4. Paris: UNESCO.

Rose, P., Sabates, R., Alcott, B. and Ilie, S. (2016) Overcoming inequalities within countries to achieve global convergence in learning. Background paper for the International Commission on Financing Global Education Opportunity Report. Cambridge: Research for Equitable Access and Learning (REAL) Centre.

Sen, A. (1999) *Development as Freedom*. Oxford: Oxford University Press.

Tomasevski, K. (2006) *Free or Fee: 2006 Global Report. The State of the Right to Education Worldwide*. Copenhagen: Report of the UN Special Rapporteur on the Right to Education.

Torche, F. (2016) Torche comment on Downey and Condron. *Sociology of Education* 89(3): 229–30.

UN (2015) *The Millennium Development Goals Report 2015*. New York: United Nations.

United Nations Educational, Scientific and Cultural Organization (UNESCO) (2017a) Accountability in education: meeting our commitments. Available at http://unesdoc.unesco.org/images/0025/002593/259338e.pdf

UNESCO (2017b) *Unpacking Sustainable Development Goal 4: Education 2030: Guide*. Paris: UNESCO.

UNESCO Institute for Statistics (UNESCO UIS) (2017) More than one-half of children and adolescents are not learning worldwide. Fact Sheet No. 46. UNESCO Institute for Statistics (UIS).

United Nations Sustainable Development (2015) Sustainable Development Goals – United Nations. Available at www.un.org/sustainabledevelopment/sustainable-development-goals/

Woldehanna, T. (2016) Inequality, preschool education and cognitive development in Ethiopia: Implication for public investment in pre-primary education. *International Journal of Behavioral Development* 40(6): 509–16.

Woldehanna, T. and Araya, M. (2016) Educational Inequalities among Children and Young People in Ethiopia. Young Lives Country Report. Oxford: Young Lives, Oxford Department of International Development.

Woldehanna, T., Mekonnen, A. and Jones, N. (2008) Education choices in Ethiopia: what determines whether poor households send their children to school? *Ethiopian Journal of Economics* 17(1). Available at https://assets.publishing.service.gov.uk/media/57a08c2ae5274a27b2001019/policy_brief2.pdf

World Bank (2019) World Development Indicators. Available at http://databank.worldbank.org/data/source/world-development-indicators/preview/on

World Bank and UNICEF (2009) *Abolishing School Fees in Africa: Lessons from Ethiopia, Ghana, Kenya, Malawi, and Mozambique.* Washington, DC: World Bank.

Young Lives (2018) Young lives survey design and sampling (round 5): Ethiopia. Oxford: Oxford Department of International Development.

3

Early Life Transitions Increase the Risk for HIV Infection: Using Latent Class Growth Models to Assess the Effect of Key Life Events on HIV Incidence Among Adolescent Girls in Rural South Africa

Audrey Pettifor, Emily Agnew, Torsten B. Neilands, Jennifer Ahern, Stephen Tollman, Kathleen Kahn and Sheri A. Lippman

Introduction

Adolescent girls and young women (AGYW) in sub-Saharan Africa are at high risk of HIV infection. HIV infection rates increase substantially among AGYW after the age of 18. In South Africa HIV prevalence rises from 6% among young women aged 15–19 years to 17% by ages 20–24. This age period marks a time of transition into adulthood and coincides with a number of key life events, such as finishing the mandatory years of schooling, leaving home, entering first sexual relationships and experiencing first pregnancies.(Human Sciences Research Council [HSRC], 2017) Key life events that include first pregnancy, coital debut, leaving school and parental death have all been found independently to be associated with an increased risk of HIV infection in young women. Young women who experience their first vaginal sex before the age of 15 are more likely to be living with

HIV, and these early events are often characterized by forced sex and sex with older male partners who are more likely to be HIV infected (Pettifor et al, 2004, 2009; Wand and Ramjee, 2012). While school attendance has multiple developmental and later life benefits, leaving school increases the risk of HIV acquisition. Girls who do not attend school as often and who drop out are more likely to acquire HIV infection than those attending and who stay in school (Stoner et al, 2017) In one study, this association appears to be explained by school environments providing safer spaces where adolescent girls are more likely to have male partners closer in age and also have fewer sexual partners than those out of school (Stoner et al, 2018) Similar patterns have been observed for young women experiencing early adolescent pregnancy (before the age of 15), whereby HIV incidence is much higher, and those who experience adolescent pregnancy also have more risk factors for HIV infection such as older partners and more sexual partners (Christofides et al, 2014). Finally, loss of a parent has been found to be associated with HIV risk in young people; orphaned youth are more likely to be living with HIV and to report riskier sexual behaviour than non-orphaned youth (Operario et al, 2011).

Despite documentation of the importance of life event to HIV risk, little is understood about the timing of key life events and how they shape HIV risk as adolescents transition into adulthood. While coital debut, pregnancy and leaving school are all key life transitions that many young people will experience as part of their expected life course (MacMillan and Copher, 2005), occurrence earlier in adolescence can result in negative outcomes for health and development (Evans et al, 2013). Life course theory highlights that the timing and sequence of life events or transitions result in different meaning and consequences (Elder, 1998). While experience of particular life events earlier may have immediate impacts on health and social factors, their impacts may also extend into the future by affecting subsequent transitions (Elder, 1998). While there is a robust body of literature documenting how adverse child events can impact health in adulthood (Hughes et al, 2017), this evidence is just starting to emerge from low- and middle-income countries (Kidman and Kohler, 2019). Further, negative life events that occur in early adolescence (ages 9–14), when major brain and social transitions are occurring, may have long-lasting consequences (Falconi et al, 2014; UNICEF, 2017). However, changes that occur in early adolescence in the brain may also provide an opportunity for intervention to improve future health and developmental trajectories (Fuhrmann et al, 2015; UNICEF, 2017). Life course research that examines how the timing of events in earlier life can impact later life health aligns well with understanding progress in meeting the Sustainable Development Goals (SDG). SDG 3, which supports ensuring healthy lives and promoting well-being for all at all ages is particularly well aligned to better understanding how earlier life events can impact health later in life. Thus, better understanding of how the timing of key events, in particular using longitudinal data, can impact HIV risk across the life course can help target prevention programmes to address vulnerable time periods in the transition to adulthood to reduce new infections, helping to achieve the SDGs which include reducing new HIV infections.

The purpose of this research was to explore the impact of key life events, specifically sexual debut, pregnancy, death of a parent and leaving school, on HIV incidence among a cohort of AGYW in rural South Africa. This research utilized latent class growth analysis (LCGA) to classify adolescent girls based on growth trajectories according to the age at which they experienced these life events. In addition, LCGA was used to examine the cumulative impact of multiple key life events within the same time period of these young women's lives, and how these events affected their risk of HIV acquisition as they aged.

Methods

Study design

The HIV Prevention Trials Network (HPTN) 068 was a phase 3 randomized controlled trial to determine whether a monthly cash transfer, conditional on school attendance, would reduce HIV incidence for adolescent girls and young women in South Africa (Pettifor et al, 2016). The study was undertaken by the Medical Research Council/ Rural Public Health and Health Transitions Research Unit, which runs the Agincourt Health and Socio-Demographic Surveillance System (HDSS) site in the rural Bushbuckridge subdistrict in Mpumalanga province, South Africa.

Women aged 13–20 years were included in the HPTN 068 study if they were enrolled in school grades 8–11 of the South African government educational system, HIV negative, not married or pregnant, able to read, able to open a bank account, and currently residing in the study area. Potential participants were identified from the Agincourt HDSS sampling frame. Each young woman and her parent or guardian provided written informed consent. Written assent was obtained for those younger than 18 years. Consent and assent forms were available in English and Shangaan.

Participants completed an interview using audio computer-assisted self-interview (ACASI) which collected information on sexual behaviour, mental health, sexual and physical abuse, pregnancy history and contraceptive use, schooling and other sociodemographic information at baseline and at 12, 24 and 36 months until the study completion date or their planned high-school completion date, whichever came first. HIV and Herpes Simplex Virus (HSV-2) testing were also conducted at each of these visits. HIV screening was done with two HIV rapid tests completed in parallel – the Determine HIV-1/2 test (Alere Medical Co, Matsudo-shi, Chiba, Japan) and the US Food and Drug Administration (FDA)-cleared Uni-gold Recombigen HIV test (Trinity Biotech, Bray, County Wicklow, Ireland). Further details of the study design can be found in the main study paper (Pettifor et al, 2016).

Institutional Review Board approval for this study was obtained from the University of North Carolina at Chapel Hill and the University of the Witwatersrand Human Research Ethics Committee.

Statistical analysis

Latent class growth models are a method for fully capturing information about between-person differences in within-person patterns of change over time. Individuals are grouped into latent classes based upon similar patterns of data over time. The method assumes that the observed distribution of values may be a combination of two or more subpopulations whose membership is unknown. As such, latent class growth analysis probabilistically assigns individuals to these subpopulations by inferring each individual's membership to latent classes from the observed growth model data. Life events at different stages in life can be classified as separate events to investigate how the event and when it happens affects the individual's risks of HIV infection.

The classes of different life event trajectories over time were categorized using LCGA, allowing the individual's variation to occur around one of multiple trajectories. After classifying life event trajectories, it was determined which trajectories were predictors of the outcome, HIV status. Each class therefore described a course over time of each of the four life events: sexual debut, pregnancy, leaving school and death of a parent. Each trajectory was determined over four time points: whether the event occurred by age 14, by age 17, by age 21 and by age 23. However, for the 'leaving school' model all participants had left by age 23 and so the trajectories are determined over only the first three time points. In addition, LCGA was applied to describe temporal patterns in multiple life events over the same time points of these young women's lives, and examine the relation of these patterns to HIV. In addition to the binary variable for whether participants had experienced one of the events by a particular age, a variable was also modelled that sums the number of events an adolescent girl had experienced by each age. All the life events in the model were included: sexual debut, first pregnancy, leaving school and the death of a parent. The analysis was conducted using Mplus version 8 (Muthén and Muthén, 2005) and Stata version 15 (StataCorp, 2017).

Models were fitted over a range of class numbers to identify the ideal number of classes in describing patterns in the timing of all life events. Models were also fitted for each of the life events – sexual debut, pregnancy, leaving school and death of a parent –, over a range of class numbers. Two to four classes were examined for the individual life events and three to six for the combined classes. The model fitting is provided in Table 3.1. Fit was assessed using the Bayesian Information Criterion (BIC), the Bootstrap likelihood ratio tests (BLRT) and entropy values (Jung and Wickrama, 2008). In addition to model fit statistics, the interpretability and practical coherence of the model classes were considered. The models were run with multiple random starting values to avoid settling on local solutions; each model was run with 100 random starts and 10 final optimizations. These values were increased when convergence was not achieved. Having determined the best fitting model, the latent classes were added to a generalized linear model (GLM), regressing HIV status on the latent class trajectories of the life events, using a binomial distributional family and log link, to estimate the risk ratio (RR) of HIV infection for each latent class.

Finally, dominance analysis, a technique which rank-ordered the relative importance or contribution of the life events classes in predicting HIV incidence, was used based on the individual variables' contribution to the overall model fit. This method is based on the average pseudo $R2$ explained by each life event across all possible subsets regression models (Azen and Traxel, 2009; Budescu, 1993).

Missing data

Parameter estimates from Mplus were adjusted for missingness using a robust full information maximum likelihood (FIML) estimator, which assumes data is missing at random. Mplus generates the covariance coverage matrix to assess the proportion of observations available for each pair of variables, the minimum recommended coverage in Mplus is 10%; the coverage proportions among the variables in this analysis were all greater than 42.5%, verifying the use of the FIML estimator for this analysis.

Measures

The study looked at events that could occur at only one time and where the timing of the event could be measured (for example, left school at age 15) so that the temporality of exposure and outcome (HIV sero-conversion) could be assessed. In order to assess time since exposure on the outcome, coital debut was measured by asking young women whether they had ever had vaginal sex and if yes, at what age they first had vaginal sex. For pregnancy, young women were asked if they had ever been pregnant and if so the age at first pregnancy. For school leaving, young women were asked if they were still attending secondary school or not and the age they left secondary school. Parental death was assessed by asking, separately, if their mother and father were alive, and if not what age the young person was when they died. Measures were adjusted for the following covariates: age at enrolment, length of study enrolment, trial arm, school attendance, anxiety, depression, interpersonal violence (IPV) and HIV knowledge.

Results

Specific life events and HIV incidence

Figure 3.1 shows the observed and expected trajectories from the LCGA model, for each of the life events. The selected models included two linear trajectory classes for leaving school and death of a parent and three linear trajectory classes for sexual debut and pregnancy.

In Figure 3.1a, the trajectories for leaving school, a two–class model fit the data best, with classes identified as those who leave school early (class 1) and those leaving later (class 2). Table 3.1 shows the unadjusted and adjusted risk ratios (RR) for the log-binomial regression of the two classes on HIV infection; the risk of HIV infection in those who leave school early (class 1) is 2.9 times higher (p-value = 0.001) than those who leave later (class 2) in the unadjusted model. When the model is adjusted for age at enrolment and length of enrolment, the participants' risk ratio increases to 4.3 (p-value < 0.001) (Table 3.1).

Figure 3.1b shows the three-class model trajectories for sexual debut, with those with an 'early' debut (class 2), those with no debut or a

Figure 3.1: Latent class growth analysis observed and expected trajectories

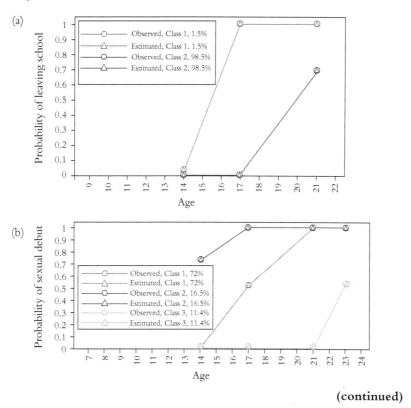

(continued)

'late' debut (class 3) and those with a debut between these (class 1). Compared to those with a 'late' debut, the risk of HIV infection of class 1 is 2.1 times higher (p-value = 0.05) and the risk of class 2 is 2.8 times higher (p-value = 0.01), when adjusted for age at enrolment and length of enrolment (Table 3.1).

Figure 3.1c shows a three-class model for pregnancy, with those with an 'early' first pregnancy (class 3), those with no pregnancy or a 'late' first pregnancy (class 2) and those with a first pregnancy between these (class 1). Compared to those with a 'late' first pregnancy, the risk of HIV infection of a neither late nor early pregnancy (class 1) is 1.6 times higher (p-value = 0.04) and the risk of an early pregnancy (class 3) is 2.8 times higher (p-value = 0.01), when adjusted for age at enrolment and length of enrolment.

Figure 3.1d shows the two-class model trajectories for the death of a parent. The two classes are those who do not experience a death or

Figure 3.1: Latent class growth analysis observed and expected trajectories (continued)

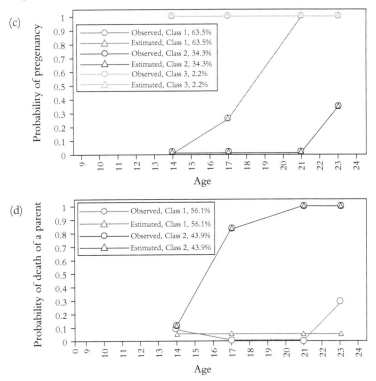

Source: Author's own

Table 3.1: Risk ratio of log-binomial regressions of classes on HIV, unadjusted, adjusted for age at enrolment and length of enrolment and adjusted for these and other covariates including study arm

Life event	Model	Variable	Risk ratio	P-value	95% CI	
Left school	Unadjusted	left school class 1	2.894	0.001	1.577	5.309
(N = 2,374)						
	Adjusted: age at entry,	left school class 1	4.275	0.000	2.313	7.900
	time enrolled	age	1.272	0.000	1.187	1.364
		enrolled_len	1.170	0.030	1.015	1.348
	Adjusted:	left school class 1	2.799	0.009	1.297	6.037

Table 3.1: Risk ratio of log-binomial regressions of classes on HIV, unadjusted, adjusted for age at enrolment and length of enrolment and adjusted for these and other covariates including study arm (continued)

Life event	Model	Variable	Risk ratio	P-value	95% CI	
		age	1.208	0.000	1.114	1.309
		enrolled_len	1.218	0.014	1.040	1.426
		arm	0.996	0.979	0.765	1.299
		attendance	0.991	0.012	0.985	0.998
		anxiety	1.039	0.092	0.994	1.085
		depression	1.055	0.041	1.002	1.110
		parental monitor	0.997	0.920	0.936	1.062
		HIV knowledge	1.054	0.738	0.776	1.432
Sexual debut	Unadjusted:	debut class 1	1.141	0.720	0.554	2.349
(N = 2,482)		debut class 2	1.498	0.305	0.693	3.238
	Adjusted: age at entry,	debut class 1	2.077	0.051	0.996	4.328
	time enrolled	debut class 2	2.781	0.010	1.276	6.058
		age	1.277	0.000	1.192	1.369
		enrolled_len	1.178	0.024	1.022	1.359
	Adjusted:	debut class 1	2.093	0.094	0.882	4.970
		debut class 2	2.462	0.054	0.986	6.148
		age	1.196	0.000	1.109	1.289
		enrolled_len	1.205	0.014	1.039	1.396
		arm	1.033	0.793	0.810	1.318
		attendance	0.991	0.001	0.985	0.996
		anxiety	1.035	0.095	0.994	1.078
		depression	1.051	0.036	1.003	1.101
		IPV	1.058	0.710	0.785	1.428
		HIV knowledge	1.040	0.791	0.781	1.384
Pregnancy	Unadjusted:	pregnancy class 1	0.764	0.185	0.513	1.138
(N = 2,447)		pregnancy class 3	1.580	0.183	0.806	3.097

(continued)

Table 3.1: Risk ratio of log-binomial regressions of classes on HIV, unadjusted, adjusted for age at enrolment and length of enrolment and adjusted for these and other covariates including study arm (continued)

Life event	Model	Variable	Risk ratio	P-value	95% CI	
	Adjusted: age at entry,	pregnancy class 1	1.633	0.042	1.017	2.623
	time enrolled	pregnancy class 3	2.832	0.007	1.336	6.006
		age	1.298	0.000	1.199	1.404
		enrolled_len	1.202	0.019	1.031	1.403
	Adjusted:	pregnancy class 1	1.525	0.062	0.979	2.377
		pregnancy class 3	2.026	0.040	1.034	3.971
		age	1.238	0.000	1.148	1.335
		enrolled_len	1.192	0.020	1.028	1.382
		arm	1.024	0.852	0.802	1.307
		anxiety	1.040	0.062	0.998	1.083
		depression	1.057	0.018	1.010	1.107
		IPV	1.150	0.349	0.859	1.539
		HIV knowledge	1.017	0.910	0.766	1.350
Parent death	Unadjusted:	parent death class 2	2.030	0.000	1.602	2.574
(N = 2,071)						
	Adjusted: age at entry,	parent death class 2	1.994	0.000	1.563	2.543
	time enrolled	age	1.252	0.000	1.170	1.339
		enrolled_len	1.145	0.055	0.997	1.316
	Adjusted:	parent death class 2	1.865	0.000	1.460	2.383
		age	1.201	0.000	1.119	1.290
		enrolled_len	1.155	0.049	1.001	1.333
		arm	1.003	0.978	0.787	1.280
		anxiety	1.036	0.080	0.996	1.078
		depression	1.061	0.012	1.013	1.110

Note: In each case the reference class is the class of the lowest probability of the event.

Figure 3.2: Latent class growth analysis trajectories for the four-class model of cumulative life events, where the events included are sexual debut, pregnancy, leaving school and death of a parent

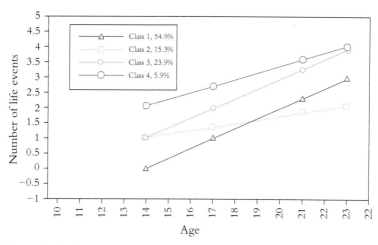

Source: Author's own

experience it later (class 1) and those who experience it earlier (class 2). The risk of HIV infection in those who experience a death earlier (class 2) is 2.0 times higher (p-value < 0.001) than those who do not or experience it later (class 1) in both the unadjusted and adjusted models.

Generally, across all of the life events, the effect of adjusting for the study arm was not significant.

Cumulative life events and HIV incidence

Figure 3.2 shows the four-class model that was selected to describe the pattern of cumulative life events. Table 3.2 shows the characteristics of each of the cumulative life event classes; class 1 ('Blue') had no one who experienced coital debut, pregnancy or school leaving by age 15 and had a relatively low percentage of participants who experienced the death of a parent by age 23 (14% compared to 80–91%). Class 4 ('Red') experienced the most negative life events by age 14. The vast majority (88.6%) had debuted by age 14, 21% had experienced a pregnancy by age 14, 90% had experienced parental death by age 14 and 3.5% had left school. Class 2 ('Green') and 3 ('Pink') started out with a similar number of events by age 14 (more than class 1 and less than class 4), however the gradient of the trajectory for class 3 is steeper than class 2, resulting in a higher number of negative events experienced by age 23. By age 23 class 3 had caught up to class 4 in

Table 3.2: Frequency of attributes by class from the model of cumulative life events

		Class 1		Class 2		Class 3		Class 4	
		N	%	N	%	N	%	N	%
HIV	Negative	974	91.1	270	89.7	408	87.9	97	85.1
	Positive	95	8.9	31	10.3	56	12.1	17	14.9
Sexual debut by 14	No	1,069	100.0	243	80.7	390	84.1	13	11.4
	Yes	0	0.0	58	19.3	74	15.9	101	88.6
	Missing	0	0.0	0	0.0	0	0.0	0	0.0
Sexual debut by 17	No	481	45.0	234	77.7	45	9.7	3	2.6
	Yes	441	41.3	67	22.3	331	71.3	110	96.5
	Missing	147	13.8	0	0.0	88	19.0	1	0.9
Sexual debut by 21	No	37	3.5	22	7.3	2	0.4	1	0.9
	Yes	590	55.2	108	35.9	350	75.4	110	96.5
	Missing	442	41.3	171	56.8	112	24.1	3	2.6
Sexual debut by 23	No	3	0.3	3	1.0	0	0.0	0	0.0
	Yes	594	55.6	109	36.2	351	75.6	110	96.5
	Missing	472	44.2	189	62.8	113	24.4	4	3.5
Pregnant by 14	No	1,069	100.0	299	99.3	449	96.8	90	78.9
	Yes	0	0.0	2	0.7	15	3.2	24	21.1
	Missing	0	0.0	0	0.0	0	0.0	0	0.0

Table 3.2: Frequency of attributes by class from the model of cumulative life events (continued)

		Class 1		Class 2		Class 3		Class 4	
Pregnant by 17	No	783	73.2	297	98.7	225	48.5	37	32.5
	Yes	127	11.9	4	1.3	124	26.7	59	51.8
	Missing	159	14.9	0	0.0	115	24.8	18	15.8
Pregnant by 21	No	95	8.9	39	13.0	15	3.2	3	2.6
	Yes	263	24.6	33	11.0	191	41.2	69	60.5
	Missing	711	66.5	229	76.1	258	55.6	42	36.8
Pregnant by 23	No	15	1.4	7	2.3	3	0.6	2	1.8
	Yes	272	25.4	35	11.6	193	41.6	70	61.4
	Missing	782	73.2	259	86.0	268	57.8	42	36.8
Left school by 14	No	1,069	100.0	301	100.0	464	100.0	110	96.5
	Yes	0	0.0	0	0.0	0	0.0	4	3.5
	Missing	0	0.0	0	0.0	0	0.0	0	0.0
Left school by 17	No	870	81.4	301	100.0	306	65.9	75	65.8
	Yes	26	2.4	0	0.0	29	6.3	15	13.2
	Missing	173	16.2	0	0.0	129	27.8	24	21.1
Left school by 21	No	84	7.9	32	10.6	35	7.5	6	5.3
	Yes	257	24.0	50	16.6	125	26.9	38	33.3
	Missing	728	68.1	219	72.8	304	65.5	70	61.4

(continued)

Table 3.2: Frequency of attributes by class from the model of cumulative life events (continued)

		Class 1		Class 2		Class 3		Class 4	
Left school by 23	No	8	0.7	2	0.7	2	0.4	0	0.0
	Yes	296	27.7	64	21.3	140	30.2	39	34.2
	Missing	765	71.6	235	78.1	322	69.4	75	65.8
Parent death by 14	No	805	75.3	46	15.3	66	14.2	8	7.0
	Yes	0	0.0	241	80.1	375	80.8	103	90.4
	Missing	264	24.7	14	4.7	23	5.0	3	2.6
Parent death by 17	No	502	47.0	46	15.3	31	6.7	5	4.4
	Yes	97	9.1	241	80.1	383	82.5	103	90.4
	Missing	470	44.0	14	4.7	50	10.8	6	5.3
Parent death by 21	No	62	5.8	6	2.0	3	0.6	0	0.0
	Yes	150	14.0	243	80.7	384	82.8	104	91.2
	Missing	857	80.2	52	17.3	77	16.6	10	8.8
Parent death by 23	No	6	0.6	0	0.0	0	0.0	0	0.0
	Yes	152	14.2	243	80.7	384	82.8	104	91.2
	Missing	911	85.2	58	19.3	80	17.2	10	8.8

Table 3.3: Risk ratios of HIV and the cumulative life event trajectories illustrated in Figure 3.2 both unadjusted and adjusted for age at enrolment and length of enrolment

Risk ratio – unadjusted						
Colour	Class	Risk ratio	Std. Err.	*p*-value	95% CI	
Blue	1-Reference	1.00				
Green	2	1.16	0.227	0.45	0.79	1.70
Pink	3	1.36	0.216	0.05	0.99	1.86
Red	4	1.68	0.410	0.03	1.04	2.71

Risk ratio – adjusted for age at enrolment and length of enrolment						
Colour	Class	Risk ratio	Std. Err.	*p*-value	95% CI	
Blue	1-Reference	1.00				
Green	2	1.11	0.22	0.59	0.76	1.63
Pink	3	1.44	0.23	0.02	1.06	1.96
Red	4	1.81	0.44	0.01	1.13	2.90

terms of number of negative life events experienced on average, while class 2, although starting in a similar place to class 3 at age 14, had experienced the fewest negative events of any class by age 23.

We then examined the risk of HIV acquisition by class. Compared to class 1, the class with the fewest events by age 14, all other classes had an increased risk of HIV infection although only class 3 and 4 have a significantly increased risk of infection (Table 3.3). While class 3 and 4 experienced the same number of negative life events by age 23, class 4, the group that experienced the most negative events by age 14, had a greater risk of HIV acquisition (RR 1.81 95% CI 1.31, 2.89) than class 3 (RR 1.44, 95% CI 1.06, 1.96). Even in class 2, where by age 23 the participants have experienced fewer events than those in class 1, the risk of HIV infection is higher, though the difference is not statistically significant. This suggests that there could be an increased impact of these life events when they occur earlier in the participants' lives as compared to later.

Dominance analysis ranked pregnancy as the most important of the life events in increasing risk of HIV infection, followed by leaving school, while sexual debut was third (Table 3.4). The death of a parent was ranked fourth of these life events.

Table 3.4: Dominance analysis of life events on risk of HIV infection

Life event	Dominance statistic	Standardized dominance statistic	Ranking
Pregnancy	0.0197	0.3185	1
Leaving school	0.0185	0.2992	2
Sexual debut	0.0173	0.2786	3
Parent death	0.0064	0.1037	4

Conclusions

It was found that adolescent girls who experienced key life events before the age of 15, specifically pregnancy, coital debut, leaving school and parental death, were at increased risk of HIV infection. Using latent growth class analysis, adolescent girls who experienced more life events before the age of 15 had the highest risk of HIV acquisition by the age of 23. Those who experienced the same number of life events by age 23 were also at increased risk of HIV but not at as great a risk as the group with the most events that occurred in early adolescence. Interestingly, the class who by age 23 had the fewest events but more life events occurring in early adolescence than the other classes also had an increased risk of HIV infection compared to the group with more events later in adolescence, although the difference was not statistically significant.

These results add to the evidence base that timing of events in the adolescent life course, not just the occurrence of the events, impact the risk of HIV acquisition and that these events have not just short-term impacts on increasing risk but long-term effects well into early adulthood. All of the events examined are part of the natural transition from adolescence into adulthood; however, when these events happen early in adolescence they may place adolescents at increased risk. All of the life events examined have been found independently to be associated with HIV infection, but few studies are longitudinal so that the evidence of these events being associated with an increased risk of future infection is limited. Importantly this work demonstrates that it is not just the occurrence of a life event or the number of life events that a young person experiences that shapes HIV risk but when they occur in the life course. This work highlights that earlier life events play a particularly important role in HIV risk over the years of transition into adulthood.

There are many pathways through which early negative life events could lead to increased HIV risk. It is likely there are direct risks for HIV associated with these exposures, such as sexual behaviour, but also other more distal risk factors such as mental health and environmental stressors that likely place young people who experience these events as they transition to adulthood at greater risk. In this analysis, both early coital debut and early pregnancy indicate early initiation of sexual behaviour, meaning adolescent girls have more time when they are at risk for HIV exposure. However, even after adjusting for time, early debut and pregnancy increase risk of HIV acquisition, suggesting that other mechanisms may be increasing risk such as older partners or unprotected sex. Earlier work in this cohort has found that low school attendance and leaving school increase HIV risk and that this risk is explained by older partners and more sexual partners.(Stoner et al, 2017, 2018). Thus school provides a protective environment from HIV infection. Loss of a parent may also lead to increased risk through similar pathways such as lack of parental monitoring and parental care and supervision (Operario et al, 2011).

There is a growing recognition of the importance of childhood and early adolescence on shaping future health. There is a large body of literature demonstrating that adverse childhood events have many negative health outcomes, including increased adult mortality, chronic disease, mental health and sexual behaviour (Hughes et al, 2017; Boullier and Blair, 2018; Balistreri and Alvira-Hammond, 2016). However, much of the work on ACEs is retrospective, asking adults about negative life events that happened before the age of 18 (including, for example, abuse, neglect, death of a parent, living in a negative household/environment). Thus, these measures often do not allow for the examination of how when these events occurred in an adolescent's life impacted future risk. There is a growing body of literature documenting early adolescence as an important time in life where negative events can have a significant impact on later life (Evans et al, 2013), but it is also a time for opportunity to intervene to counter negative future outcomes (Fuhrmann et al, 2015). While negative experiences during early adolescence can set up negative patterns of behaviour that continue into adulthood, it also provides an opportunity to intervene to prevent these risky trajectories from continuing (UNICEF, 2017). In addition, the life events measured do not occur in isolation but within a larger environment that adolescents and their caregivers operate in; cultural expectations and the social consequences of life events may have differential impacts for youth in different settings (UNICEF, 2017). Further, events such as early coital debut, pregnancy and leaving school are associated, and one event may lead to an adolescent experiencing another (for example, pregnancy leads to leaving school) which is consistent with life course theory. Thus, identifying these events when they happen and intervening early with supportive, evidence-based interventions so that more events do not occur is important.

The implications of these findings are that HIV prevention programmes need to not only screen for current risk factors but take into account earlier life events that may place adolescents on a trajectory of increased risk into adulthood and perhaps beyond that. Successfully meeting SDG goal 3.1, ending the HIV epidemic by 2030, will require a holistic view of prevention over the life course and understanding that events that happen to individuals earlier in their lives impact their future HIV risk. While HIV incidence does not increase rapidly until after age 18, experiences that happen in early adolescence and even childhood put young women at increased risk well into early adulthood. A two-fold approach to HIV prevention programming and policy in adolescents involves both intervening with younger adolescents to prevent negative early life events, working with young adolescents experiencing negative life events to prevent future negative health outcomes and also working with older adolescents who have also experienced negative life events to address trauma, coping and resilience skills to support prevention behaviours. In particular, programmes and policies that support young women staying in secondary school and completing school and those providing comprehensive, adolescent health services to prevent early pregnancies and comprehensive sexuality education in schools are some of the key steps that may help provide safety nets to help adolescents transition safely to adulthood.

References

Azen, R. and Traxel, N. (2009) Using dominance analysis to determine predictor importance in logistic regression. *Journal of Educational and Behavioral Statistics* 31(3): 293–318.

Balistreri, K.S. and Alvira-Hammond, M. (2016) Adverse childhood experiences, family functioning and adolescent health and emotional well-being. *Public Health* 132: 72–8.

Boullier, M. and Blair, M. (2018) Adverse childhood experiences. *Paediatrics and Child Health* 28(3): 132–7.

Budescu, D.V. (1993) Dominance analysis: a new approach to the problem of relative importance of predictors in multiple regression. *Psychological Bulletin* 114(3): 542–51.

Christofides, N.J., Jewkes, R.K., Dunkle, K.L., Nduna, M., Shai, N.J. and Sterk, C. (2014) Early adolescent pregnancy increases risk of incident HIV infection in the Eastern Cape, South Africa: a longitudinal study. *Journal of the International AIDS Society* 17(1): 18585.

Elder, G.H. (1998) The life course as developmental theory. *Child Development* 69(1): 1–12.

Evans, G.W., Li, D. and Whipple, S.S. (2013) Cumulative risk and child development. *Psychological Bulletin* 139(6): 1342–96.

Falconi, A., Gemmill, A., Dahl, R.E. and Catalano, R. (2014) Adolescent experience predicts longevity: evidence from historical epidemiology. *Journal of Developmental Origins of Health and Disease* 5(3): 171–7.

Fuhrmann, D., Knoll, L.J. and Blakemore, S.J. (2015) Adolescence as a sensitive period of brain development. *Trends in Cognitive Sciences* 19(10): 558–66.

Hughes, K., Bellis, M.A., Hardcastle, K.A., Sethi, D., Butchart, A., Mikton, C. et al (2017) The effect of multiple adverse childhood experiences on health: a systematic review and meta-analysis. *The Lancet Public Health* 2(8): e356–66.

Human Sciences Research Council (HSRC) (2017) The fifth South African national HIV prevalence, incidence, behaviour and communication survey, 2017: HIV impact assessment summary report. Cape Town.

Jung, T. and Wickrama, K.A.S. (2008) An introduction to latent class growth analysis and growth mixture modeling. *Social and Personality Psychology Compass* 2(1): 302–17.

Kidman, R. and Kohler, H.P. (2019) Adverse childhood experiences, sexual debut and HIV testing among adolescents in a low-income high HIV-prevalence context. *AIDS* 33(14): 2245–50.

MacMillan, R. and Copher, R. (2005) Families in the life course: interdependency of roles, role configurations, and pathways. *Journal of Marriage and Family* 67(4): 858–79.

Muthén, L. and Muthén, B. (2005) Mplus: statistical analysis with latent variables: user's guide.

Operario, D., Underhill, K., Chuong, C. and Cluver, L. (2011) HIV infection and sexual risk behaviour among youth who have experienced orphanhood: systematic review and meta-analysis. *Journal of the International AIDS Society* 14: 25.

Pettifor, A.E., Van Der Straten, A., Dunbar, M.S., Shiboski, S.C. and Padian, N.S. (2004) Early age of first sex: a risk factor for HIV infection among women in Zimbabwe. *AIDS* 18(10): 1435–42.

Pettifor, A., O'Brien, K., MacPhail, C., Miller, W.C. and Rees, H. (2009) Early coital debut and associated HIV risk factors among young women and men in South Africa. *International Perspectives on Sexual and Reproductive Health* 35(2): 74–82.

Pettifor, A., MacPhail, C., Hughes, J.P., Selin, A., Wang, J., Gómez-Olivé, F.X. et al (2016) The effect of a conditional cash transfer on HIV incidence in young women in rural South Africa (HPTN 068): a phase 3, randomised controlled trial. *The Lancet Global Health* 4: e978–88.

StataCorp (2017) Stata Statistical Software: Release 15, 2017.

Stoner, M.C.D., Pettifor, A., Edwards, J.K., Aiello, A.E., Halpern, C.T., Julien, A. et al (2017) The effect of school attendance and school dropout on incident HIV and HSV-2 among young women in rural South Africa enrolled in HPTN 068. *AIDS* 31: 2127–34.

Stoner, M.C.D., Edwards, J.K., Miller, W.C., Aiello, A.E., Halpern, C.T., Julien, A. et al (2018) Does partner selection mediate the relationship between school attendance and HIV/Herpes Simplex Virus-2 among adolescent girls and young women in South Africa. *Journal of Acquired Immune Deficiency Syndromes* 79(1): 20–27.

United Nations International Children's Emergency Fund (UNICEF) (2017) *The Adolescent Brain: A Second Window of Opportunity*. Florence: UNICEF.

Wand, H. and Ramjee, G. (2012) The relationship between age of coital debut and HIV seroprevalence among women in Durban, South Africa: a cohort study. *BMJ Open*. https://doi.org/10.1136/bmjopen-2011-000285

4

Achieving the Sustainable Development Goals: Evidence from the Longitudinal Parenting Across Cultures Project

Jennifer E. Lansford, W. Andrew Rothenberg, Sombat Tapanya, Liliana Maria Uribe Tirado, Saengduean Yotanyamaneewong, Liane Peña Alampay, Suha M. Al-Hassan, Dario Bacchini, Marc H. Bornstein, Lei Chang, Kirby Deater-Deckard, Laura Di Giunta, Kenneth A. Dodge, Sevtap Gurdal, Qin Liu, Qian Long, Patrick S. Malone, Paul Oburu, Concetta Pastorelli, Ann T. Skinner, Emma Sorbring and Laurence Steinberg

Introduction

This chapter uses evidence from the Parenting across Cultures (PAC) project to illustrate ways in which longitudinal data can help achieve the Sustainable Development Goals (SDGs; https://sustainabledevelopment.un.org/). The chapter begins by providing an overview of the research questions that have guided PAC as well as a description of the participants, procedures and measures. Next, empirical findings from PAC are summarized to illustrate implications for six specific SDGs. Then the chapter describes how longitudinal data offer advantages over cross-sectional data in operationalizing SDG targets and implementing the SDGs. Finally, limitations, future research directions and conclusions are provided.

PAC was developed in response to concerns that understanding of parenting and child development was biased by the predominant focus in the literature on studying families in Western, educated, industrialized, rich and democratic (WEIRD) societies and that findings in such countries may not generalize well to more diverse populations around the world (Henrich et al, 2010). In an analysis of the sample characteristics in the most influential journals in six subdisciplines of psychology from 2003 to 2007, 96% of research participants were from Western industrialized countries, and 68% were from the United States alone (Arnett, 2008), which means that 96% of research participants in these psychological studies were from countries with only 12% of the world's population (Henrich et al, 2010). When basic science research is limited to WEIRD countries, knowledge of human development becomes defined by a set of experiences that may not be widely shared in different cultural contexts, so studying parenting and child development in a wide range of diverse cultural contexts is important to understand development more fully.

PAC has been conceptualized and funded as a consecutive series of three five-year grants, each covering a different developmental period and guided by different research questions. In the first project period, participants were aged 8 to 12. The main research questions focused on cultural differences in links between discipline and child adjustment, warmth as a moderator of links between harsh discipline and child outcomes, and cognitive and emotional mediators of effects of harsh discipline on children's aggression and anxiety. In the second period, target participants were 13 to 17 years old. The main research questions focused on how biological maturation and socialization interact in the development of risk-taking behaviour; psychological mechanisms through which biological maturation, parenting and culture alter the development of adolescent risk-taking behaviour; and how cultural normativeness of parenting behaviours and culturally shaped opportunity for risk-taking behaviours moderate the relation between parenting and adolescents' risk-taking. In the third and current period, target participants are aged 18 to 22. The main research questions focus on parenting influences on risky behaviours, cultural context moderators of associations between early parenting factors and the development of both competence and maladaptation during the transition to adulthood, and child-level and family-level mediators of links between childhood risk factors and young-adult competence and maladaptation.

Participants

Participants included 1,432 families with a child ranging in age from 7 to 10 years ($M = 8.28$, $SD = 0.65$; 51% girls) at the time of recruitment.

Families were drawn from Jinan, China (n = 120), Shanghai, China (n = 122), Medellín, Colombia (n = 108), Naples, Italy (n = 100), Rome, Italy (n = 109), Zarqa, Jordan (n = 114), Kisumu, Kenya (n = 100), Manila, Philippines (n = 120), Trollhättan/Vänersborg, Sweden (n = 103), Chiang Mai, Thailand (n = 120) and Durham, North Carolina, United States (n = 112 European Americans, n = 104 African Americans, n = 100 Hispanic Americans). Participants were recruited through public and private schools to increase socioeconomic diversity and representativeness of the sample. Response rates varied from 24% to nearly 100%, primarily because of differences in the schools' roles in recruiting. For example, in China, once schools agreed to participate, the parents agreed to participate as well, and interviews were conducted at the schools, leading to participation rates of nearly 100%. In the United States, after schools agreed to help with recruitment, our interview team was allowed to leave letters explaining the study at the school to send home with students. Parents then returned a letter to the school indicating their willingness to participate. Our team then contacted them directly to arrange an interview at a convenient time and place.

Most parents lived together (82%) and were biological parents (97%); non-residential and non-biological parents also provided data. Sampling included families from each country's majority ethnic group, except in Kenya where we sampled Luo (third largest ethnic group, 13% of population), and in the United States, where we sampled equal proportions of White, Black and Latino families. Socioeconomic status was sampled in proportions representative of each recruitment area. For example, six well-defined socioeconomic strata in Colombia were used as a basis for recruiting families to our sample in proportion to their representation in the socioeconomic strata in Medellín, our recruitment city. The samples are not nationally representative, but our goal was to sample families in each recruitment city such that residents would deem the sample locally representative. Child age and gender did not vary across cultural groups.

With one exception, retention of the original sample exceeded 75% and approached 100% in some sites through the most current wave of data collection, ten years after initial recruitment. We retained the sample and minimized attrition over time by maintaining detailed contact information (including email addresses, mobile phone numbers, street addresses and social media contacts) for mothers, fathers and adolescents. We also obtained contact information for family members or friends who do not live with the participants who would know how to find them. Periodic newsletters are sent to families with information about the project as well as birthday and holiday cards to keep families engaged. Participants are given incentives specific to individual sites, either payments in cash or gift cards that are deemed locally motivating but not coercive or gifts to children's schools. On occasion, our project has been an important resource for the participating families. For example, when a flood in the Philippines destroyed a participating family's home, our project records of their address served as the documentation they provided to local authorities to prove where they had once lived.

Procedure and measures

Annual interviews are conducted with target participants, their mothers and their fathers. Until age 10, children completed in-person oral interviews in which interviewers would ask children questions and record their responses, showing children visual representations of response scales to aid in their responding. After age 10, children were given the choice of continuing with oral interviews or completing interviews in writing. Parents completed oral interviews in the first project year and were given the choice of completing oral or written interviews in subsequent years. Completing online interviews was added as an option when advances in technology and internet access made this option feasible. To maximize retention, we have been flexible about offering several ways for participants to complete the interviews, including over the telephone or in writing to be mailed back to our project in-country offices, especially if families have moved too far to make an in-person interview in their home or the university possible. Interviews generally last one to two hours.

Measures have assessed a wide range of parenting variables (for example, discipline, monitoring, warmth, control) and a wide range of child adjustment variables (for example, social competence, school performance, prosocial behaviour, internalizing and externalizing problems). In project years 3, 6 and 9 children completed computerized batteries in the form of games to assess aspects of executive functioning, such as reward sensitivity and impulse control. Measures were administered in the predominant language of each country, following forward- and back-translation and meetings to resolve any item-by-item ambiguities in linguistic or semantic content. In addition to translating the measures, translators noted and suggested improvements to items that did not translate well, were inappropriate for the participants, were culturally insensitive or elicited multiple meanings. Site coordinators and the translators reviewed the discrepant items and made appropriate modifications. A full list of project measures is available at parentingacrosscultures.org.

Implications of select PAC findings for the SDGs

Findings from the PAC project inform understanding of how to realize six SDGs. However, realization of many SDGs is interconnected. For example, both SDG 1 (no poverty) and SDG 3 (good health and well-being) are more attainable with higher levels of quality education (advanced in SDG 4).

SDG 1: Ending poverty in all its forms

A large body of international research has demonstrated that poverty has detrimental effects on children's growth and physical health. Using longitudinal data from PAC, this international focus was extended to children's emotional and behavioural development. It was found that higher household income was related to decreases in children's internalizing and externalizing problems from age 8 to age 10, above and beyond effects of mothers' and fathers' education (Lansford et al, 2019). For families with household incomes at or below the mean, mother-reported child externalizing behaviour declined modestly over time, but for families with household incomes above the mean, mother-reported child externalizing behaviour remained fairly stable over time, and always lower than mother-reported child externalizing for families with incomes at or below the mean. This means that even just a little increase in income for families at the lowest levels of income makes the biggest difference in terms of decreasing children's externalizing problems over time. The findings highlight that family-level income is important for child development regardless of macro-level poverty in low-, middle- and high-income countries. The longitudinal data made it possible to examine how poverty related to children's internalizing and externalizing behaviours at a single point in time and how poverty related to changes in internalizing and externalizing behaviours over time.

It was also found that even when household income remained stable over time, parents' perceptions of material deprivation predicted their use of psychological aggression towards their child and children's self- and parent-reported externalizing behaviour problems (Schenck-Fontaine et al, forthcoming). These findings were consistent across, high-, middle- and low-income countries, suggesting that perceived material deprivation likely influences children's outcomes regardless of actual income level.

SDG 3: Ensure healthy lives and promote well-being for all at all ages

SDG target 3.4 is to promote well-being and mental health. Positive social relationships are among the best predictors of well-being and mental health, and harsh treatment by parents, peers and others predicts poorer mental health and behavioural adjustment. For example, in PAC it was found that children's perceptions of their parents' rejection predicted increases in children's mother- and father-reported internalizing and externalizing behaviour problems and decreases in parent-reported school performance and child-reported prosocial behaviour across three years, controlling for concurrent associations between parenting and child adjustment, stability across time in parenting and child adjustment, parental age, parental education and parents' likelihood of responding in socially desirable ways (Putnick et al, 2015). More similarities than differences were found across cultures in links between mothers', fathers' and children's reports of five aspects of parenting (expectations regarding family obligations, monitoring, psychological control, behavioural control and parental warmth) and five aspects of child well-being (social competence, prosocial behaviour, academic achievement, externalizing behaviour and internalizing behaviour); whether each aspect of parenting was culturally normative affected the strength of some of these links (Lansford et al, 2018b). For example, children were more socially competent when their mothers held higher expectations regarding the child's family obligations, particularly if high expectations regarding family obligations were culturally normative.

Both individual- and culture-level predictors of the development of externalizing behaviour problems were found, such as aggression and delinquency, from age 7 to 14 (Lansford et al, 2018a). For example, not only did individual mothers' and children's endorsement of aggression and authoritarian attitudes predict higher initial levels of externalizing behaviour problems and growth in externalizing behaviours over time, but cultural norms endorsing aggression and authoritarian attitudes exacerbated these effects. These findings suggest that intervention efforts to change cultural norms that increase the risk of children's behavioural problems may be a necessary part of promoting children's well-being to achieve the SDGs.

SDG 4: Inclusive quality education for all

Collaborators from the nine PAC countries have compiled an edited volume that provides an overview of each country's current school system, discusses parenting in light of the school system, and provides evidence from that country regarding links between parenting and students' academic performance (Sorbring and Lansford, 2019). Several themes relevant to realizing the goal of inclusive quality education for all emerged across countries. First, even when public education is theoretically free, hidden costs often keep young people out of school. For example, families may not be able to afford to pay for uniforms, books and activity fees, or may be able to afford these expenses for only some of their children, keeping the others out of school. Second, access to quality education often varies as a function of social class, ethnicity, urban versus rural residence and other within-country demographic differences. Third, with the increased focus, especially in low- and middle-income countries, on access to free primary and secondary education, the quality of available education may have decreased in some countries, largely because of an insufficient number of trained teachers, books and other educational materials to serve the higher numbers of enrolled students. For example, in Colombia, to accommodate the large volume of students, half rather than full school days are the norm so that students can attend in shifts. Only 11% of public school students in Colombia are able to attend even one full day of school per week, which puts them at a severe disadvantage compared to Colombian students who attend private schools, which are more often full-day programmes, as well as compared to students from other countries in scores on international standardized tests of reading, mathematics and science (Di Giunta and Uribe Tirado, 2019).

Understanding different countries' education systems, policies, programmes that countries have implemented to improve access to and quality of education, and how parents can facilitate students' academic achievement makes it possible for countries to learn from one another ways to realize educational targets. For example, school enrolment in the Philippines has increased by 9% among those eligible for a cash transfer programme (Chaudhury and Okamura, 2012), suggesting a model that could be used in other countries to make it financially feasible for families to keep their adolescents in secondary school. Likewise 'mother tongue' programmes in which 12 local languages have been added as languages of instruction in the first years of primary school in the Philippines have shown promise in enhancing children's and parents' comprehension (Alampay and Garcia, 2019), providing another avenue that could be adopted by other countries where students have many different native languages. Children living in poverty are particularly vulnerable to a lack of quality education, so would especially benefit from scholarships and macro-level supports such as better staffing and infrastructure. Longitudinal data are essential for evaluating the impact of education reforms. Without baseline data prior to a reform and follow-up data after implementing reforms, it is impossible to know whether changes in policies or educational practices are having their desired effects.

SDG 5: Gender parity and equitable life chances

Longitudinal studies can advance understanding of ways in which boys and girls may benefit from different supports for their development and ways in which they typically develop similarly. For example, consistent with many other studies, in PAC it was found that boys report more physical aggressive than girls; however, boys and girls did not differ in their reported use of relationally aggressive behaviour (that is, excluding another child from a group, saying mean things about that person, and saying things about another child to make people laugh; Lansford et al, 2012).

It was found that both mothers' and fathers' positive evaluations of aggressive responses to hypothetical childrearing vignettes at one time predicted parents' subsequent self-reported use of corporal punishment and harsh verbal discipline (Lansford et al, 2014b). Mothers and fathers make similar attributions for successes and failures in caregiving situations, but fathers hold more authoritarian attitudes than do mothers (Bornstein et al, 2011). Within the same family, mothers' and fathers' attitudes are moderately correlated with each other.

Many similarities were also found in the ways in which mothers' and fathers' parenting is related to children's development. For example, no differences were found between mothers and fathers in the ways in which their warmth toward children was related to increases in children's prosocial behaviour over the course of three years (Putnick et al, 2018) or the ways in which mothers' and fathers' reports of their use of corporal punishment were related to an increase in children's self- or parent-reported externalizing behaviours over time (Alampay et al, 2017). It was also found that parental warmth and behavioural control reported by mothers, fathers and children convey similarly protective effects on child externalizing and internalizing behaviours (also reported by mothers, fathers and children) from ages 8 to 13, but that both mother and father effects convey unique protections over and above one another (Rothenberg et al, 2020). In other words, it appears that both mothers' and fathers' parenting play important and, for some child outcomes, unique roles in child development in similar ways across cultures. Therefore, our collective findings argue for the importance of increasing gender parity by including both mothers and fathers in parenting programmes that are designed to change parents' knowledge, attitudes and behaviours.

SDG 11: Create safe, secure and sustainable cities and communities

It was found, using mothers', fathers' and children's reports, that children who live in unsafe neighbourhoods, have chaotic home environments, have fluctuating household incomes and experience stressful life events behave more aggressively and perform more poorly in school later in childhood and adolescence (Chang et al, 2019). The longitudinal data in PAC made it possible for us to understand mechanisms through which unsafe and insecure families and communities contribute to poor developmental outcomes for children and adolescents, again using reports from mothers, fathers and children. For example, household chaos and neighbourhood danger when children are 13 years old predicted harsher maternal parenting when they were 14 years old, which predicted more externalizing, internalizing and scholastic problems when they were 15 years old (Deater-Deckard et al, 2019). Additionally, it was found that 9-year-old children whose families experienced financial difficulties and whose parents used corporal punishment exhibited more aggressive and delinquent behaviour at age 12 than children who did not experience those adversities, in part because children who experienced early adversities developed poorer impulse control and became more likely to attribute hostile intent to others in ambiguous social situations (Lansford et al, 2017). Even when parents reported monitoring their child's whereabouts, activities and companions, the link between perceptions of living in a dangerous neighbourhood and more child aggression remained (Skinner et al, 2014a). All of these findings highlight the importance of creating safe and secure communities to promote positive child development.

Children were presented with hypothetical vignettes depicting an ambiguous social situation in which the main character experiences a negative outcome and asked children why the provocateur in the vignette behaved as they did (Dodge et al, 2015). Responses were coded as either hostile (for example, he was being mean) or benign (for example, it was an accident) intent. Children also indicated how likely they would be to respond with aggression in that situation, and children and mothers rated children's aggression in real-life situations. It was found that cultural groups that were above average in children's propensity for making hostile attributions were also above average in

Figure 4.1: The relation between attribution of intention and probability of aggressing, by cultural group

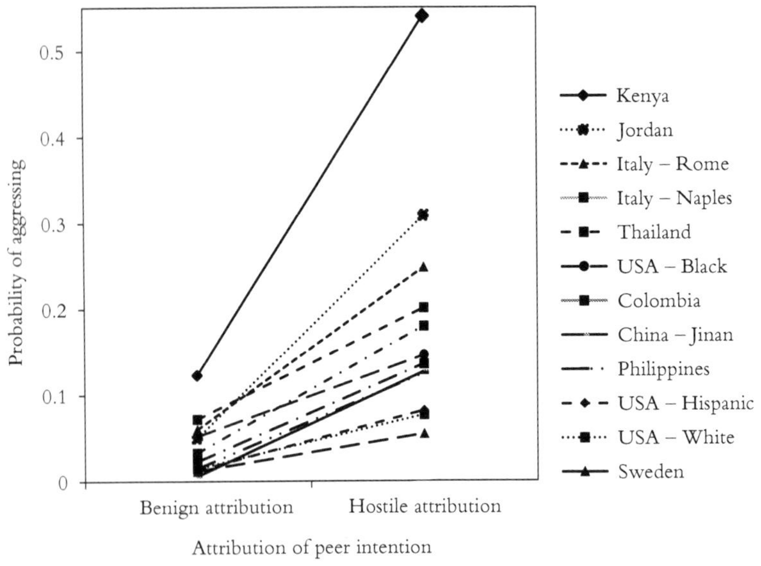

Source: Adapted from Dodge et al, 2015

children's aggression, according to mothers' and children's reports. In addition, it was found that within a cultural group, children who were above average for their cultural group in their likelihood of making hostile attributions also were above average for their cultural group in aggressive behaviour. Finally, it was found that individual children were more likely to indicate they would respond to aggression in vignettes for which they made a hostile attribution than in vignettes for which they made a benign attribution (see Figure 4.1). Identifying this psychological mechanism in children's aggressive behaviour suggests that aggressive behaviour could be reduced at a societal level by focusing on how groups socialize children to respond to provocations with hostile or benign attributions and to generate non-aggressive solutions in provocative situations.

SDG 16: Achieve peace, justice and strong institutions

Target 16.2 is to end abuse, exploitation, trafficking and all forms of violence against and torture of children. Indicator 16.2.1 is the proportion of children aged 1–17 years who experienced any physical punishment and/or psychological aggression by caregivers in the past month. In PAC, it was found that across the nine participating countries, 54% of girls' and 58% of boys' parents reported that their child had experienced corporal punishment by their parents or someone in their household in the last month (Lansford et al, 2010). Across countries, 17% of parents reported believing that using corporal punishment is necessary to rear their child properly, but that ranged from none of the parents in Sweden to 48% and 54% of the parents in Kenya believing that corporal punishment is necessary to rear their daughter or son, respectively. Use and endorsement of different forms of discipline show larger between-country differences than most other aspects of parenting and child development in PAC (Deater-Deckard et al, 2018; see Figure 4.2).

It has been found that parents' perceptions of the severity and justness of corporal punishment do not moderate the relation between corporal punishment and negative child outcomes (Alampay et al, 2017). That is, corporal punishment is related to more child internalizing and externalizing behaviour problems, even when it is mild and when parents believe they are justified in using it. Likewise, it was found that more frequent corporal punishment is related to more child self- and mother-reported anxiety and aggression even when parents also show warmth towards their child; indeed, children were most anxious when parents used corporal punishment in conjunction with warmth, perhaps because it was difficult for children to reconcile parental warmth with the experience of being hit by their parents (Lansford et al, 2014a; see Figure 4.3). Parents' use of corporal punishment is predicted by both individual-level factors (especially child externalizing behaviours, because children who misbehave more often elicit more discipline from their parents in response) as well as cultural-level factors (especially normativeness of corporal punishment in the community, because parents tend to behave in ways that are endorsed and practised by their cultural group; Lansford et al, 2015).

The analyses focusing on links between corporal punishment and different aspects of child development exclude Sweden, which outlawed all forms of corporal punishment in 1979. Despite measures taken to ensure that Swedish participants could report corporal punishment if they or their parents were using it (for example, having the questions about discipline separate from other measures and mailing them directly to the United States rather than to the investigators in Sweden), almost none of the Swedish parents reported using corporal punishment. As of November 2019, corporal punishment has been outlawed by 58 countries and is one of the chief means by which countries are trying to realize SDG Target 16.2. Kenya outlawed corporal punishment in 2010, providing a natural experiment because data were collected for

Figure 4.2: Percentage of variance accounted for by between-culture, between-person within-culture, and residual effects for mother-reported variables

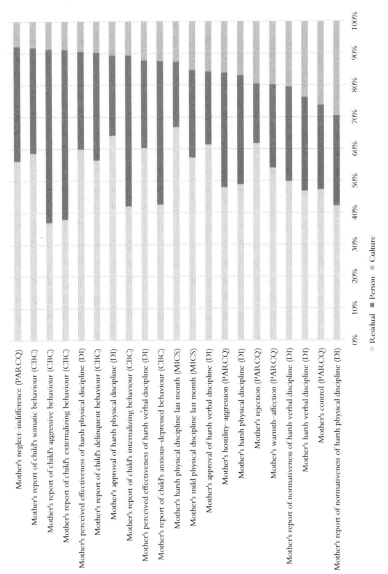

Note: CBC = Child Behaviour Checklist, DI = Discipline Interview, MICS = Multiple Indicator Cluster Survey, PARCQ = Parental Acceptance-Rejection/Control Questionnaire

Source: Adapted from Deater-Deckard et al, 2018

Figure 4.3: Model-implied slopes representing change in anxiety over three years at different levels of corporal punishment and maternal warmth

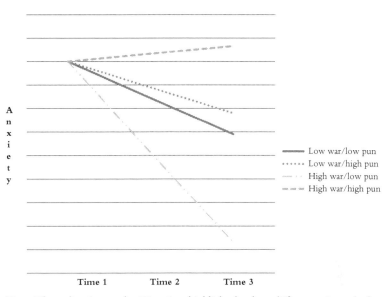

Note: The scaling is zeroed at Time 1 to highlight the slope differences, instead of confounding them with intercept differences. The y-axis is an effect size scale, relative to standard deviations of the slope.

Source: Adapted from Lansford et al, 2014a

PAC both before and after the legal ban. Preliminary analyses conducted suggest a decrease in reported use of corporal punishment following the legal ban in 2010 that is not reflected in other PAC countries that did not ban corporal punishment. Additional longitudinal analyses will clarify the extent to which legally banning corporal punishment results in desired changes in parenting and child outcomes.

Important policy decisions related to the realization of SDG Target 16.2 sometimes involve decisions regarding ages at which children should be treated as adults in legal systems, including when they should be criminally tried as an adult. In an extension of the PAC study that included data from 10- to 30-year-olds in Cyprus and India in addition to the PAC countries, evidence was found that in all 11 countries, individuals' sensation-seeking increased through adolescence and peaked around age 19 before declining, whereas self-regulation continues to develop into early adulthood before reaching a plateau between the ages of 23 and 26 (Steinberg et al, 2018). These findings provide cross-national support for the dual-systems theory, which has likened brain development in adolescence and early adulthood to a car that has a functioning engine before brakes are in place (Steinberg, 2008). However, risk-taking propensity in laboratory-based tasks was more consistent across countries than risk-taking in real-world settings, suggesting that, although reward sensitivity peaks in adolescence across cultures, opportunities for and constraints on risk-taking may promote or limit risky behaviour in real life (Duell et al, 2018). In an explicit consideration of the implications of these findings for legal systems, it was concluded that a maturity gap exists between the age at which adolescents are able to engage in complex reasoning in controlled settings and the age at which adolescents can exercise self-restraint in emotional situations. In legal systems, adolescents may be capable of making decisions in situations that involve careful deliberation at an age younger than when they can be held responsible for decisions made quickly in emotionally charged situations (Icenogle et al, 2019).

How longitudinal data offer advantages over cross-sectional data

The design of the PAC project, with family members nested within families, which are nested within cultures and assessed over time is optimal for understanding whether variance is explained by within-individual factors that change over time, by within-family factors, by within-culture factors or by between-culture factors. In an analysis parsing these different sources of variance for a large number of parenting and child adjustment variables, it was found that more variance is explained by within-culture than between-culture factors (Deater-Deckard et al, 2018). That is, the variation in parenting and child adjustment within cultural groups is greater than the variation in parenting and child adjustment between cultural groups. Some of the within-culture variation is accounted for by factors that change over time, such as by changes in how parents treat children as they develop, and other within-culture variation is accounted for by factors to which some but not other members of a cultural group are exposed, such as a traumatic life event or the presence of a supportive parent.

Longitudinal data also make it possible to examine reciprocal relations between children and parents over time. Using cross-sectional data, one would be able to say whether a particular aspect of parenting (or another aspect of the child's environment) is correlated with a particular child outcome, but could not determine the direction of effects. To speak definitively about cause and effect, one would need to use an experimental design. But, using longitudinal data, it is possible to control for early parenting or child variables in the statistical prediction of these variables at a later point in time to determine whether a change in parenting predicts a change in child outcomes (see Figure 4.4). In addition, longitudinal models are able to test directions of effects from children to parents and parents to children (Putnick et al, 2018). In PAC, for example, it was found that effects of parental warmth and control on children's externalizing and internalizing behaviours are more pronounced in childhood than in adolescence and that effects of children's externalizing and internalizing behaviours on parents' subsequent warmth and control are stronger and more consistent than parents' effects on children's externalizing and internalizing behaviours (Lansford et al, 2018c). Similarly, children who behave prosocially elicit subsequently positive discipline and have warmer relationships with their mothers than do children who are initially low in prosocial behaviour (Pastorelli et al, 2016). Longitudinal findings about the importance of child effects on parents have significant implications for the development of parenting programmes, which are often implemented in an attempt to alter child behaviours. In PAC analyses, the robustness of findings is enhanced by the inclusion of data reported by mothers, fathers and children rather than relying only on a single source of data, which can artificially inflate relations through same-source biases.

Because political, environmental and other societal-level circumstances change over time, it may become necessary to operationalize SDG targets in different ways over time and in different cultural groups so as to capture the changing environments to which families are exposed. For example, during the course of the PAC project, a disputed political election in Kenya resulted in more than 1,200 deaths, thousands of internal displacements, and destroyed homes and businesses. Recognizing the opportunity to understand how exposure to political violence was related to parenting and child outcomes both in close temporal proximity to the election and at more distal times, questions were added to the PAC measure regarding exposure to political violence for the interviews with Kenyan mothers and fathers, who reported whether they had experienced each of 14 forms of violence and whether their child had been exposed to these forms of violence. It was found that children who were exposed to more post-election violence exhibited more externalizing behaviour problems the following year, which in turn predicted parents' use of more childrearing violence in the next year (Skinner et al, 2014b). These findings suggest that exposure to even short-term political violence can set in motion negative, reciprocal developmental trajectories for children and their parents.

Figure 4.4: Framework for analyses examining longitudinal associations between a parent's behaviour and a child's behaviour across different cultural groups (Source: Adapted from Lansford et al, 2018c)

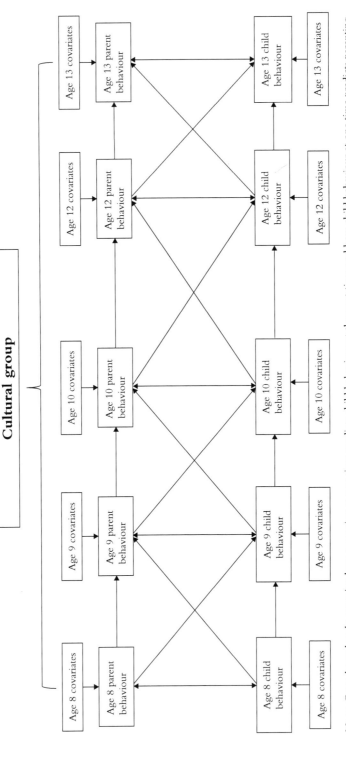

Note: Cross-lagged paths examine how parenting at one time predicts child behaviour at the next time and how child behaviour at one time predicts parenting at the next time. The model controls for time-specific associations with study covariates (child gender, parent education), stability in parent and child behaviour over time (as depicted by the autoregressive paths), and contemporaneous associations between parent and child behaviour. Associations between measures at non-adjacent time points (for example, child behaviour at age 8 and 10) can also be controlled.

Limitations and future directions

Despite its strengths in having longitudinal data available from mothers, fathers and children from age 8 into early adulthood from nine countries, the PAC project also has limitations. The samples are not nationally representative so cannot be used to make claims about national prevalence rates of particular aspects of parenting or child outcomes. Recruiting nationally representative samples from several countries and following them annually over several years would exceed the budgets of most funding agencies. The Multiple Indicator Cluster Surveys include nationally representative samples from dozens of low- and middle-income countries and have been administered at several points in time, albeit with different participants at each time point rather than following the same participants over time (http://mics. unicef.org/). Several high-income countries have recruited nationally representative samples to follow longitudinally over time (for example, the Millennium Cohort Study in the United Kingdom, the National Longitudinal Survey of Youth in the United States), but these surveys cannot compare across countries. Combining the advantages of nationally representative samples with longitudinal data collection in many high-, middle- and low-income countries remains an aspiration for future research.

The PAC project also is limited to development from middle childhood through early adulthood. Early childhood typically has received more attention than middle childhood and adolescence in international development work. Future research that includes the full developmental range from birth (or even prenatally) through early adulthood will be important to understand developmental trajectories that often are set in motion early in life, as well as how later risks and supports may alter these developmental trajectories.

Ecological momentary assessments (EMA) are a relatively new mode of data collection that can be used to advance realization of the SDGs. In a typical design using ecological momentary assessments, brief questions are sent to participants' mobile phones two or three times per day over a period of several days or weeks. As part of PAC, questions were sent three times per day for 15 days to the mobile phones of adolescents in Rome. Across the two-week study period, adolescents responded to 90% of the questions (Rothenberg et al, 2019). Because the majority of adolescents globally now have mobile phones, using EMA offers the potential in future research to monitor a number of indicators related to the SDGs (such as school attendance, experiences of violence) in real time and to assess change over time for less expense than other forms of data collection would entail. EMA also drastically reduce the typical length of time between assessment points compared to annual data collection in more traditional longitudinal designs, making it possible to assess changes that occur more rapidly and to look at variation over relatively short periods of time.

Another important direction for future research will be to capitalize on advances in neuroscience and biomarkers to enhance understanding of ways to realize the SDGs. To date in PAC, functional magnetic resonance imaging has been used in the United States sample to examine how exposure to poverty, neurobiological circuitry connected to emotion dysregulation, later exposure to stressful life events and symptoms of psychopathology develop over time. Exposure to poverty at age 10 was related to changes in the resting state coupling between the amygdala and ventromedial prefrontal cortex, two brain structures centrally involved with emotion processing and regulation, at age 15. Lower coupling of these two brain regions, in combination with early poverty and concurrent exposure to stressful life events, predicted mental health problems at age 16 (Hanson et al, 2019). Costs of and access to equipment for conducting brain imaging can pose a barrier to neuroscientific studies in low- and middle-income countries, but it is possible to collect biomarkers in hair, saliva and blood for lower costs. Findings from brain imaging and biomarkers often are especially influential with policy makers so can be used to garner financial and political support for interventions, practices or policies that would advance the SDGs in ways that are connected to improvements in biological functioning.

Conclusions

The Parenting Across Cultures project provides evidence regarding the development of children and adolescents in nine countries that vary widely in sociodemographic and cultural factors that can be used to inform understanding of how to achieve the SDGs. The longitudinal design makes possible analyses that examine bi-directional influences between children and their parents, taking into account stability of children's mental health, behavioural adjustment, academic performance and features in their environment, such as parenting and household income. If changes in parenting or income, for example, predict subsequent changes in children's well-being, these suggest particularly meaningful targets for achieving the SDGs. Realization of some of the SDGs depends directly on accurately measuring children's experiences, such as with the operationalization of Indicator 16.2.1 as the proportion of children aged 1–17 years who experienced any physical punishment

Table 4.1: Highlights for policy makers and practitioners

- The Parenting Across Cultures project recruited 8-year-old children, their mothers and fathers in nine countries (China, Colombia, Italy, Jordan, Kenya, Philippines, Sweden, Thailand and United States) and continues with annual interviews through early adulthood.

- **SDG 1 (Ending poverty in all its forms):** Living in poverty and perceptions of material deprivation are risk factors for increases in children's behaviour and mental health problems over time.

- **SDG 3 (Ensure healthy lives and promote well-being for all at all ages):** Positive social relationships are among the best predictors of well-being and mental health, and harsh treatment by parents, peers and others predicts poorer mental health and behavioural adjustment.

- **SDG 4 (Inclusive quality education for all):** Even when public education is theoretically free, costs of uniforms, books and fees keep students out of school. Decreased quality may accompany increased access if an insufficient number of trained teachers, books and other materials cannot serve the higher numbers of enrolled students.

- **SDG 5 (Gender parity and equitable life chances):** Mothers' and fathers' parenting each relates to children's development in many similar ways, arguing for the importance of including both mothers and fathers in programmes that are designed to change parents' knowledge, attitudes and behaviours.

- **SDG 11 (Create safe, secure, and sustainable cities and communities):** Children who live in an unsafe neighbourhood, have chaotic home environments, have fluctuating household income and experience stressful life events behave more aggressively and perform more poorly in school than do children without these difficulties.

- **SDG 16 (Achieve peace, justice, and strong institutions):** As of August 2019, corporal punishment is outlawed by 56 countries and is one means by which countries try to realize SDG 16. Decisions regarding ages at which children should be criminally tried as an adult or jailed with adult offenders should be informed by findings regarding adolescent brain development.

and/or psychological aggression by caregivers in the past month. Realization of other aspects of SDG 16 involving just social institutions is only possible with a solid understanding of adolescent brain development because of the implications of differences in the developmental timeframes of sensation-seeking and self-regulation for understanding adolescents' propensity for risky behaviours, suggesting they should not be treated as legally responsible for their actions committed in emotion-charged situations. Understanding the development of children and adolescents is important for achieving the international development agenda set forth in the SDGs.

References

Alampay, L.P. and Garcia, A.S. (2019) Education and parenting in the Philippines. In E. Sorbring and J.E. Lansford (Eds) *School Systems, Parent Behavior, and Academic Achievement: An International Perspective* (pp 79–94). Cham, Switzerland: Springer.

Alampay, L.P., Godwin, J., Lansford, J.E., Bombi, A.S., Bornstein, M.H., Chang, L. et al (2017) Severity and justness do not moderate the relation between corporal punishment and negative child outcomes: a multicultural and longitudinal study. *International Journal of Behavioral Development* 41(4): 491–502.

Arnett, J.J. (2008). The neglected 95%: why American psychology needs to become less American. *American Psychologist* 63(7): 602–14.

Bornstein, M.H., Putnick, D.L. and Lansford, J.E. (2011) Parenting attributions and attitudes in cross-cultural perspective. *Parenting: Science and Practice* 11(2–3): 214–37.

Chang, L., Lu, H.J., Lansford, J.E., Skinner, A.T., Bornstein, M.H., Steinberg, L., Dodge, K.A. et al (2019) Environmental harshness and unpredictability, life history, and social and academic behavior of adolescents in nine countries. *Developmental Psychology* 55(4): 890.

Chaudhury, N. and Okamura, Y. (2012) Conditional cash transfers and school enrollment: impact of the conditional cash transfer program in the Philippines. World Bank Social Protection Policy Note No. 6. Washington, DC: World Bank. Available at http://documents. worldbank.org/curated/en/479681468093580402/Conditional-cash-transfers-and-school-enrollment-impact-of-the-conditional-cash-transfer-program-in-the-Philippines

Deater-Deckard, K., Godwin, J., Lansford, J.E., Bacchini, D., Bombi, A.S., Bornstein, M.H. et al (2018) Within- and between-person and group variance in behavior and beliefs in cross-cultural longitudinal data. *Journal of Adolescence* 62(1): 207–17.

Deater-Deckard, K., Godwin, J., Lansford, J.E., Uribe Tirado, L.M., Yotanyamaneewong, S., Alampay, L.P. et al (2019) Chaos, danger, and maternal parenting in families: links with adolescent adjustment in low- and middle-income countries. *Developmental Science* 22(5): e12855.

Di Giunta, L. and Uribe Tirado, L.M. (2019) Education and parenting in Colombia. In E. Sorbring and J.E. Lansford (Eds) *School Systems, Parent Behavior, and Academic Achievement: An International Perspective* (pp 29–42). Cham, Switzerland: Springer.

Dodge, K.A., Malone, P.S., Lansford, J.E., Sorbring, E., Skinner, A.T., Tapanya, S. et al (2015) Hostile attributional bias and aggressive behavior in global context. *Proceedings of the National Academy of Sciences* 112(30): 9310–15.

Duell, N., Steinberg, L., Icenogle, G., Chein, J., Chaudhary, N., Di Giunta, L. et al (2018) Age patterns in risk taking across the world. *Journal of Youth and Adolescence* 47(Suppl 2): 1052–72.

Hanson, J.L., Albert, W.D., Skinner, A.T., Shen, S.H., Dodge, K.A. and Lansford, J.E. (2019) Resting state coupling between the amygdala and ventromedial prefrontal cortex is related to household income in childhood and indexes future psychological vulnerability to stress. *Development and Psychopathology* 31(3): 1053–66.

Henrich, J., Heine, S.J. and Norenzayan, A. (2010) The weirdest people in the world? *Behavioral and Brain Sciences* 33(2–3): 61–83.

Icenogle, G., Steinberg, L., Duell, N., Chein, J., Chang, L., Chaudhary, N. et al (2019) Adolescents' cognitive capacity reaches adult levels prior to their psychosocial maturity: evidence for a 'maturity gap' in a multinational, cross-sectional sample. *Law and Human Behavior* 43(1): 69–85.

Lansford, J.E., Alampay, L., Al-Hassan, S., Bacchini, D., Bombi, A.S., Bornstein, M.H. et al (2010) Corporal punishment of children in nine countries as a function of child gender and parent gender. *International Journal of Pediatrics* 2010: 672780.

Lansford, J.E., Skinner, A.T., Sorbring, E., Di Giunta, L., Deater-Deckard, K., Dodge, K.A. et al (2012) Boys' and girls' relational and physical aggression in nine countries. *Aggressive Behavior* 38(4): 298–308.

Lansford, J.E., Sharma, C., Malone, P.S., Woodlief, D., Dodge, K.A., Oburu, P. et al (2014a) Corporal punishment, maternal warmth, and child adjustment: a longitudinal study in eight countries. *Journal of Clinical Child and Adolescent Psychology* 43(4): 670–85.

Lansford, J.E., Woodlief, D., Malone, P.S., Oburu, P., Pastorelli, C., Skinner, A.T. et al (2014b) A longitudinal examination of mothers' and fathers' social information processing biases and harsh discipline in nine countries. *Development and Psychopathology* 26(3): 561–73.

Lansford, J.E., Godwin, J., Uribe Tirado, L.M., Zelli, A., Al-Hassan, S.M., Bacchini, D. et al (2015) Individual, family, and culture level contributions to child physical abuse and neglect: a longitudinal study in nine countries. *Development and Psychopathology* 27(4): 1417–28.

Lansford, J.E., Godwin, J., Bornstein, M.H., Chang, L., Deater-Deckard, K., Di Giunta, L. et al (2017) Reward sensitivity, impulse control, and social cognition as mediators of the link between childhood family adversity and externalizing behavior in eight countries. *Development and Psychopathology* 29(5): 1675–88.

Lansford, J.E., Godwin, J., Bornstein, M.H., Chang, L., Deater-Deckard, K., Di Giunta, L. et al (2018a) Parenting, culture, and the development of externalizing behaviors from age seven to 14 in nine countries. *Development and Psychopathology* 30(5): 1937–58.

Lansford, J.E., Godwin, J., Zelli, A., Al-Hassan, S.M., Bacchini, D., Bombi, A.S. et al (2018b) Longitudinal associations between parenting and youth adjustment in twelve cultural groups: cultural normativeness of parenting as a moderator. *Developmental Psychology* 54(2): 362–77.

Lansford, J.E., Rothenberg, W.A., Jensen, T.M., Lippold, M.A., Bacchini, D., Bornstein, M.H. et al (2018c) Bidirectional relations between parenting and behavior problems from age 8 to 13 in nine countries. *Journal of Research on Adolescence* 28(3): 571–90.

Lansford, J.E., Malone, P.S., Tapanya, S., Uribe Tirado, L.M., Zelli, A., Alampay, L.P. et al (2019) Household income predicts trajectories of child internalizing and externalizing behavior in high-, middle-, and low-income countries. *International Journal of Behavioral Development* 43(1): 74–9.

Pastorelli, C., Lansford, J.E., Luengo Kanacri, B.P., Malone, P.S., Di Giunta, L., Bacchini, D. et al (2016) Positive parenting and children's prosocial behavior in eight countries. *Journal of Child Psychology and Psychiatry* 57(7): 824–34.

Putnick, D.L., Bornstein, M.H., Lansford, J.E., Malone, P.S., Pastorelli, C., Skinner, A.T. et al (2015) Perceived mother and father acceptance-rejection predict four unique aspects of child adjustment across nine countries. *Journal of Child Psychology and Psychiatry* 56(8): 923–32.

Putnick, D.L., Bornstein, M.H., Lansford, J.E., Chang, L., Deater-Deckard, K., Di Giunta, L. et al (2018) Parental acceptance–rejection and child prosocial behavior: developmental transactions across the transition to adolescence in nine countries, mothers and fathers, and girls and boys. *Developmental Psychology* 54(10): 1881–90.

Rothenberg, W.A., Di Giunta, L., Lansford, J.E., Lunetti, C., Fiasconaro, I., Basili, E. et al (2019) Examining daily associations between anger, sadness, and psychopathology symptoms in adolescence: the mediating and moderating role of emotion dysregulation. *Journal of Youth and Adolescence* 48: 2207–21.

Rothenberg, W.A., Lansford, J.E., Alampay, L.P., Al-Hassan, S.M., Bacchini, D., Bornstein, M.H. et al (2020) Examining effects of mother and father warmth and control on child externalizing and internalizing problems from age 8 to 13 in nine countries. *Development and Psychopathology* 32: 1113–37.

Schenck-Fontaine, A., Lansford, J.E., Skinner, A.T., Deater-Deckard, K., Di Giunta, L., Dodge, K.A. et al (2020) Associations between perceived material deprivation, parents' discipline practices, and children's behavior problems: an international perspective. *Child Development* 91(1): 307–26.

Skinner, A.T., Bacchini, D., Lansford, J.E., Godwin, J., Sorbring, E., Tapanya, S. et al (2014a) Neighborhood danger, parental monitoring, harsh parenting, and child aggression in nine countries. *Societies* 4(1): 45–67.

Skinner, A.T., Oburu, P., Lansford, J.E. and Bacchini, D. (2014b) Childrearing violence and child adjustment after exposure to Kenyan post-election violence. *Psychology of Violence* 4(1): 37–50.

Sorbring, E. and Lansford, J.E. (Eds) (2019) *School Systems, Parent Behavior, and Academic Achievement: An International Perspective.* Cham, Switzerland: Springer.

Steinberg, L. (2008) A social neuroscience perspective on adolescent risk-taking. *Developmental Review* 28(1): 78–106.

Steinberg, L., Icenogle, Shulman, E.P., Breiner, K., Chein, J.M., Bacchini, D. et al (2018) Around the world, adolescence is a time of heightened reward seeking and immature self-regulation. *Developmental Science* 21(2): e12532.

5

Achieving Gender Equality: Understanding Gender Equality and Health Among Vulnerable Adolescents in the Sustainable Development Goals Era

Leah R. Koenig*, Mengmeng Li* and Robert W. Blum

Introduction

The goal of global gender equality is articulated in the fifth Sustainable Development Goal (SDG 5). This objective signifies the global community's recognition, for the first time, of the central role that gender equality plays in sustainable development. However, the importance of gender equality in the Sustainable Development Goals goes beyond SDG 5. Issues of equality, and specifically gender equality, are interwoven throughout the SDGs and are central to both SDG targets and their related efforts that range in scope from the individual through macro-national and global political institutions.

Independent of the SDGs, adolescent health and well-being have recently emerged as national and global priorities (Patton et al, 2016). For some, the increased importance of adolescents and youth reflects the impressive child survival successes under the MDGs (Bhutta et al, 2019). It is also an acknowledgement that this segment of the population represents a political and social force; there is a critical need to support young people's growth and development if they are to participate in national growth and development. The SDG era (2015–30) provides an opportunity to highlight the needs of adolescents worldwide, by putting a growing body of longitudinal evidence into practice in the evaluation of SDG-relevant programmes, tracking the achievement of SDG targets among adolescents, and ultimately developing policies that ensure no one, especially this next generation of national and global leaders, is left behind. In order to ensure just and sustainable global development, policy makers must understand the experiences and concerns of adolescents around the world. However, despite their critical role in global development, adolescents are essentially absent from most SDG indicators (Guglielmi and Jones, 2019).

The work of the Global Early Adolescent Study (GEAS) is especially compelling within the SDG context because, until recently, little was known about the first five years of adolescence. Most research began at age 15 and approached young adolescents with assumptions about their experiences, rather than evidence. We know now that early adolescence is not only a time of rapid pubertal development but also of neurological development that impacts social and cognitive functioning (Dahl et al, 2018).

These developmental changes take place within the context of dramatic shifts in social expectations, and in adolescents' relationships with family, friends and romantic partners as they mature (Cohen et al, 2003). We also know that gender norms become more solidified in this period. If gender norm change programming is to be successful, beginning in the early adolescent years appears to have the greatest promise (Blum, in press; Blum et al, 2017; Galambos et al, 1990). However, little remains known about the influence of gender-unequal perceptions on behaviours, health and overall well-being in adolescence and across life stages.

The Global Early Adolescent Study

The GEAS grew out of an awareness in 2010 that while international research had examined the health of children and of older adolescents and youth, few studies at that time had focused on gender norms or on health among early adolescents (World Health Organization, 2011). To address this gap, the GEAS was initiated to understand how young people living in low-resource urban environments experience gender expectations, how these perceptions evolve with age, and the pathways through which these beliefs influence health and behaviours over time. With a longitudinal design, the GEAS will demonstrate over time the factors that influence gendered perspectives and health across adolescence. Ultimately, this expanded understanding of gender socialization beginning in the early adolescent period will inform policy makers around the world about the consequences of gender inequality and how early interventions can shift toward positive trajectories in gender attitudes, health and development.

Sampling

The Global Early Adolescent Study focuses on adolescents living in some of the most disadvantaged sections of the world's major urban areas. It highlights the experiences of young people living in low-resource urban environments because by 2050, 70% of the world's population will live in cities (UNICEF, 2012). These young people, who are navigating the lowest economic strata of their societies, face the greatest adversities, including the impacts of gender inequality (Boyce and Dallago, 2004; Cagatay, 1998). By focusing on adolescents living in disadvantaged urban areas, the GEAS explores the intersection of gender inequality with poverty and other forms of social disadvantage.

Formative research

The Global Early Adolescent Study began as a self-funded collaboration of six institutions around the world dedicated to understanding the relationship between gendered expectations and health among young adolescents. Over time and with the support of a global network of donors, the United Nations Population Fund and the World Health Organization, the network expanded to 15 sites and conducted mixed-methods formative research with adolescents and their caregivers in settings across Europe, North America, Africa, South America and Asia. The GEAS formative qualitative research involved interactive interviews, discussions and activities to understand the social structures of young people's worlds and to give voice to their perceptions about the future and their personal expectations as they progress to adulthood.

This qualitative research, undertaken between 2014 and 2017, led to the development of quantitative measures that assess perceptions of gender norms and empowerment among young adolescents – a unique set of cross-cultural tools piloted and internationally validated for this age group. All tools developed as part of the GEAS are made publicly available, including its survey instruments, qualitative guides and training materials (The Global Early Adolescent Study, 2019).

Longitudinal study

Informed by this formative research, the GEAS began a longitudinal study phase in 2017 in order to understand how gender norms, attitudes and beliefs impact adolescent health outcomes over time. To achieve this, the GEAS follows adolescents in ten countries on five continents, allowing for global comparisons of these processes. Study sites are highlighted in Figure 5.1 and include: Kinshasa, DRC, Blantyre, Malawi and Cape Town, South Africa in Africa; Shanghai, China, Denpasar, Bandar Lampung and Semarang, Indonesia in Asia; Cuenca, Ecuador, Santiago, Chile and São Paulo, Brazil in South America; New Orleans, USA in North America; and Flanders, Belgium in Europe (Figure 5.1).

While the longitudinal follow-up periods vary, adolescents in the GEAS are followed each year for up to five years. The GEAS longitudinal study design, as well as its central indicators, is depicted in Figure 5.2.

Longitudinal intervention impact evaluation

Though all sites in the GEAS examine changes in gender norms over time and their associated health impacts, in half, the GEAS survey is used to conduct a longitudinal impact evaluation of gender-transformative interventions. There, in addition to the observation study, we seek to understand the impact of interventions that address attitudes and norm changes, with the hypothesis that those shifts may improve health behaviours and outcomes (Figure 5.2). Interventions are carried out in Bandar Lampung, Semarang and Denpasar, Indonesia; New Orleans, USA; Kinshasa, DRC; and Blantyre, Malawi. While all interventions hold central this gender-transformative aim, the approach and curricula of each intervention vary.

Growing Up GREAT! is an intervention designed and implemented by Save the Children in Kinshasa, DRC, that aims to improve young adolescents' gender-equitable perceptions, knowledge of puberty and reproductive development, and use of reproductive health services as they transition into older adolescence. The intervention, informed by other programmes successful in improving gender-equal expectations, uses an ecological framework to address restrictive gender norms.

In recognition of the multiple spheres of influence on social norms at this age, Growing Up GREAT! includes activities that address sexual and reproductive health and gender inequality at the individual, family,

Figure 5.1: Map of global early adolescent study settings

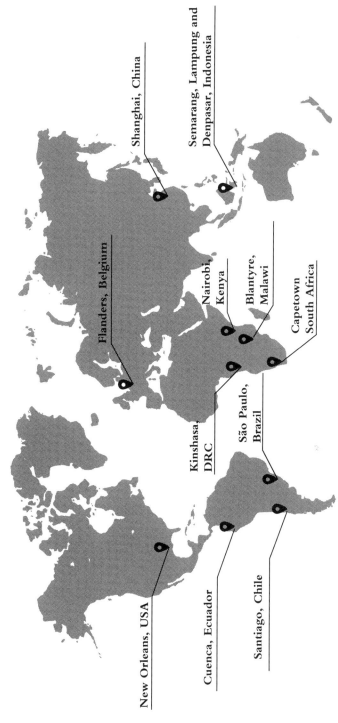

Source: Author's own

Figure 5.2: Global early adolescent longitudinal study research activities

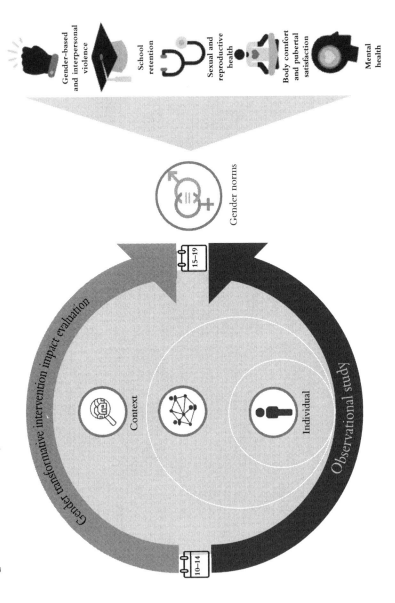

Source: Author's own

school and community levels. Participants engage in weekly club meetings that involve games, stories and materials to promote reflection on and discussion of these topics. Their parents attend community video and discussion sessions that feature testimonials of other parents in their community. Teachers interact with intervention materials, and community members engage in discussions about gender-equal expectations for adolescents. The intervention hypothesizes that these activities will shift perceptions about gender roles, delay sexual debut and pregnancy, and promote family planning use.

In New Orleans, USA, in addition to a focus on changing gender norms, the intervention targets gender norms together with other forms of social disadvantage to promote well-being. There, the Institute for Women and Ethnic Studies implements Creating a Future Together, a trauma-informed comprehensive sexuality education programme for young people with modules that address social justice and engagement, coping and healthy relationships. In Indonesia, Rutgers, Netherlands is carrying out Semangat Dunia Remaja or Teen Aspirations (SETARA), a comprehensive sexuality education curriculum that seeks to support healthy sexual development by teaching about sexuality, puberty and relationships, as well as life skills such as critical thinking, communication, negotiation and assertiveness, in addition to promoting critical reflection upon gender norms. In Blantyre, Malawi, Promundo and Rutgers, Netherlands are implementing Get Up Speak Out!, an intervention that focuses on challenging gender stereotypes, raising awareness about adolescents' rights and building critical thinking skills. To a larger extent than most interventions, young adolescent participants are involved in programmatic development and decision making.

The data from these longitudinal evaluations will promote understanding about the activities that are effective in shifting perceptions of gender norms and promoting healthy behaviours. These evaluations will allow us to go beyond associations to determine the extent to which the interventions contribute to the changes observed. Evaluating different interventions with common elements will allow us to identify the core elements across contexts that appear to have the greatest impact. This information will aid policy makers as well as donors to make informed programmatic investments at regional or national levels.

Measurement

In order to better understand the circumstances in which young adolescents live, participants report contextual information at the individual, family, peer, school and neighbourhood levels. The study's key outcomes of interest are adolescents' mental health, experiences of violence, body comfort, school completion, and sexual and reproductive health. Over time, it will examine changes in these indicators of health and well-being, their relationship to gender equality, and how social factors impact these outcomes. These processes can also be compared among both boys and girls.

Beyond evaluating differences by sex, the GEAS measures allow for the assessment of young people's perceptions of gendered norms towards romantic and sexual relationships in early adolescence (Moreau et al, 2019). The first scale measures the extent to which adolescents ascribe to a sexual double standard, a construct that socially benefits boys for engaging in romantic and sexual relationships while penalizing girls for the same behaviours. The second assesses the acceptability of romantic relationships in adolescence. Both scales have been validated across diverse cultural settings. Two additional gender norm constructs are under development, one that assesses adolescents' perceptions of the gendered nature of traits or affects, and the other that examines expectations of gender-stereotypical roles in the household. Beyond these individual constructs of gender norms, the creation of a global index of perceived gender equality is underway that, once completed, can be applied across cultural contexts.

The GEAS has also developed a method of measuring adolescents' gendered perceptions about relationships with peers, parents and romantic partners using vignettes. These scenarios were developed by young adolescents through multi-day focus group discussions and role-play activities in each of 15 participating sites. Participants role-played these situations and discussed potential responses, centred on differences in reactions between boys and girls. The articulated scenarios were then recorded as vignettes and corresponding response options in the quantitative survey, male and female protagonists separately. During the process, drafts were reviewed and critiqued by the adolescent participants before being finalized. After pilot testing, the finalized vignettes described: approaching a romantic interest, social inclusion of gender-atypical peers, reactions to pubertal onset, and decision making about unintended pregnancy. Baseline findings from three sites suggest that young adolescents can respond to these vignettes and differentiate their own projected response from that of a protagonist, answering both from the perspective of their own sex and the opposite sex (Blum et al, 2019a). These findings suggest a promising role for vignettes as a measurement tool to assess gender equality and projected reactions to various scenarios among adolescents.

Empowerment scales were also created as part of the GEAS, drawing from existing measurement and theory to tailor constructs to the lives of young adolescents. Most existing measures of empowerment – which focus on dimensions of power in the political, economic, family and family planning spheres – have been designed to evaluate empowerment among adults (Cornwall, 2016; Malhotra, 2002; Samman and Santos, 2009; Hindin and Muntifering, 2011; Narayan, 2005; Pulerwitz, 2000; Schuler et al, 1997). No existing studies to our knowledge have investigated the measurement of empowerment among early adolescents, which likely manifests differently from empowerment in an adult population. Historically, much greater attention has been paid to understanding and increasing the empowerment of women and girls. Few have paid equal attention to understanding manifestations of power among both boys and girls, though understanding and addressing both is critical to promoting gender equality (Kato-Wallace et al, 2016).

The GEAS embraces a multi-level and multi-dimensional concept of empowerment that takes into account not only adolescents' intrinsic capacities but also the environmental forces that shape these attributes. These agency scales assess the extent to which young adolescents feel they have freedom of movement in their communities, their capacity to voice their mind and be heard, and their decision making about everyday choices, such as what to wear when not in school (Zimmerman et al, 2019).

The landscape of global longitudinal research in adolescence

From a life-course perspective, studying young people beginning in early adolescence offers an opportunity to close the gap between existing research on children and on older adolescents and youth. Among these older populations, a number of studies have been conducted to date that link gendered perspectives and health, predominantly with cross-sectional designs (Ahmed et al, 2016; Basu et al, 2017; Higgins et al, 2010; Pallitto and O'Campo, 2005).

Among early adolescents, researchers have demonstrated the presence of gender-unequal perceptions across settings (Heise and Kotsadam, 2015; Kågesten et al, 2016; Landry et al, 2019; Vu et al, 2017). A limited body of evidence has highlighted links between gender norms and certain health outcomes in adolescence. Researchers have found relationships between unequal gender norms and violence perpetration and victimization (Das et al, 2014; McCauley et al, 2014; Reed et al, 2011; Reyes et al, 2016; Zuo et al, 2018 Stark and colleagues have demonstrated associations between community gender-equal norms and increased self-esteem for girls living in refugee settings in Ethiopia. (Stark et al, 2018 Gender equality at the country level has been associated with contraceptive use among adolescents in European countries (de Looze et al, 2019).

As awareness of gender inequality's role in health increases against the backdrop of the SDGs, evaluations of gender norm targeting programmes, and specifically efforts to understand their influence on the health of young people, have also emerged in recent years. Haberland's review of sexual education programmes that aim to protect against HIV and promote sexual and reproductive health among young people found that curriculums with elements that addressed gender inequality and power differentials were more likely to be effective in improving sexual and reproductive health outcomes compared to those without (Haberland, 2015). Levy and colleagues' systematic review of gender transformative interventions found that most evaluated studies effected attitudinal, awareness or behaviour shifts among young people. However, we do not yet know about the 'sticking power' of these programmes on long-term health, or their ability to change community (Levy et al, 2019).

However, this predominantly cross-sectional evidence draws largely from data in high-income settings and, for the most part, is unable to differentiate the directionality of associations detected. Few studies have employed a longitudinal design to investigate these relationships among young people. In light of this literature that has described gender norms and their links to health in the adolescent period, there is an emerging recognition of the importance of the power of longitudinal research to guide programmatic investments and policy decisions.

The National Longitudinal Study of Adolescent to Adult Health (Add Health)

In the United States, the National Longitudinal Study of Adolescent to Adult Health (Add Health) has followed a nationally representative sample of 7th–12th graders in the United States, beginning in 1992 (Harris, 2018). Add Health researchers have developed measures to assess gender expression. Fleming and colleagues (2017) described a technique to measure feminine and masculine behaviours, which has subsequently been used to demonstrate influences of such gender expressions on adult outcomes as diverse as social mobility, substance use, chronic disease and violence (Domingue et al, 2019; Shakya et al, 2019; Wilkinson et al, 2018).

The Young Lives study

One of the longest running international studies is Oxford University's Young Lives study. Young Lives has followed over 12,000 adolescents in Ethiopia, India, Peru and Vietnam over the course of 15 years and continues today (Barnett et al, 2013; Young Lives, 2017). Initially, two Young Lives cohorts were enrolled at ages 1 and 8, respectively, providing two periods of insight into the transitions into and out of adolescence. This longitudinal data from four low- and middle-income countries allows for cross-site comparisons of indicators on emerging health and development outcomes as well as other important insights over time, such as the impact of poverty on nutrition and growth (Young Lives, 2008). Young Lives has described the emergence of gender inequalities in well-being among adolescents, including those related to nutrition, future expectations and education (Aurino, 2017; Young Lives, 2015). A mixed-methods study of Young Lives data also highlighted the role of gender-discriminatory norms in shaping sex disparities in school retention (Singh and Mukherjee, 2018).

Gender and Adolescence: Global Evidence (GAGE)

GAGE is a longitudinal adolescent health study with a central focus on gender and adolescence. GAGE conducts mixed-methods research, following adolescents in Ethiopia, Rwanda, Bangladesh, Nepal, Jordan, Lebanon and Palestine. The study collects data from a diverse group of adolescents, including those who live in both rural and urban areas. Qualitative data drawing from GAGE in Ethiopia and Rwanda have highlighted the role of gendered norms in inhibiting access to sexual and reproductive health access for young people (Coast et al, 2019). Baseline data has also demonstrated links between traditional gendered perceptions and adverse physical and mental health (Baird et al, 2019). While data collection is ongoing, GAGE's longitudinal evidence will elucidate adolescents' experiences of gender and reaction to gendered messages from people and institutions influential in their lives.

Add Health, Young Lives and GAGE are among the relatively small number of longitudinal studies that assess gendered norms, attitudes, beliefs or behaviours and their relationships to health among adolescents. While each of these studies represents an important contribution to the field of adolescent health and to the objective of understanding gender as a social driver of health, longitudinal evidence about transitions into adolescence remains sparse. It is imperative to further understand the emergence of these gendered perspectives in adolescence, and how these perspectives regulate other developmental milestones.

Given its longitudinal design, global perspective, emphasis on young adolescents in vulnerable urban settings and central focus on gender norms, the GEAS is poised to expand global understanding about the role of gender in promoting health trajectories for the world's vulnerable adolescents. Ultimately, these data can inform the activities and achievement of SDG 5.

The Global Early Adolescent Study and the Sustainable Development Goals

The GEAS is shedding light on the experiences of socioeconomically disadvantaged youth around the world. In keeping with the SDGs' focus on equity, the GEAS can play an important role in identifying the key factors that enable or impede the achievement of gender equality for adolescents living in urban low-resource settings, who will be entering adulthood at a time when the success of the SDG indicators will be evaluated. To ensure 'no one is left behind', policy makers, researchers and programme implementers must understand the complex forces that shape risk and poor health among the most disadvantaged. The extensive picture of adolescents' lives captured in the GEAS can help to expand understanding about the experiences of growing up in poverty, what works in promoting health and well-being in this period and, in particular, the realization of gender equality.

Early GEAS data suggest that, across cultures, adolescents hold very traditional norms about relationships and ascribe to hegemonic gender traits and roles. Recent findings have also demonstrated that by the age of 10–12, adolescent boys and girls already endorse a number of gendered beliefs regarding how boys and girls should appear and behave, as well as the dominant role of men within the family. In many GEAS sites, girls endorse these gender-stereotypical norms to an equal or greater extent than boys.

We have also observed that dimensions of gender norms are heterogeneous. While an adolescent may hold a gender-equal view about romantic relationships, they may simultaneously express unequal expectations about household roles. Analysing these perceptions at the root of gender discrimination will help policy makers and programme specialists understand the dimensions of the gender system and the points of inflection most amenable to change.

The empowerment of girls and women is inseparable from the achievement of gender equality, and is reflected in the fifth SDG. Across the sites that participated in the GEAS formative research, a gap in freedom of movement is observed between boys and girls in most countries, as girls' mobility is restricted while boys' worlds expand. Sex differences in voice and decision making, however, are less pronounced at this young age (Zimmerman et al, 2019).

SDG 5 also emphasizes universal access to sexual and reproductive health and promotion of reproductive rights. Early experiences of sexual and reproductive health, skills, knowledge and experiences are integral to understanding later outcomes. In our baseline data, sexual and reproductive health knowledge is limited among young adolescents across sites (Explore 4 Action, 2019; Global Early Adolescent Study, 2018, 2019; Growing up GREAT!, 2018). For example, only half know that a girl can get pregnant at the first time of sexual intercourse, or that taking birth control pills or injections can prevent girls from pregnancy. Adolescents also reported limited knowledge about HIV prevention. Roughly two thirds of adolescents across sites did not know HIV can be contracted at first sex, or that condoms can protect against HIV. This lack of important SRH knowledge is often more pronounced among girls than boys. With longitudinal data, we can assess how early sexual and reproductive health skills predict later sexual behaviours and exposures. We can also evaluate whether gender-equal norms protect against sexual and reproductive health risks, and the efficacy of various interventions in promoting sexual and reproductive health.

Although most of the GEAS study sites are early in the cycle of longitudinal data collection, as of early 2020 two waves of data collection have been completed in Kinshasa, DRC and Shanghai, China. Preliminary data analysis on the Kinshasa data over a one-year interval suggests increased endorsement of unequal gender norms, and a persistent greater endorsement among girls than boys. We also observed small gains in three empowerment agency domains. In addition, over a one-year time frame, we observed an increase in knowledge of pregnancy and HIV prevention among both boys and girls and increased awareness of how to access condoms among adolescents enrolled in school. However, greater proportions of boys and girls reported they felt embarrassed to seek out family planning services at follow-up than at baseline, suggesting perhaps that knowledge alone is not sufficient to overcome other barriers to obtaining and using contraception.

With extended longitudinal follow-up, the GEAS will provide greater perspective on gender norms, empowerment and their impacts on health outcomes, enabling donors and policy makers to better target programmes and services to the most vulnerable. As the fields of social determinants of health and adolescent health research intersect, the GEAS can establish important links between context, social experiences and health at this critical juncture.

As is true for the SDGs, the GEAS contributes to a vision of a just and equal future by researching gender inequalities in resource-constrained urban settings where adolescents are at greatest risk of harm, including child marriage, homicide and sexual violence (Browning et al, 2008; Chapman et al, 2011; International Center for Research on Women, 2006; Males, 2015; Warner and Weist, 1996). By highlighting the unique challenges and opportunities facing young adolescents, the GEAS calls attention to existing disadvantages and enriches knowledge about what can contribute to upward trajectories in relation to socioeconomic disadvantage, well-being and gender equality. By doing this, the GEAS evidence makes a powerful contribution to the SDGs' commitment to leave no one behind and to create a world of gender equality.

However, the contribution of the GEAS to the SDGs will not be realized without advocacy at the country and global policy levels. Advocacy efforts are ongoing at local and national levels as data are collected, to reflect upon key findings and ensure policy makers are informed about the circumstances of vulnerable young people's lives in a timely manner. At the global level, the GEAS is committed to sharing cross-cultural findings with audiences working in gender, adolescent and public health research, funding, programmatic and policy institutions.

In 2018, the GEAS convened a panel of experts to develop a work plan to address the gap in indicators and research that approach adolescence as central to achieving SDG 5 (Blum et al, 2019b). The panel recommended a set of targeted indicators to assess progress towards SDG 5 among adolescents and produced an international report (Blum, 2019c).

Challenges of conducting longitudinal research with vulnerable adolescents

Conducting longitudinal research with young adolescents poses a number of challenges as well as unique opportunities. The paucity of research in this age group attests to some of the barriers. Ethical or institutional review boards (IRBs) are often reluctant to approve of research questions they perceive as too sensitive for young adolescents. A lack of understanding about adolescent development can hamper realistic assessments of young adolescents' exposures. IRBs may fear pushback from gatekeepers such as policy makers, school administrators and parents, who they reason may object to questions being asked. In turn, parents are at times reluctant to enrol their children in a study that addresses issues like experiences of abuse and sexual activity. They may fear disclosure or may not understand the safeguards afforded to study participants. As a result, young adolescents are often excluded from research even though the resulting data would draw attention to the important issues they observe and experience.

Researchers also face barriers originating from adolescents themselves. At ages and in urban settings with great mobility, longitudinal follow-up of our cohorts can prove very challenging. After one year of follow-up two GEAS sites have been able to attain retention rates of approximately 90% of baseline participants; however, the financial and human resource costs far exceeded expectations since participants change schools, neighbourhoods or even cities. To address this, online data collection holds promise of novel acceptable and cost-effective ways to survey young people who may have moved. Despite ethical committee or legal requirements, as adolescents grow in maturity they may resist their parents' involvement in their participation in research. Such discordance poses complex ethical issues for researchers pertaining to consent, referrals and reporting. Finally, adolescents may be reluctant to share information when they are aware that their disclosures of abuse or distress may not remain anonymized.

Within cross-cultural research, standardizing research protocols may prove challenging, including aligned sampling, protocols and surveys. These standardizations become even more complex as local legal regulations, ethical standards and research interests vary. Longitudinal survey design, an already complex process, grows more difficult as these questionnaires need to reflect multiple facets of adolescent development, remain cross-culturally relevant and minimize the survey burden for participants. Finding common ground across cultures even in defining terms can prove challenging. One that arose in the GEAS was defining the experiences that constitute abuse. In certain cultures and legal jurisdictions, any hitting or slapping of a child is deemed abuse, while elsewhere such practices are seen as normative child disciplinary actions.

Limitations of the Global Early Adolescent Study

The GEAS is not without limitations. The sampling of the longitudinal cohort study varies between settings to meet site constraints and objectives and therefore is not identical across sites. Second, given the

GEAS funding model, in which each site seeks funding with support from a coordinating centre based at Johns Hopkins University, some sites are in an on-going quest for financial support to maintain the cohort. Finally, while gender norms are influenced by interpersonal and community influences (Kågesten et al, 2016), the GEAS does not have the capacity to collect data about gender norms perceptions at the family or community levels.

Policy recommendations

In the Sustainable Development Goal era, improving the health and well-being of adolescents has emerged as a critical global development objective, for the well-being of this young cohort and for the ramifications for national development that will resonate through future generations. This chapter has briefly reviewed a few of the major longitudinal adolescent studies globally and has highlighted some of the key gender-related findings from that work. From that work and from the GEAS we come away with a few recommendations for policy makers, donors and programme specialists:

- Gender inequality is maintained by gender norms that shape sex disparities in health. Research has demonstrated the influence of gender norms not only in adolescence but also into adulthood. Therefore, if the SDGs are to be realized it is imperative to better understand the predictors of and barriers to gender-equal attitudes, community norms and policies both locally and globally.
- Good policy starts with sound evidence. Longitudinal research with adolescents is critical to the development of a comprehensive understanding of adolescents' lives. From a life-course perspective, expanded longitudinal research during the early adolescent period will fill a significant gap in global knowledge but will also provide vital information on the drivers of attitudes, beliefs and behaviours that will set individual life-course trajecotries and pathways for national development.
- While the GEAS has contributed substantially to the measurement of gender norms, empowerment and relationships in early adolescence, there remains a need for increased investment in the development of measures that capture contextual, social, behavioural and health aspects of adolescents' lives, as existing measures for other age groups may not apply to adolescents' experiences. These measures can be used to document young people's experiences and to optimize policies that address their needs.

- Start early to tackle unequal gender norms. Across the GEAS study sites, we have already witnessed strong endorsements of traditional gender norms among young adolescents. There is also good evidence that early adolescence is a window of opportunity to challenge these norms and to shift attitudes of young people toward greater equality.

Conclusions

Longitudinal research is a powerful tool to help realize the global policy objectives of the Sustainable Development Goals. The experiences and perspectives of young adolescents living in poverty around the world remain understudied. As research subjects, young people are best positioned to teach researchers, programme implementers and policy makers about the realities of their worlds. If the world is to realize the goal of global gender equality and truly 'leave no one behind', then we must better understand the unique vulnerabilities and opportunities that vulnerable young adolescents face. Only then can we understand how to best support progress and equality in just development for future generations. This will put us in the best position to achieve the vision of gender equality and of the SDGs.

Note
* These authors contributed equally to this work.

References

Aurino, E. (2017) Do boys eat better than girls in India? Longitudinal evidence on dietary diversity and food consumption disparities among children and adolescents. *Economics and Human Biology* 25: 99–111.

Ahmed, T., Vafaei, A., Auais, M., Guralnik, J., and Zunzunegui, M.V. (2016) Gender roles and physical function in older adults: cross-sectional analysis of the International Mobility in Aging Study (IMIAS). *PLOS One* 11(6): e0156828.

Baird, S., Bhutta, Z.A., Hamad, B.A., Hicks, J.H., Jones, N. and Muz, J. (2019) Do restrictive gender attitudes and norms influence physical and mental health during very young adolescence? Evidence from Bangladesh and Ethiopia. *SSM – Population Health* 9: 100480.

Barnett, I., Ariana, P., Petrou, S., Penny, M.E., Duc, L.T., Galab, S. et al (2013) Cohort profile: the Young Lives study. *International Journal of Epidemiology* 42: 701–8.

Bhutta, Z.A., Victora, C., Boerma, T., Kruk, M.E., Patton, G., Black, M.M. et al (2019) Optimising the continuum of child and adolescent health and development. *The Lancet* 393: 1080–82.

Blum, R.W. (2019) *Achieving Gender Equality By 2030: Putting Adolescents at the Center of the Agenda*. Baltimore, MD: Johns Hopkins University Press.

Blum, R.W. (2020) Gender norm transformative programming: where are we now? Where do we need to be? *Journal of Adolescent Health* 66(2): 135–6.

Blum, R.W., Mmari, K. and Moreau, C. (2017) It begins at 10: how gender expectations shape early adolescence around the world. *Journal of Adolescent Health* 61: S3–S4.

Blum, R.W., Sheehy, G., Li, M., Basu, S., El Gibaly, O., Kayembe, P. et al (2019a) Measuring young adolescent perceptions of relationships: a vignette-based approach to exploring gender equality. *PLOS One* 14: e0218863.

Blum, R.W., Boyden, J., Erulkar, A., Kabiru, C. and Wilopo, S. (2019b) Achieving gender equality requires placing adolescents at the center. *Journal of Adolescent Health* 64: 691–3.

Boyce, W. and Dallago, L. (2004) Socioeconomic inequality. In C. Currie (Ed) *Young People's Health in Context: Health Behaviour in School-Aged Children (HBSC) Study: International Report from the 2001/2002 Survey, Health Policy for Children and Adolescents* (pp 13–25). Copenhagen: World Health Organization, Regional Office for Europe.

Browning, C.R., Burrington, L.A., Leventhal, T. and Brooks-Gunn, J. (2008) Neighborhood structural inequality, collective efficacy, and sexual risk behavior among urban youth. *Journal of Health and Social Behavior* 49: 269–85.

Cagatay, N. (1998) Gender and Poverty (No 5). United Nations Development Programme.

Chapman, C., Laird, J., Ifill, N. and KewalRamani, A. (2011) Trends in high school dropout and completion rates in the United States: 1972–2009. Washington DC: National Center for Education Statistics, US Department of Education.

Coast, E., Jones, N., Francoise, U.M., Yadete, W., Isimbi, R., Gezahegne, K. and Lunin, L. (2019) Adolescent sexual and reproductive health in Ethiopia and Rwanda: a qualitative exploration of the role of social norms. *SAGE Open* 9: 215824401983358.

Cohen, P., Kasen, S., Chen, H., Hartmark, C. and Gordon, K. (2003) Variations in patterns of developmental transitions in the emerging adulthood period. *Developmental Psychology* 39, 657–69.

Cornwall, A. (2016) Women's empowerment: what works? *Journal of International Development* 28: 342–59.

Dahl, R.E., Allen, N.B., Wilbrecht, L. and Suleiman, A.B. (2018) Importance of investing in adolescence from a developmental science perspective. *Nature* 554: 441–50.

Das, J.K., Salam, R.A., Lassi, Z.S., Khan, M.N., Mahmood, W., Patel, V. and Bhutta, Z.A. (2016) Interventions for adolescent mental health: an overview of systematic reviews. *Journal of Adolescent Health* 59(4): S49–S60.

de Looze, M., Madkour, A.S., Huijts, T., Moreau, N. and Currie, C. (2019) Country-level gender equality and adolescents' contraceptive use in Europe, Canada and Israel: findings from 33 countries. *Perspectives on Sexual and Reproductive Health* 51(1): 43–53.

Domingue, B.W., Cislaghi, B., Nagata, J.M., Shakya, H.B., Weber, A.M., Boardman, J.D. et al (2019) Implications of gendered behaviour and contexts for social mobility in the USA: a nationally representative observational study. *The Lancet Planetary Health* 3: e420–28.

Explore 4 Action (2019) Gender norms and adolescent development, health and wellbeing in Indonesia. Available at https://rutgers.international/sites/rutgersorg/files/media/E4A%20National%20Report%2015%20Januari%202020.pdf

Fleming, P.J., Harris, K.M. and Halpern, C.T. (2017) Description and evaluation of a measurement technique for assessment of performing gender. *Sex Roles* 76: 731–46.

Galambos, N.L., Almeida, D.M. and Petersen, A.C. (1990) Masculinity, femininity, and sex role attitudes in early adolescence: exploring gender intensification. *Child Development* 61(6): 1905–14.

Global Early Adolescent Study (2018) Global Early Adolescent Study: Blantyre baseline report. Johns Hopkins University.

Global Early Adolescent Study (2019) Global Early Adolescent Study: Shanghai baseline report. Johns Hopkins University.

Growing up GREAT! (2018) Baseline report. Johns Hopkins University, Institute for Reproductive Health, Georgetown University, and Save the Children for the US Agency for International Development and Bill & Melinda Gates Foundation, Washington, DC.

Guglielmi, S. and Jones, N. (2019) The invisibility of adolescents within the SDGs 8. Available at https://www.gage.odi.org/wp-content/uploads/2020/01/The-invisibility-of-adolescents-within-the-SDGs_report.pdf

Haberland, N.A. (2015) The case for addressing gender and power in sexuality and HIV education: a comprehensive review of evaluation studies. *International Perspectives on Sexual and Reproductive Health* 41(1): 31–42.

Harris, K. (2018) Overview of add health for new data users. In *Add Health Users Conference, Bethesda, MD.*

Heise, L.L., and Kotsadam, A. (2015) Cross-national and multilevel correlates of partner violence: an analysis of data from population-based surveys. *The Lancet Global Health* 3(6): e332–40.

Higgins, J.A., Hoffman, S. and Dworkin, S.L. (2010) Rethinking gender, heterosexual men, and women's vulnerability to HIV/AIDS. *American Journal of Public Health* 100(3): 435–45.

Hindin, M.J. and Muntifering, C.J. (2011) Women's autonomy and timing of most recent sexual intercourse in Sub-Saharan Africa: a multi-country analysis. *Journal of Sexual Research* 48(6): 511–19.

International Center for Research on Women (2006) Child marriage and poverty. Fact sheet available at https://www.icrw.org/files/images/Child-Marriage-Fact-Sheet-Poverty.pdf

Kågesten, A., Gibbs, S., Blum, R.W., Moreau, C., Chandra-Mouli, V., Herbert, A. and Amin, A. (2016) Understanding factors that shape gender attitudes in early adolescence globally: a mixed-methods systematic review. *PLOS One* 11(6): e0157805.

Kato-Wallace, J., Barker, G., Sharafi, L., Mora, L. and Lauro, G. (2016) *Adolescent Boys and Young Men: Engaging Them as Supporters of Gender Equality and Health and Understanding Their Vulnerabilities.* Washington, DC and New York City: Promundo-US and UNFPA.

Landry, M., Vyas, A., Malhotra, G. and Nagaraj, N. (2020) Adolescents' development of gender equity attitudes in India. *International Journal of Adolescence and Youth* 25(1): 94–103.

Levy, J.K., Darmstadt, G.L., Ashby, C., Quandt, M., Halsey, E., Nagar, A. and Greene, M.E. (2019) Characteristics of successful programmes targeting gender inequality and restrictive gender norms for the health and wellbeing of children, adolescents, and young adults: a systematic review. *The Lancet Global Health* 8(2): e225–36.

Males, M. (2015) Age, poverty, homicide, and gun homicide: is young age or poverty level the key issue? *SAGE Open.* https://doi.org/10.1177/2158244015573359

Malhotra, A. (2002) Measuring women's empowerment as a variable in international development. Available at https://www.academia.edu/17726621/Measuring_womens_empowerment_as_a_variable_in_international_development

McCauley, H.L., Dick, R.N., Tancredi, D.J., Goldstein, S., Blackburn, S., Silverman, J.G. et al (2014) Differences by sexual minority status in relationship abuse and sexual and reproductive health among adolescent females. *Journal of Adolescent Health* 55(5): 652–8.

Moreau C., Li M., De Meyer S., Manh L.V., Guiella G., Acharya R., Bello B., Maina B. and Mmari K. (2019) Measuring gender norms about relationships in early adolescence: results from the global early adolescent study. *Social Science Medicine* 7: 100–314.

Narayan-Parker, D. (Ed) (2005) *Measuring Empowerment: Cross Disciplinary Perspectives.* World Bank Publications.

Pallitto, C.C., and O'Campo, P. (2005) Community level effects of gender inequality on intimate partner violence and unintended pregnancy in Colombia: testing the feminist perspective. *Social Science & Medicine* 60(10): 2205–16.

Patton, G.C., Sawyer, S.M., Santelli, J.S., Ross, D.A., Afifi, R., Allen, N.B. et al (2016) Our future: a Lancet commission on adolescent health and wellbeing. *The Lancet* 387: 2423–78.

Pulerwitz, J. (2000) Measuring sexual relationship power in HIV/STD research. *Sex Roles* 42: 637–60.

Reed, J.L. and Huppert, J.S. (2011) Adolescent sexually transmitted infections: a community epidemic. *Journal of Prevention & Intervention in the Community* 39(3): 243–55.

Reyes, H.L.M., Foshee, V.A., Niolon, P.H., Reidy, D.E. and Hall, J.E. (2016) Gender role attitudes and male adolescent dating violence perpetration: normative beliefs as moderators. *Journal of youth and adolescence* 45(2): 350–60.

Samman, E. and Santos, M.E. (2009) Agency and empowerment: a review of concepts, indicators and empirical evidence. Oxford Poverty & Human Development Initiative.

Shakya, H.B., Domingue, B., Nagata, J.M., Cislaghi, B., Weber, A. and Darmstadt, G.L. (2019) Adolescent gender norms and adult health outcomes in the USA: a prospective cohort study. *The Lancet Child & Adolescent Health* 3: 529–38.

Schuler, S.R., Hashemi, S.M. and Riley, A.P. (1997) The influence of women's changing roles and status in Bangladesh's fertility transition: evidence from a study of credit programs and contraceptive use. *World Development* 25: 563–75.

Singh, R. and Mukherjee, P. (2018) 'Whatever she may study, she can't escape from washing dishes': gender inequity in secondary education – evidence from a longitudinal study in India. *Compare: A Journal of Comparative and International Education* 48(2): 262–80.

Stark, L., Asghar, K., Seff, I., Cislaghi, B., Yu, G., Gessesse, T.T. et al (2018) How gender-and violence-related norms affect self-esteem among adolescent refugee girls living in Ethiopia. *Global Mental Health*, 5.

The Global Early Adolescent Study (2019) Available at www.geastudy. org/

UNICEF (2012) State of the world's children: children in an urban world. Report available at https://www.unicef.org/sowc2012/pdfs/ SOWC-2012-Main-Report_EN_21Dec2011.pdf

United Nations International Children's Emergency Fund (UNICEF) State of the world's children. Available at https://www.unicef. org/sowc2012/pdfs/SOWC-2012-Main-Report_EN_21Dec 2011.pdf

Vu, L., Pulerwitz, J., Burnett-Zieman, B., Banura, C., Okal, J. and Yam, E. (2017) Inequitable gender norms from early adolescence to young adulthood in Uganda: tool validation and differences across age groups. *Journal of Adolescent Health* 60(2): S15–S21.

Warner, B.S. and Weist, M.D. (1996) Urban youth as witnesses to Longitudinal intervention impact evaluation Longitudinal intervention impact evaluation violence: BEGINNING assessment and treatment efforts. *Journal of Youth and Adolescence* 25: 361–77.

Wilkinson, A.L., Fleming, P.J., Halpern, C.T., Herring, A.H. and Harris, K.M. (2018) Adherence to gender-typical behavior and high-frequency substance use from adolescence into young adulthood. *Psychology of Men and Masculinity* 19: 145–55.

World Health Organization (2011) The sexual and reproductive health of young adolescents in developing countries: reviewing the evidence, identifying research gaps, and moving the agenda (Expert Consultation Report No 11.11). Human Reproduction Programme, World Health Organization.

Young Lives (2008) An international study of childhood poverty: overall summary findings. Oxford University.

Young Lives (2015) How gender shapes adolescence: diverging paths and opportunities (Policy Brief No 22). Oxford University.

Young Lives (2017) A guide to young lives research section 3: what can longitudinal research tell us about children's life-chances? Oxford University.

Zimmerman, L.A., Li, M., Moreau, C., Wilopo, S. and Blum, R. (2019) Measuring agency as a dimension of empowerment among young adolescents globally: findings from the Global Early Adolescent Study. *SSM Population Health* 8: 100454.

Zuo, X., Lou, C., Gao, E., Lian, Q. and Shah, I.H. (2018) Gender role attitudes, awareness and experiences of non-consensual sex among university students in Shanghai, China. *Reproductive Health*: 15(1): 49.

6

Capturing the Complexities of Adolescent Transitions Through a Mixed Methods Longitudinal Research Design

Sarah Baird, Nicola Jones, Bassam Abu Hamad, Maheen Sultan and Workneh Yadete

Introduction

Adolescence is a time of rapid change, not only in physical, cognitive and psychological competencies but also in social roles and expectations (Patton et al, 2012; Steinberg, 2015; Viner et al, 2015). Yet we still know relatively little about the patterning of these changes, and the types of support young people need in order to reach their full human capabilities (Patton et al, 2016). Given that many of the Sustainable Development Goals (SDGs) rest on investments in adolescents (Sheehan et al, 2017) – from eliminating harmful traditional practices (including child marriage and female genital mutilation) to ensuring quality education and training – investing in a more robust evidence base and improved measurement is critical.

The Gender and Adolescence: Global Evidence (GAGE) research programme addresses these evidence and measurement gaps. This chapter discusses the design and methodological choices made by the GAGE study – to date, the largest longitudinal study (covering nine years, 2015–24) focusing on adolescents (10–19 years) in the Global South. GAGE is following 18,000 adolescent girls and boys in three regions: East Africa, the Middle East and North Africa (MENA) and

South Asia. Using mixed methods, the study is weaving together survey findings from adolescents and their caregivers with in-depth qualitative research with adolescents, caregivers and siblings, as well as community leaders, service providers and policy officials.

This chapter highlights key features of GAGE's longitudinal design: (1) working with two distinct age cohorts (younger adolescents aged 10–12 and older adolescents aged 15–17) to capture the dynamism of this life stage; (2) involving girls and boys to explore gender dynamics; (3) surveying primary female caregivers to understand intergenerational dynamics; (4) purposely sampling disadvantaged adolescents (those who married early, have a disability, or are internally displaced or refugees); and (5) working across diverse geographies (urban, rural, pastoralist, refugee camps) to understand the role of livelihood options, service access and infrastructural factors in shaping adolescent trajectories.

GAGE's approach was informed by the need to address questions around adolescent experiences and perceptions, alongside questions on the impact of policies and programmes in mediating these experiences. The research design twins observational longitudinal research across six key capability domains closely linked to the SDGs (education and learning; bodily integrity and freedom from violence; health, nutrition and sexual and reproductive health (SRH); psychosocial well-being; voice and agency; and economic empowerment) with nested experimental and quasi-experimental evaluations of adolescent programming to explore the impact of different support packages.

The chapter concludes by reflecting on the strengths and challenges of longitudinal research, while also highlighting how research funders could do more to enhance the value, relevance and uptake of such research in academic, policy and programming circles, including in terms of achieving the SDGs.

Why adolescence needs a longitudinal lens

The confluence of the major changes that adolescence brings (see Box 6.1) is increasingly recognized by scientists, development actors and policy makers as a vital window in which to accelerate progress against the effects of poverty, inequity and discrimination, and to foster positive development trajectories (United States Agency for International Development [USAID], 2016; Sheehan et al, 2017; Lansford and Banati, 2018). However, the evidence base on the patterning of these changes and adolescents' evolving capacities – and how they are shaped by gender, geography, political context, (dis)ability, sexuality, marital status and ethnicity, among other identities – is growing but still limited,

---

Box 6.1: Multidimensional changes during adolescence

Biological changes: during adolescence the body achieves its maximum potential in terms of fitness, physical strength and reproductive capacity (De Sanctis et al, 2014). Growth during adolescence is faster than at any other time of life, with a 15–20% increase in height, and individuals gaining up to 50% of their adult body weight. With puberty (typically between 8 and 14 years), hormone changes lead to the development of secondary sex characteristics and, for girls, the onset of menstruation (Lerner and Steinberg, 2004).

Neurodevelopmental changes: early adolescence sees developments in the limbic system – the area of the brain responsible for pleasure-seeking and reward-processing, emotional responses and sleep regulation (Crone and Dahl, 2012). While risk-taking in adolescence may be perceived negatively, it can also lead to adaptive behaviours that promote acquisition of new skills and autonomy and long-term survival (Suleiman and Dahl, 2017). Later in adolescence, changes take place in the pre-frontal cortex – the area responsible for decision making, organization, impulse control and future planning (World Health Organization [WHO], 2018).

Socio-emotional changes: while parental support is critical to adolescent well-being, during adolescence young people typically become more independent from their families and interact more with their peers, valuing opportunities for peer socialization (Saxbe et al, 2015; UNICEF Innocenti, 2017).

Norm changes: in many low- and middle-income country (LMIC) contexts, gender norms and role expectations become more entrenched and personally salient during adolescence. This is manifested in increasing restrictions on adolescent girls' mobility, and the framing of their future through the lens of marriage and motherhood only (Islam, 2012; Jones et al, 2015; Basu and Acharyam, 2016). By contrast, though adolescent boys tend to have more freedom and status within the family, gender norms around masculinity put them at greater risk of physical violence, substance use and even suicide (as men are discouraged from expressing emotions) (Pinheiro, 2006; UNICEF, 2017).

Legal changes: adolescence typically involves shifts in legal status. Internationally, 18 is recognized as the year of legal maturity (officially entering adulthood), but in many countries, 16-year-olds can legally work, marry and be conscripted (UNESCO, 2015).

---

as is evidence on what works to fast-track social change during this window (GAGE, 2019).

A longitudinal lens is critical to capture the dynamism and diversity of adolescent transitions and to understand what works in improving adolescents' outcomes and trajectories (Morrow and Crivello, 2015; Lansford and Banati, 2018). Given the particular 'stickiness' of gender norms, programmes such as GAGE can play an important role in exploring how gender norms shape adolescent development trajectories through observational research, while systematically disentangling the mediating roles that particular programme interventions can play in this process and at different stages of adolescence, through the impact evaluation component.

GAGE overview and conceptual framing

GAGE[1] follows the lives of 18,000 adolescent girls and boys in six LMICs in Africa (Ethiopia and Rwanda), Asia (Bangladesh and Nepal) and the Middle East (Jordan and Lebanon) (Jones et al, 2018b). Three core research questions underlie the mixed-methods approach:

- How do adolescents in diverse LMICs experience transitions from childhood to adulthood? How do these differ by age, gender, disability, geographic location?
- What effects do adolescent-focused programmes have on adolescent capabilities in the short and longer term?
- What programme design and implementation characteristics matter for effective delivery and scalability? (Jones et al, 2018b)

GAGE research builds on and complements seminal studies like Young Lives (Boyden et al, 2019). However, GAGE studies a larger and different set of countries (though it includes Ethiopia), focuses on marginalized populations (adolescents with disabilities, married adolescents, and refugee or internally displaced adolescents), and emphasizes understanding of what works to improve adolescents' lives through embedded impact evaluations. This dimension of programme evaluation adds significant value to the research design, but also complicates longitudinal data collection in numerous ways (discussed later).

Conceptual framework

The GAGE conceptual framework (Figure 6.1) is based on a capabilities approach, which explores the economic, human, political, emotional

Figure 6.1: The Global Early Adolescent Study conceptual framework (Source: GAGE Consortium, 2017, p 6)[2]

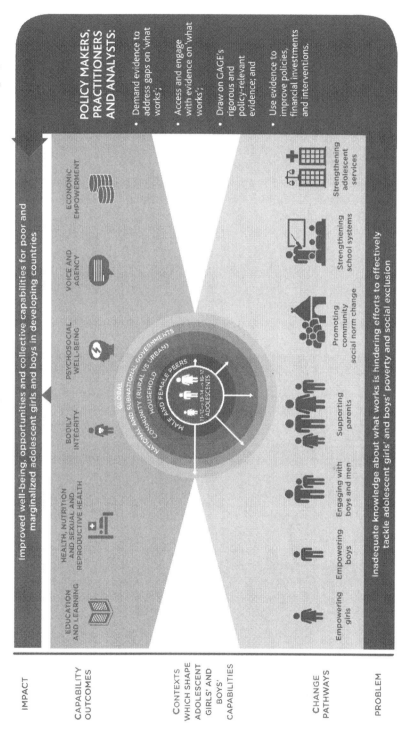

and social assets that increase adolescents' capacities (Kabeer, 2003; Sen, 2004; Nussbaum, 2011). The '3 Cs' are: adolescents' *capabilities*, meaning young people's individual and collective well-being in the six GAGE domains; *change* strategies, which explores how to maximize programme impacts by simultaneously intervening at the individual, family, community, service and system levels; and *context*, which investigates how adolescents' local, national and international environments shape their lives and development trajectories (GAGE Consortium, 2019). The conceptual framework pays particular attention to the role of micro-, meso- and macro-level context factors, gender norms and programmes. The 3 Cs are the thread that creates a coherent narrative and ensures that the overall GAGE research agenda is substantially more than the sum of its parts.

As Alkire and Deneulin (2018) argue, the capabilities approach is highly compatible with the SDG agenda. First, both the SDGs and the capabilities approach assess a country's development based on how well their people are doing, rather than on income or consumption levels. 'What ultimately matters are the types of lives that people are able to live – whether they can function well as human beings, and be and do things they value and have reason to value' (Alkire and Deneulin, 2018, p 2). Both approaches also adopt a multidimensional perspective on poverty and inequality, recognizing multiple and overlapping forms of deprivation. Second, Alkire and Deneulin argue that the SDGs and the capabilities approach both recognize the interconnectedness of targets across dimensions, including between environmental, economic, social and political domains. Third, the capabilities approach, as advanced by Martha Nussbaum (2011), calls for a common set of capabilities to be strived towards for all individuals irrespective of gender, ability or citizenship – reflecting a shared emphasis on ensuring that no one is left behind. This is also reflected in the SDGs' emphasis on disaggregated data, whether by ethnicity, disability, age, gender or geographical location. Finally, both approaches underscore the importance of agency and processes, with a strong emphasis on empowering people as agents of change in their own lives and communities, as well as on robust institutions and state action to address structural barriers to tackling poverty and inequality.

Globally, today's adolescent population is the largest ever (estimated at 1 billion). With appropriate support, it is possible to offset childhood disadvantage, help adolescents transition successfully into adulthood, and contribute to national efforts to reap the demographic dividend that a youthful population offers. As such, investing in adolescent well-being will be a critical part of achieving the SDGs (UNICEF,

2016); yet, to date, the targets and indicators pay limited attention to the specific challenges facing young people. While the 17 goals and 169 targets are now linked to 230 individual indicators, only 15 of those are disaggregated by gender and age, and they relate to just four goals (SDG 3 on health and well-being, SDG 4 on education and learning, SDG 5 on gender equality and SDG 8 on decent work) (UN Statistics Division, 2016; Guglielmi and Jones, 2019). Given its multi-capability focus, GAGE is therefore well positioned to contribute to monitoring progress around these 15 existing indicators, but also to advance thinking on the adolescent-specific dimensions of other targets, including those related to justice, innovation, urban spaces and climate change.

GAGE research methods

In order to understand the lived realities of adolescent girls and boys, GAGE's mixed-methods research uses quantitative and qualitative data (described in more detail later). An overview is then given of the nested impact evaluations the study is conducting in Bangladesh, Ethiopia, Jordan, Nepal and Rwanda.

GAGE quantitative data

GAGE aims to collect at least three rounds of quantitative data in each country, ensuring that data can be analysed for questions of cross-sectional interest (such as the association between gender norms and health), panel data questions (such as what factors are associated with school dropout) and impact evaluation questions (such as what is the causal impact of gender transformative programming in Ethiopia). The focus is on younger adolescents (10–12 years), who are often overlooked by demographic and health surveys (DHS) and labour market surveys, but a smaller older cohort (15–17 years) is also included to be able to understand transitions into early adulthood.

Unlike many studies that focus solely on representative samples, GAGE oversamples certain vulnerable populations to provide more evidence on these understudied groups. The programme also focuses on fragile and conflict-affected contexts (where young people's specific needs tend to be invisible), and on adolescents living in remote rural areas (those least likely to be reached by services). Finally, GAGE also oversamples adolescents with disabilities (for whom the knowledge base is exceedingly fractured) and never-married girls and boys (whose realities tend to be studied only retrospectively, through DHS questions

---

Box 6.2: Child marriage findings from GAGE Ethiopia

To achieve SDG target 5.3 on eliminating harmful traditional practices (including child marriage) by 2030, strengthening the evidence base to inform programme interventions is critical. The Ethiopian Demographic and Health Survey (2016) shows that child marriage is still common, but GAGE baseline findings underscore stark regional variation in child marriage practices and age at marriage, which has important implications for programme design. In Amhara, for example, the data shows that age at marriage has been climbing sharply, and older girls are now negotiating with their parents about their marriage partner, although very young girls may still be forced to accept arranged marriages. By contrast, key informants and married adolescents in Oromia confirmed that age at marriage has been falling in some communities, mainly due to the fact that child marriage has become more adolescent driven (due to peer pressure, the involvement of brokers and limited educational opportunities beyond primary school). In Afar, where the national family law has still not been adopted, *absuma* marriage (mandatory marriage to a maternal cousin) is a deeply entrenched norm, and girls have little say in the choice of marriage partner or timing of marriage.

---

with women in their twenties, or ignored, given a disproportionate programming focus on child marriage prevention rather than response) (see Box 6.2). For more details, see Jones and colleagues (2018a).

GAGE uses three core quantitative instruments, with both common and country-specific questions and modules. The Primary Female Caregiver module aimed to interview the main caregiver in each household (although secondary female caregivers or male caregivers were substituted as needed). Questions focus on the household structure, family background, assets, durables, dwelling and other household-level characteristics. It also has a specific focus on parenting of the younger cohort, as well as asking about attitudes and norms, mental health, financial inclusion, time allocation, exposure to violence, fertility, marriage and use of technology (with significantly more detail for parents of young adolescents). The core respondent module involves a face-to-face interview with the adolescent, exploring education, time allocation, paid work, health and nutrition, mental health, mobility, voice and agency, social inclusion, programme support, financial inclusion, economic empowerment, technology, marriage and relationships, SRH and violence. The questions are tailored to the age of the respondent.

Finally, GAGE quantitative survey instruments include community, health facility and school surveys. These surveys are closely linked to the conceptual framework to collect detailed data across all six capability areas, focusing on gender as a cross-cutting domain (see Baird et al, 2019b, for the baseline instruments from Ethiopia).

Qualitative and participatory research methods

The quantitative survey is complemented by in-depth qualitative and participatory research with a subset of adolescents, their parents and siblings to better understand the experiences and perspectives of young people in diverse contexts. The study uses a qualitative toolkit designed to mirror the '3 Cs' framework, and the specific tools used are now described in more depth (see also Jones et al, 2018a, 2019b).

Capabilities

A Few of My Favourite Things – a tool originally used in longitudinal qualitative research with UK adolescents (Thomson et al, 2011; Thomson and Hadfield, 2014) – was adapted to explore adolescent capabilities. Some talked about objects they would like to have (such as a bicycle, radio or mobile phone) rather than what they already have. Others chose objects that highlight the challenges facing disadvantaged young adolescents (for example, a piece of paper among visually impaired students so that they can take Braille notes during class, or a small table in the case of a newly married adolescent girl now responsible for keeping an independent household). Interviewers were able to probe the object's significance in the adolescent's life and how it relates to GAGE's six capability domains. To explore psychosocial well-being and voice and agency, interviewers also used a Social Support Network exercise, asking who the respondent enjoys spending time with (and why), who they can confide in, and who they avoid.

GAGE has also set up participatory research groups that meet more regularly (at least once a quarter) for vulnerable adolescents (for example, those with disabilities, married or divorced adolescents, or internally displaced/refugee adolescents). These groups offer a space for these young people to explore and capture, using participatory photography, the experiences and perspectives of young people at risk of being left behind.

Contexts

GAGE also included tools to explore the family, community and state-level contexts as well as gender and age dynamics that shape the development of adolescents' capabilities. A sibling timeline explores how a sibling's life compares with that of the focal adolescent, and why. A parent timeline explores key influences in the parents' lives and how their experiences have shaped their approach to parenting, and their aspirations for their children. A similar exercise for grandparents focuses on intergenerational similarities and differences around social norms related to age, adolescent development, and gendered expectations, roles and responsibilities. Together, the individual interviews with family members across three generations provide a rich picture of intergenerational changes and their underlying drivers.

The toolkit includes a number of group-based exercises to explore community-level influences. A community timeline is constructed, with older adults who can remember changes over time. A social norms change tool is also used to explore key opportunities and challenges facing adolescents in each capability domain. These adult-focused discussions are complemented by community mapping with younger and older adolescent girls and boys, to identify the key places and spaces in the community where adolescents can and cannot go, as well as their favourite or secret places, dangerous places and places they aspire to access as adults.

To explore more sensitive issues (with individuals or groups), researchers can use body mapping (a visual tool) to facilitate discussions around emotional and psychosocial well-being, relationships, pubertal development, SRH and gender-based violence. It is also a helpful way to explore similarities and differences between adolescents who are able-bodied and those living with different types of disabilities. Vignette exercises – for instance, a girl about to be subject to forced marriage, or a child who is bullied due to having a disability – are read out to the group, which then discusses whether such a scenario could happen in their community (why it could or could not).

Change strategies

GAGE undertook a wide range of key informant interviews with government officials and civil society representatives at community, district and regional levels. Each interview began by exploring the main opportunities and challenges facing adolescents from the interviewee's perspective – where possible, mapped against the six capability domains.

The tool then explores the key informant's role and organizational mandate, and the extent to which they have been able to contribute to tackling adolescent vulnerabilities and promoting their capability development. The interviewer ended by probing priority changes and possible 'quick wins' in the interviewee's area of expertise, and what barriers would need to be overcome to maximize the development of adolescents' capabilities.

A set of experimental and quasi-experimental impact evaluations embedded within the panel data collection activities allows investigators to complement panel data analysis with causal questions on programme impact. Alongside quasi-experimental research in Jordan (Makani) and Nepal (Room to Read), GAGE has three ongoing randomized control trials (RCTs): the Act With Her and Her Spaces programmes in Ethiopia; the 12+ girls' empowerment programme in Rwanda; and the Adolescent Girls Programme (AGP) in Bangladesh (see Table 6.1).

Emerging findings that have promise for longitudinal follow-up

Alongside impact evaluation questions of interest, GAGE's mixed-methods dataset will allow for a large set of interesting longitudinal questions. Here, we discuss just a few, and highlight key baseline findings that motivate future longitudinal research. The conceptual framework highlights the interconnectedness of domains, which is clearly reflected in the baseline findings. In Ethiopia, for example, it is found that in Afar, where many very young adolescents are already out of school, they are more vulnerable to child marriage, gender-based violence and poor psychosocial well-being (Jones et al, 2019b). Understanding how this interconnectedness evolves over time will highlight how specific vulnerabilities or capabilities either persist or evolve.

The longitudinal data will also provide critical insight into how gender attitudes and norms change (or stay the same) over time, and how this change is associated with outcomes across the GAGE capability domains. This will build on baseline analysis showing strong associations between gender attitudes and norms and GAGE outcomes. For example, Baird and colleagues (2019a) find that restrictive gender attitudes and norms are associated with poorer physical and mental health outcomes for younger adolescents (aged 10–12) in Bangladesh and Ethiopia. Surprisingly, they find little difference in this association for boys compared with girls, and find stronger results in urban locations. Seeing whether similar findings manifest when we look at changes in attitudes and norms over time – and particularly how this

Table 6.1: Overview of RCT programmes evaluated by GAGE

Act With Her (Ethiopia)	*Funder*	Bill & Melinda Gates Foundation (BMGF)
	Delivery partner	Pathfinder & Care International and Pathfinder Ethiopia and Care Ethiopia
	Focal regions	Act With Her: Amhara, Oromia, Afar Her Spaces: Afar, Amhara, Harari, Oromia and Tigray
	Value/project size	$16,700,000 50,000 direct beneficiaries and 1.7 million indirect beneficiaries.
	Objectives	Act With Her aims to enable adolescent girls (aged 11–16 at project start) to successfully navigate transitions to adulthood by addressing pervasive and harmful gender inequalities, empowering girls, enabling their capabilities and ensuring that girls are able to access essential services.
	Interventions	Act With Her: Clubs (curriculum-based, led by 'near peers'), interventions with boys, parental engagement, community and systems engagement – especially with ministries of Health and Women, Children and Youth. Her Spaces: A scaled-down 10-month girls' club focused on life skills and safe spaces.
	GAGE evaluation approach	Mixed-methods longitudinal RCT evaluation design – sample size of approximately 7,000 adolescents and caregivers.
Investing in Adolescent Girls (Rwanda)	*Funder*	Department for International Development (DFID) Rwanda
	Delivery partner	Non-governmental organization (NGO) partners (procurement process is still ongoing)+ Ministry of Gender and Family Promotion (MIGEPROF)

Table 6.1: Overview of RCT programmes evaluated by GAGE (continued)

	Focal regions	All regions – 26 out of 31 districts
	Value/project size	£12.5 million. 200,000 adolescents (150,000 girls and 50,000 boys)
	Objectives	To equip young adolescents with the knowledge and capabilities needed to achieve their full potential.
	Interventions	Delivering out-of-school life skills lessons to 200,000 11-year-old girls and boys, covering basic health, nutrition and hygiene behaviours, sexual health and family planning, puberty, gender and violence, economic opportunities.
	GAGE evaluation approach	Mixed-methods longitudinal RCT evaluation design – sample size of approximately 3,000 adolescents and caregivers.
Adolescent Student Programme (Bangladesh)	Funder	World Bank
	Delivery partner	Government of Bangladesh (Ministries of Education and Health) and partner NGOs.
	Focal regions	Eventually nationwide but currently in Chittagong and Sylhet.
	Value/project size	SEDP for Bangladesh $500 million; HSSP $500 million.
	Objectives	The ASP Adolescent Girls Programme (AGP) aims to enhance cycle completion, gender equity in secondary school outcomes, improved voice and agency, and economic empowerment.

(continued)

147

Table 6.1: Overview of RCT programmes evaluated by GAGE (continued)

	Interventions	AGP interventions will include: sexual harassment training and support in schools, outreach to teachers on adolescent physical health (including SRH and nutrition), mental health and bullying prevention. Awareness, guidance and community participation on adolescent health to delay age at marriage and timing of first birth.
	GAGE evaluation design	Mixed-methods longitudinal RCT evaluation design – sample size of approximately 5,000 adolescents and caregivers.
Makani/ My space (Jordan)	*Funders*	Multiple
	Delivery partner	UNICEF, Ministry of Social Development and local NGOs
	Focal regions	Camps, host communities, informal tented settlements across Jordan.
	Value/project size	90,000 beneficiaries annually.
	Objectives	Makani aims to support the development and well-being of refugee and vulnerable host community children and adolescents through an out-of-school one-stop-shop model.
	Interventions	Makani provides safe spaces for children and adolescents aged 6–18 years, learning support, psychosocial support and child protection.
	GAGE evaluation design	Mixed-methods longitudinal quasi-experimental design involving 4000 adolescents, with half in Makani and half not.
Room to Read, Nepal	*Funder*	Room to Read
	Delivery partner	Room to Read Nepal Country Office

Table 6.1: Overview of RCT programmes evaluated by GAGE (continued)

Focal regions	Tanahun and Nukawot
Value/project size	4,800 girls total; 571 beneficiaries in the GAGE study.
Objectives	Exploring the impact of the Girls' Education. Programme support for adolescent girls' access to quality education and transitions.
Interventions	Curriculum-based life skills programme facilitated by social mobilizers focused on: self-confidence, problem solving, critical thinking. Focus also on reproductive health, nutrition, financial literacy and career choices. Programme includes mentoring, family and community support, and needs-based material support.
GAGE evaluation design	Quantitative quasi-experimental design with control and intervention groups. Sample size of 1200 adolescent girls.

plays out by gender – will shed important light on the role of attitudes and norms as children progress from early to later adolescence.

Given our focus on parenting, the longitudinal data will also illuminate the evolving relationship between parents and adolescents and how this drives adolescent outcomes. Baseline analysis on parent–adolescent communication about future marital and fertility expectations from urban Bangladesh and Ethiopia shows that increases in the primary female caregiver's desired age at marriage or first birth for their adolescent child is associated with similar increases among adolescents themselves. The results also show that intergenerational dynamics matter, as the gendered attitudes of the primary female caregiver are associated with a lower desired age at first birth for the adolescent (Baird et al, 2019a). The longitudinal data will help unpack the continued role of parents, exploring whether adolescents' attitudes and behaviours evolve to be closer to those of their parents or, as context and culture change, move further apart.

GAGE data (quantitative and qualitative) has a specific focus on refugees and internally displaced adolescents. In Jordan, the GAGE sample includes approximately 3,000 Syrian adolescent refugees in camp and host communities, and in Bangladesh approximately 1,000 Rohingya adolescent refugees in Cox's Bazar (see Guglielmi and Jones, 2019; Jones et al, 2019a); there are also samples of indigenous populations in the host communities. Understanding the dynamics between refugee and host communities will highlight both the specific vulnerabilities of refugees, and how their presence affects host populations. Moreover, given uncertainty over the future of these refugees in the host countries, there is potential for rapid change, which the GAGE panel dataset is well placed to capture.

GAGE also focuses on the experiences of adolescents with disabilities (see Box 6.3) – a group for whom it is rare to have quantitative data, and especially panel data. As documented in Muz and colleagues (2019), to ensure a large enough sample of adolescents with disabilities within the overall sample, various strategies were used throughout the data collection process. These included adding a screening question on disability to the household census form prior to selecting the survey sample, identifying adolescents with disabilities during fieldwork by talking to knowledgeable community members, and including in the quantitative survey a set of questions (endorsed by the Washington Group) designed to identify disability.

The short case studies from Bangladesh and MENA (see boxes 6.4 and 6.5) provide examples of emerging baseline findings that can

---

Box 6.3: Contributing to the evidence base on adolescents with disabilities in Ethiopia

SDG 4 calls for quality and inclusive education, including for persons with disabilities, yet approximately one third of children who are not in school (19 million) have a disability (Saebones et al, 2015; Male and Wodon, 2017). Other studies suggest a close relationship between poverty and disability, but evidence gaps obscure the specific mechanisms for this (Filmer, 2008; Mont, 2014). However, we still know relatively little about access to education for children with disabilities in low- and middle-income countries (LMICs), partly due to chronic underreporting (Lewis, 2009). In Ethiopia, the evidence base is especially fragmented due to an absence of routine gender-, age- and disability-disaggregated data collection systems. Indeed, while the World Health Organization (WHO) estimates that about 10% of the world's population is affected by disability, Ethiopia's most recent census puts the national total at just 1.09% (ACPF, 2011).

GAGE baseline data (collected in 2017 and 2018) highlights that adolescents with disabilities in Ethiopia face many interrelated challenges, not least in accessing quality and inclusive education. The quantitative findings show that adolescents with disabilities are less likely to be enrolled (64% versus 85%) than those without disabilities and have completed fewer years of education (3.5 versus 4.6). The type and severity of the disability also shape school enrolment: those with intellectual and hearing impairments are mostly out of school, and this gap increases by grade level and age (such that accessing upper primary and secondary education becomes a critical problem). Barriers to accessing inclusive education include inadequate infrastructure and education facilities, limited training and recruitment of suitably qualified teachers, lack of materials, and discriminatory attitudes from parents, teachers, peers and the wider community.

---

inform policy and practice, which, alongside longitudinal data, will significantly advance the knowledge base.

Learning so far

GAGE has generated some important learning so far, with implications for longitudinal work more generally. Here we discuss three lessons: (1) the promise and perils of embedded RCTs; (2) a truly mixed-methods approach; and (3) ensuring that the sample includes the most vulnerable.

Box 6.4: Threats facing adolescents in urban spaces: emerging findings from Bangladesh

Almost one fifth of Greater Dhaka's 20 million people are adolescents (18.8%) (Index Mundi, 2018), yet there is little understanding of young people's experiences in this rapidly changing context. Here, we briefly reflect on two examples from our baseline findings: adolescent drug use (in line with SDG target 3.5 on preventing and treating substance use) and internet connectivity (in line with target 9.3 on access to information technology), which will be key issues to track longitudinally.

Drug use: Substance abuse in Bangladesh has risen to prominence largely in the context of the government's 'war on drugs', such that most studies on drug use in the country are couched in terms of crime rather than addiction (see Coyne and Hall, 2017; Gupta and Pokharel, 2018; Islam, 2019). Estimates of drug addiction levels nationwide range from 2.5 million (Shazzad et al, 2013) to 7 million (Haider, 2018), with youth disproportionately affected (comprising up to 80% of all Bangladeshi drug users). Almost half of all drug use is in the capital, Dhaka (Gaffar and Deeba, 2017). While recent evidence demonstrates a relationship between unemployment and drug use (Rahman et al, 2016), patterns of substance abuse among urban adolescents and the social dynamics that lead to increased risk remain poorly understood (Islam, 2019).

Although only about 10% of adolescent respondents in the GAGE baseline survey said they had smoked and only about 5% said they had ever had alcohol, the community focus group discussions, key informant interviews and interviews with boys revealed how common and accessible drugs have become, and how inextricably they are linked with violence and unemployment. Selling drugs is an easy source of income for adolescents who become users, often after they start out earning an initial income from acting as carriers. Interviews with adolescent girls also highlighted the fear and risks of sexual harassment in public spaces by young boys and men who are unemployed and sometimes using drugs. Not only is substance abuse a mental health issue, it is also related to violence and lack of security for girls, boys, women and men in urban settings.

Internet connectivity: Bangladesh has one of the world's highest rates of internet coverage – 145 million sim cards for a population of 160 million – but there are significant disparities in access and use. As of 2013, national survey results indicated a pronounced gender disparity in internet usage among adolescents, with only 3% of adolescent girls surveyed having used the internet in the past year (Bangladesh Bureau of Statistics (BBS) and UNICEF, 2015), and significant differences between rural and urban access to information and communication technology (ICT) (BBS, 2012). GAGE 2018 baseline data highlight similar gender disparities: 56% of older adolescent boys compared to just 30% of older girls have their own phones, while 75% of the older boys have gone online (versus 35% of the older girls).

Box 6.5: Complexities of psychosocial needs among adolescents in humanitarian contexts

SDG 3 on health and well-being for all has brought much-needed attention to this important issue, including among young people (target 3.4). Findings from GAGE, echoing studies in other parts of the Middle East and North Africa region (Okasha et al, 2012; Pocock, 2017), indicate that adolescents' psychosocial needs are often acute, as they are disadvantaged by age- and gender-related hierarchies, political turbulence, poverty, and lack of resources and skills that would help them cope with these multiple stressors (Samuels et al, 2017; Jones et al, 2019c). The literature indicates that many adolescents in the region have developed anxiety-related disorders, depression, loss of hope and susceptibility to risky behaviours, including suicidal ideation and substance abuse (Abu Hamad et al, 2015; Saymah et al, 2015; WHO and Palestinian National Institute of Public Health, 2017). The GAGE baseline survey in Jordan found that 32% of respondents meet the threshold for 'caseness' on the General Health Questionnaire (GHQ) (Jones et al, 2019a), while 46.2% of adolescents in Gaza reported psychosocial ill-being (Hamayel and Ghandour, 2014).

GAGE findings suggest that older girls are 11% more likely than older boys to exhibit emotional distress, mostly attributed to their greater social isolation, anxiety about being forced to marry young, subsequent experiences with child marriage, and limited access to psychosocial services (Jones et al, 2019c). In terms of context, poorer adolescents living in highly conservative informal tented settlements were especially likely to exhibit distress (40% versus 33% in host communities and 29% in camps) (Jones et al, 2019c).

While most studies on psychosocial well-being in the MENA region are medically/epidemiology oriented (focusing on prevalence of illnesses), GAGE uniquely focuses on the gendered experiences and perceptions of adolescents about their psychosocial well-being. For example, conforming to expectations of 'family honour' is a source of considerable stress for older girls, while physical violence was a major concern among boys.

GAGE also fills an important gap by exploring the extent to which age- and gender-sensitive psychosocial support is available to adolescents, and their experiences accessing such services. Adolescent uptake of formal services is limited by lack of knowledge about service availability as well as stigma attached to mental illness (Samuels et al, 2017). Boys reported that social norms around masculinity and self-sufficiency restrict their participation in psychosocial activities, and that they tend to resort to substance use and/or violence as a coping strategy (Samuels et al, 2017). By contrast, social norms around marriageability tend to preclude adolescent girls from accessing psychosocial services.

Overall, at the system level, our findings highlight that such services are fragmented, poorly governed and monitored, reactive in nature, and are neither gender- nor age-sensitive, while access to specialist services is limited (Samuels et al, 2017). It is therefore essential to launch cross-sectoral interventions, including but not restricted to strengthening the links between psychosocial support and health services, education systems and social protection programmes (Jones et al, 2019c).

Embedded RCTs

While these RCTs are an essential part of GAGE, they have also introduced complications that other researchers doing similar work could learn from. First and foremost, as GAGE funding did not include any funding for implementation, GAGE researchers had to find implementing partners willing to work with a research team on an evaluation design without any additional financial support. Also, the timing of implementation had to line up with the research (and vice versa) – with some, but limited, flexibility given GAGE's reporting commitments to funders. The original plan (to find existing programming to work with) was ultimately thwarted, largely due to these two constraints. The exception is 12+ in Rwanda – also funded by DFID – but even in this case, GAGE delayed data collection for more than two years to accommodate programme delays (baseline is now scheduled for 2020).

For the other two RCTs, GAGE was ultimately able to operate within these constraints by working closely with partners to bring in additional money for implementation. This is exemplified in the Ethiopia case, where GAGE worked closely with Pathfinder International to secure implementation funds from the Bill & Melinda Gates Foundation for programming that aligned with the GAGE conceptual framework. In

Bangladesh, GAGE partnered with the World Bank and a local NGO to evaluate the AGP, which will ultimately be scaled up nationally. While we believe these collaborations further GAGE's work and reach, building these partnerships demanded many hours of work by the GAGE team outside of the study's original mandate.

Incorporating programming and developing RCTs has had some drawbacks though. As mentioned, aligning GAGE data collection with programming led to long delays in data collection (Rwanda) or less than ideal timing between data collection and programming (in Ethiopia, for example, baseline data collection took place in late 2017 but programming only started in mid-2019). It also complicates some of the panel aspects of the data collection, in terms of comparisons within and across countries. In Ethiopia, for example, Act With Her focuses on 10–13-year-olds in rural areas, so in order to have sufficient sample size for the RCT, GAGE data collection focused solely on young adolescents in these areas. However, GAGE is also interested in adolescent transitions in urban locations in Ethiopia, where data was collected on both younger and older adolescents. This data structure implies that we cannot distinguish whether certain findings among 15–17-year-old urban adolescents are due to age or the urban environment.

There are similar challenges with comparisons across countries. Due to delays in programming, as well as differences in target age groups and/or duration, data collection sometimes focuses on different age groups (for instance, 11-year-olds in Rwanda versus 14–15-year-olds in Bangladesh and 11–13-year-olds in Ethiopia); nor are these groups aligned in terms of timings (for example, adolescents in Ethiopia were 10–12 years in 2017, while those in Rwanda will be 11 in 2020). While we believe the added value of the impact evaluation component outweighs the drawbacks, maintaining a perfect multi-country panel data structure while at the same time nesting impact evaluations is probably impossible, except perhaps if a funder funded both research and implementation (although the reality of fieldwork would still make this a challenge).

Mixed methods

While other longitudinal research claims some level of a mixed-methods approach, almost inevitably one approach takes priority over the other. GAGE puts equal emphasis on quantitative and qualitative methods, which is reflected in the research team composition. This ensures that quantitative data is appropriately contextualized and that qualitative data is forced to confront issues around lack of representativeness. Yet it also presents some major challenges: first, funding is fixed, so both sides must make compromises, particularly given the additional cost of coordination; second, this leads to almost constant ongoing fieldwork, which makes managing the workload challenging at times; and third, this makes publication of findings more challenging, as there are fewer journals that publish mixed-methods work.

Vulnerable adolescents

As already mentioned, GAGE's central focus is on the most vulnerable but typically under-researched young people – adolescents with disabilities, adolescents who have experienced child marriage, and refugee and internally displaced adolescents. Again, though, there are important trade-offs. First, adolescents with disabilities and those who experience child marriage are often not reached by traditional quantitative methods, so we undertook complementary purposeful sampling. This not only adds costs, but raises the question of whether conventional 'census'-style listing misses key populations, or whether GAGE is actually over-representing these populations in our research (we believe the former to be the case). Second, both of these groups are usually left out of programming or, if they are included, programmes are not tailored to their needs, so including them in the sample is at odds with exploring programme impact. Third, given taboos around child marriage, quantitative and qualitative data may record an individual's marriage status differently, leading to challenges in triangulating data. Finally, tracking respondents over time is already a challenge with adolescents as they are a very mobile population; when you add in refugees and internally displaced populations, these challenges become very considerable, particularly as some may return to their home countries.

Implications of longitudinal research design for policy and programming impacts

What lessons can we draw from GAGE's experience of longitudinal research design and implementation, and how does this approach strengthen the evidence base on gender and adolescence and inform the SDGs?

First, given the relative rarity of longitudinal research funding but the huge potential of such research, public goods research arguably has an obligation to seek to balance demands for methodologically robust social science with practice- and policy-relevant research evidence.

In this regard, GAGE's hybrid design combining observational longitudinal research with nested impact evaluations is innovative. The observational longitudinal research tells a broader story but also helps to contextualize the impact evaluation findings, situating the potential impact of a given programme against a more complex backdrop of political, social and economic change.

Second, research and programming teams within the same funding entities need to design this work jointly from the outset if investments into longitudinal research are to have maximum use for policy and programming. While productive partnerships can be forged across programmes with different funding streams, GAGE's experience to date suggests that these are often complex, time-intensive and imperfect; many of the obstacles faced could (arguably) have been avoided through joint design and mutual contractual mandates.

Third, longitudinal research evaluations of programming typically rely on programme stability, but in reality, programming is often more dynamic; indeed, there is growing evidence that an adaptive management approach is critical for context-responsive programme implementation. In this regard, GAGE is exploring how to harness its hybrid research design to allow for programming adaptations in response to emerging findings while maintaining a panel study and continuing to learn about the medium- and longer-term legacy effects of the original design on adolescents' lives.

Fourth, given the rapid cognitive and psychosocial shifts that adolescence brings, research instruments over successive rounds need to be adapted to be age-responsive while maintaining sufficient continuity so as to assess impact. This requires considerable investments in developing research instruments and piloting.

Fifth, in order to contribute to the breadth of the SDG agenda as it pertains to adolescent lives, considerable resources are needed to develop research instruments that cut across thematic areas. This is in turn compounded by efforts in line with the 'leave no one behind' agenda to ensure an inclusive sample that encompasses married adolescents and adolescent parents, those in remote rural areas, adolescents with disabilities and those who are internally displaced or refugees.

Finally, there is a need to educate stakeholders about the increasing value of longitudinal research insights over time. Because the start-up costs (resources and time) are considerable, managing expectations in the early years and in monitoring and evaluation of such programmes is critical. When the focus is on finding out 'what works?' it is important to understand that expectations around baseline and first follow-up should be appropriately modest. Ultimately, the rationale for a nine-year programme is precisely because it takes this kind of timeframe to answer this question comprehensively.

Acknowledgments

The authors wish to thank Eric Neumeister and Kate Pincock for research assistance for this chapter.

Notes

[1] The GAGE Consortium, managed by the Overseas Development Institute (ODI), includes 35 partner organizations from around the world known for their expertise in research, policy and programming in the fields of adolescence, gender and social inclusion. GAGE is funded by UK aid from the UK government. For more details see www.gage.odi.org.

[2] Available at https://www.gage.odi.org/wp-content/uploads/2019/01/Gender-and-Adolescence-CF-FINAL-1.pdf

References

Abu Hamad, B., Jones, N., Al Bayoumi, N. and Samuels, F. (2015) *Mental Health and Psychosocial Support Service Provision for Adolescent Girls in Post-Conflict Settings: The Case of the Gaza Strip.* London: Overseas Development Institute.

African Child Policy Forum (2011) The African report on child wellbeing 2011. Available at https://resourcecentre.savethechildren.net/library/african-report-child-wellbeing-2011-budgeting-children

Alkire, S. and Deneulin, S. (2018) The real wealth of nations. SDGs: delivering change. Blog, 19 March. Available at www.sustainablegoals.org.uk/real-wealth-nations

Baird, S., Bhutta, Z., Hamad, B., Hicks, J., Muz, J. and Jones, N. (2019a) Do restrictive gender attitudes and norms influence physical and mental health during very young adolescence? Evidence from Bangladesh and Ethiopia. *SSM – Population Health* 9: 100480.

Baird, S., Hicks, J., Jones, N., Muz, J. and GAGE Consortium (2019b) Ethiopian baseline survey 2017/2018. Core respondent module. London: Gender and Adolescence: Global Evidence.

Bangladesh Bureau of Statistics (BBS) (2012) Population and housing census 2011. Socio-economic and demographic report. National series, vol 4. Dhaka: Bangladesh Bureau of Statistics.

BBS and UNICEF (2015) Bangladesh: multiple indicator cluster survey 2012–2013. Progotir Pathey, final report. Dhaka: Bangladesh Bureau of Statistics and UNICEF.

Basu, S. and Acharyam, R. (2016) Gendered socialization of very young adolescents: perceptions and experiences of adolescents and their parents from a disadvantaged urban community of Delhi, India. Paper presented at conference on Adolescence, Youth and Gender: Building Knowledge for Change, 8–9 September, Oxford.

Boyden, J., Dawes, A., Dornan, P. and Tredoux, C. (2019) *Tracing the Consequences of Child Poverty: Evidence from the Young Lives Study in Ethiopia, India, Peru and Vietnam.* Bristol: Policy Press.

Coyne, C.J. and Hall, A. (2017) Four decades and counting: the continued failure of the war on drugs. CATO Institute, Policy Analysis No. 811.

Crone, E.A. and Dahl, R.E. (2012) Understanding adolescence as a period of social-affective engagement and goal flexibility. *Nature Reviews Neuroscience* 13(9): 636–50.

De Sanctis, V., Soliman, A.T., Fiscina, B., Elsedfy, H., Elalaily, R., Yassin, M. et al (2014) Endocrine check-up in adolescents and indications for referral: a guide for health care providers. *Indian Journal of Endocrinology and Metabolism* 18 (Suppl 1): S26–38.

Filmer, D. (2008) Disability, poverty, and schooling in developing countries: results from 14 household surveys. *World Bank Economic Review* 22(1): 141–63.

GAGE Consortium (2019) *Gender and Adolescence: Why Understanding Adolescent Capabilities, Change Strategies and Contexts Matters.* London: Gender and Adolescence: Global Evidence.

Gaffar, M.B. and Deeba, F. (2017) Mental health conditions among adolescents of substance dependent parents. *South East Asia Journal of Public Health* 7(1): 48–50.

Guglielmi, S. and Jones, N. (2019) *The Invisibility of Adolescents within the SDGs: Assessing Gaps in Gender and Age Disaggregation to Leave No Adolescent Behind.* London: Gender and Adolescence: Global Evidence.

Gupta, S. and Pokharel, S. (2018) Bangladesh defends war on drugs as body count mounts. *CNN*, 8 June. Available at https://edition. cnn.com/2018/06/08/asia/bangladesh-drug-war-intl/index.html

Haider, L. (2018) Bangladesh has 7 million drug addicts, 'over half of them are addicted to yaba'. *Bdnews24.com*, 21 May. Available at https://bdnews24.com/bangladesh/2018/05/21/bangladesh-has-7-million-drug-addicts-over-half-of-them-are-addicted-to-yaba

Hamayel, L. and Ghandour, R. (2014) *Assessment of the Psychosocial Health Status of Adolescents 12–18 Years Old in the Occupied Palestinian Territory.* Ramallah: Birzeit University, Institute of Community and Public Health.

Index Mundi (2018) Bangladesh demographics profile 2018. Available at www.indexmundi.com/bangladesh/demographics_profile.html

Islam, N. (2019) War on drugs: the case of Bangladesh. *Harvard Public Health Review* 25. Available at http://harvardpublichealthreview.org/bangladesh

Islam, T. (2012) Causes and consequences of eve-teasing in urban Bangladesh: an empirical study. *SUST Studies* 15(1): 10–20.

Jones, N., Tefera, B., Presler-Marshall, E., Gupta, T., Emirie, G., Gebre, B. and Berhanu, K. (2015) *'Now I Can Propose Ideas That Can Solve Any Problem': The Role of Community Awareness Interventions in Tackling Child Marriage in Ethiopia*. London: Overseas Development Institute.

Jones, N., Camfield, L., Coast, E., Samuels, F., Abu Hamad, B., Yadete, W., et al (2018a) *GAGE Baseline Qualitative Research Tools*. London: Gender and Adolescence: Global Evidence.

Jones, N., Baird, S. and Lunin, L. (2018b) *GAGE Research Design, Sample and Methodology*. London: Gender and Adolescence: Global Evidence.

Jones, N., Gebeyehu, Y. and Hamory-Hicks, J. (2019a) Exploring the role of evolving gender norms in shaping adolescents' experiences of violence in pastoralist Afar, Ethiopia: victim, perpetrator, or what else? *Sociological Studies of Children and Youth* 25: 125–47.

Jones, N., Presler-Marshall, E., Małachowska, A., Jones, E., Sajdi, J., Baniaweda, K. et al (2019b) *Qualitative Research Toolkit: GAGE's Approach to Researching with Adolescents*. London: Gender and Adolescence: Global Evidence.

Jones, N., Baird, S., Presler-Marshall, E., Małachowska, A., Kilburn, K., Abu Hamad, B. et al (2019c) Adolescent well-being in Jordan: exploring gendered capabilities, contexts and change strategies – a synthesis report on GAGE Jordan baseline findings. London: Gender and Adolescence: Global Evidence.

Kabeer, N. (2003) Gender equality, poverty eradication and the millennium development goals: promoting women's capabilities and participation. Gender and development discussion paper series (13). New York: United Nations.

Lansford, J. and Banati, P. (2018) *Handbook of Adolescent Development Research and Its Impact on Global Policy*. Oxford: Oxford University Press.

Lerner, R. and Steinberg, L. (2004) *Handbook of Adolescent Psychology* (2nd edn). Hoboken, NJ: John Wiley.

Lewis, I. (2009) Education for disabled people in Ethiopia and Rwanda. Background paper prepared for the Education For All Global Monitoring Report 2010.

Male, C. and Wodon, Q. (2017) *Disability Gaps in Educational Attainment and Literacy*. The Price of Exclusion: Disability and Education Series. Washington, DC: World Bank and Global Partnership for Education.

Mont, D. (2014) Childhood disability and poverty. Working Paper 25. London: Leonard Cheshire Disability and Inclusive Development Centre, University College London.

Morrow, V. and Crivello, G. (2015) What is the value of qualitative longitudinal research with children and young people for international development? *International Journal of Social Research Methodology* 18(3): 267–80.

Muz, J., Baird, S., Hicks, J., Rashid, S., Sultan, M., Yadete, W., Jones, N. (Eds) (2019) *A Mixed Methods Approach to Including Adolescents with Disabilities in Survey Research*. Comparative Research Programme on Poverty (CROP). Available at https://expert.gwu.edu/individual/doc-3e9ba5a32d4dc2f0e4e8a7dc157af5bb

Nussbaum, M. (2011) *Creating Capabilities: The Human Development Approach*. Cambridge, MA: Harvard University Press.

Okasha, A., Karam, E. and Okasha, T. (2012) Mental health services in the Arab world. *World Psychiatry* 11(1): 52–4.

Patton, G.C., Coffey, C., Cappa, C., Currie, D., Riley, L., Gore, F. et al (2012) Health of the world's adolescents: a synthesis of internationally comparable data. *The Lancet* 379(9826): 1665–75.

Patton, G., Sawyer, S.M., Santelli, J.S., Ross, D.A., Afifi, R., Allen N.B. et al (2016) Our future: a *Lancet* commission on adolescent health and wellbeing. *The Lancet* 387(10036): 2423–78.

Pinheiro, P.S. (2006) *World Report on Violence against Children*. Geneva: United Nations.

Pocock, L. (2017) Mental health issues in the Middle East: an overview. *Middle East Journal of Psychiatry and Alzheimers* 8(1): 10–15.

Rahman, F.N., Ahmad, M. and Ali, M. (2016) Socio-economic status of drug addicted young people in Dhaka City. *Journal of Armed Forces Medical College* 12(2): 15–20.

Sæbønes, A.M., Bieler, R.B., Baboo, N., Banham, L., Singal, N., Howgego, C. et al (2015) Towards a disability inclusive education. Background paper for the Oslo Summit on Education for Development, 6–7 July.

Samuels, F., Jones, N. and Abu Hamad, B. (2017) Psychosocial support for adolescent girls in post-conflict settings: beyond a health systems approach. *Health Policy and Planning* 32(5): 40–51.

Saymah, D., Tait, L. and Michail, M. (2015) An overview of the mental health system in Gaza: an assessment using the World Health Organization's Assessment Instrument for Mental Health Systems (WHO-AIMS). *International Journal of Mental Health Systems* 9(41): 1–8.

Saxbe, D., Del Piero, L., Immordino-Yang, M.H., Kaplan, J. and Margolin, G. (2015) Neural correlates of adolescents' viewing of parents' and peers' emotions: associations with risk-taking behavior and risky peer affiliations. *Social Neuroscience* 10: 592–604.

Sen, A. (2004) Elements of a theory of human rights. *Philosophy & Public Affairs* 32(4): 315–56.

Shazzad, M.N., Abdal, S.J., Majumder, M.S.M., Ali, S.M.M. and Ahmed, S. (2013) Drug addiction in Bangladesh and its effect. *Medicine Today* 25(2): 84–9.

Sheehan, P., Sweeny, K., Rasmussen, B., Wils, A., Friedman, H.S., Mahon, J. et al (2017) Building the foundations for sustainable development: a case for global investment in the capabilities of adolescents. *The Lancet* 390(10104): 1792–806.

Steinberg, L. (2015) *Age of Opportunity: Lessons from the New Science of Adolescence.* New York: Eamon Dolan/Mariner Books.

Suleiman, A.B. and Dahl, R.E. (2017) Leveraging neuroscience to inform adolescent health: the need for an innovative transdisciplinary developmental science of adolescence. *Journal of Adolescent Health* 60(3): 240–48.

The Palestinian National Institute of Public Health (2017) *Estimating the Extent of Illicit Drug Use in Palestine.* Ramallah: The Palestinian National Institute of Public Health/UNODC/KOICA (Korea International Cooperation Agency).

Thomson, R. and Hadfield, L. (2014) Day-in-a-life microethnographies and favourite things interviews. In V. Johnson, R. Hart and J. Colwell (Eds) *Steps to Engaging Young Children in Research: Volume 2: The Researcher Toolkit* (pp 126–30). Brighton: University of Brighton. Available at https://bernardvanleer.org/publications-reports/steps-engaging-young-children-research-volume-2-researcher-toolkit/steps-for-engaging-young-children-in-research-volume-2-the-researcher-toolkit7591

Thomson, R., Kehily, M., Hadfield, L. and Sharpe, S. (2011) *Making Modern Mothers.* Bristol: Policy Press.

United States Agency for International Development (USAID) (2016) *Acting on the Call. Ending Preventable Child and Maternal Deaths: A Focus on Equity.* Washington, DC: USAID. Available at www.usaid.gov/sites/default/files/Final-AOTC-file-v2.pdf

UN Statistics Division (2016) *The Sustainable Development Goals Report 2016*. New York: United Nations. Available at https://unstats.un.org/sdgs/report/2016

UNESCO (2015) *EFA Global Monitoring Report 2015. Education for All 2000–2015: Achievements and Challenges*. Paris: UNESCO.

UNICEF (2016) *Harnessing the Power of Data for Girls: Taking Stock and Looking Ahead to 2030*. New York: UNICEF. Available at https://data.unicef.org/resources/harnessing-the-power-of-data-for-girls

UNICEF (2017) *A Familiar Face: Violence in the Lives of Children and Adolescents*. New York: UNICEF.

UNICEF Innocenti (2017) The adolescent brain: a second window of opportunity. A compendium. Florence: UNICEF Office of Research, Innocenti.

Viner, R., Ross, D., Hardy, R., Kuh, D., Power, C., Johnson, A. et al (2015) Life course epidemiology: recognising the importance of adolescence. *Journal of Epidemiology & Community Health* 69(8): 719–20.

WHO (2018) *Guideline: Implementing Effective Actions for Improving Adolescent Nutrition*. Geneva: World Health Organization. Available at www.who.int/nutrition/publications/guidelines/effective-actions-improving-adolescent/en

7

Child Well-being Across the Life Course: What Do We Know, What Should We Know?

Gary Pollock, Haridhan Goswami and Aleksandra Szymczyk

Introduction

The 2030 Agenda for Sustainable Development, which includes 17 global goals, charts an ambitious course for the coming decade and beyond. Attached to the goals are 169 targets, which lay out the specific aims towards which the global community is working. In total, 95 of the targets are either directly (48) or indirectly (47) connected to children. The SDGs can only deliver on the promise of equity if the world knows which children and families are thriving and which are being left behind (UNICEF, 2017). Understanding the situation of children in relation to the SDGs is, therefore, crucial both for the well-being of children and for reaching the targets of the global goals.

Childhood well-being has an impact on a range of outcomes such as adult health, educational attainment, and employment and socioeconomic status in adulthood (Statham and Chase, 2010). Even though there is general agreement that policies to ensure child well-being are necessary there are disparities in the practical implementation of policy between countries and on regional levels. In some countries, a lack of financial resources may be the main reason for not having an appropriate monitoring system that has the potential to inform politicians on a regular and reliable basis; on the other hand, it could be a question of competing priorities. There is, however, an acknowledged need for high-quality data on child and youth well-being, necessary to inform policy making aimed at addressing the 2030 Agenda for Sustainable Development Global Goals.

A longitudinal survey design has the unique capacity to capture the dynamics of childhood and young person development and helps to capture the impact of major life events, such as starting school, reaching adolescence and leaving home as well as giving a rare insight into the effects of socio-political changes and historical events that take place during their lifetime. This crucial phase of the life course is included in the focus of SDG 4 – Quality Education and SDG 8 – Quality Work (UN, 2020). Birth cohort surveys across the world have been central to our understanding of the factors which contribute to enhancing child well-being. These longitudinal data sets provide the highest quality data, which reveal demographic patterns of difference, changes over time and factors associated with high levels of well-being. They are an important source of evidence for policy makers seeking to protect and enhance the lives of children as they grow up. However, until now such surveys have been developed independently and, while there are some common features, in order to compare data in different countries there are many challenges in post hoc data harmonization. The merits of collecting national longitudinal data are widely recognized, and yet the current studies are not easily comparable as they contain different questions and are conducted at different times and on different age groups.

The European Commission (2012) recognizes that there is a significant gap in European data on children. These European data needs present a clear case-input harmonized comparative birth cohort survey. The European Cohort Development Project has been funded by the EU and has developed the design and business case for such a survey since 2018. The proposed survey – EuroCohort – comprises a common questionnaire, common sampling and fieldwork procedures and will thus allow a direct comparison of the well-being of children as they grow up across Europe in different national contexts. In the future, researchers the world over will be able to learn from the lived experiences of children and young people as they grow up in a diverse range of European countries.

This chapter begins with an overview of the development of child well-being research perspectives over the past few decades, including debates on models of participation for children and measurement debates on child well-being research. Secondly, it discusses birth cohort surveys as increasingly popular tools of measuring individual change over time and the growing desire to undertake comparisons and associated analytic challenges. Thirdly, it demonstrates the value of internationally comparable longitudinal data for evidence-based policy making on all levels of policy geography. Finally, it presents the design of and case for EuroCohort, an input-harmonized comparative birth cohort study, as a solution for addressing the European data needs.

Perspectives on and the measurement of child well-being

This section focuses on the development of child well-being research perspectives over the past few decades. It starts with debates on models of participation for children in research. It then focuses on measurement debates on child well-being research. Finally it discusses the development of research on child well-being demonstrating the gradual shift from tokenistic participation of children to co-creative model which appears to be aligned with the move in using subjective over objective measures of well-being. In academic literature, well-being is used as an overarching concept to indicate the quality of life of people in society (Rees et al, 2010a). From a hedonic point of view, it refers to a 'person's cognitive and affective evaluations of his or her life' (Diener et al, 2002, p 63).

Models of participation in research with children

There are a number of models of how children and young people can/ should be involved in a study. Depending on the degree of control and participation children may have in a study, Shaw and colleagues (2011) identified four models (ranging from the lowest to the highest level of participation): children are sources of research data, children are consulted about the research, children are collaborators in the study, and children are owners of the research. Hart (1992) also developed a 'Ladder of Participation' to describe the level of children and young people's participation, going from rung 1, where young people are manipulated, to rung 8, where young people and adults share decision making. Current best practice for involving children in research focuses on a stronger and more active involvement, one that empowers them (Goswami et al, 2016).

Since childhood is not static and children's abilities to participate vary by their age, the participation model used for research with children in a longitudinal design must be flexible. Lansdown (2001), a long-standing advocate of children's participation in democratic decision making, argued for different levels of support and to use a variety of methods of working and expression to enable all children to participate to the maximum. In the context of longitudinal research, a number of parallel child advisory panels composed of children from different age groups could provide a solution to these issues as it creates room for evolving the framework to guide participation across age groups as suggested by Lansdown (2001).

Objective versus subjective measures of well-being

In child well-being research, a distinction is made between objective and subjective measures. *Objective* measures of social reality are those which are not filtered by perceptions and are independent from personal evaluations. On the other hand, *subjective* measures are supposed to explicitly express subjective states, such as perceptions, assessments and preferences (Noll, 2013).

The use of objective measures such as GDP, household income, household wealth and income distribution, the proportion of children in education, educational attainment, life expectancy and crime rates are well established in research with children and young people's well-being. Although objective measures provide useful information on well-being at the macro level, there are many criticisms and caveats to be taken into account when confronting such measures (McGillivray, 2007). For example, Hicks (2011) terms the approach to using objective well-being measures as 'paternalistic'. This approach, he argues, assumes that certain things are good or bad for well-being and these are included in any indicator set; although there may be a model underpinning the choice, there is the danger that what is measured becomes what matters rather than what matters being measured. Some researchers (for example, Pollard and Lee, 2003) argue that the growth of the 'developmental perspective' in analysing childhood well-being has influenced the research on child well-being by objective indicator-based measures. The major UK birth cohort surveys (1958 National Child Development Study, 1970 British Cohort Study, 2000 Millennium Cohort Survey) have been guided by this perspective. A developmental perspective, they suggest, tends to adopt measures associated with deficits, such as poverty, ignorance and physical illness. While such indicators are important to begin to redress issues of inequalities and social exclusion which negatively impact on children's health and well-being – for example, lower family socioeconomic position is linked to poor educational for children in schools (see the review by Blanden and Gregg, 2004) – they tend to ignore the potential, attributes and strengths of children.

In order to explain the usefulness of subjective measures in well-being research, Kroll and Delhey (2013) used the famous Thomas theorem (Thomas and Thomas, 1928, p 572) grounded in symbolic interactionism: 'If men [sic] define situations as real, they are real in their consequences.' Thus, subjective measures draw on human perception: individuals themselves decide what is crucial in assessing their lives. In spite of some methodological issues such as the problems of measurement, bias, and divergence (see Veenhoven, 2002), they provide important additional information over and above objective measures on the quality of people's lives (Hicks, 2011). There is growing consensus in support for considering subjective well-being as a necessary complement to objective indicators (Guillén-Royo and Velazco, 2006, Stiglitz et al, 2009) and they together can create a rounded picture of the condition of well-being (Children's Worlds, 2019).

This holistic approach (Goswami et al, 2016) to measuring children's well-being is adopted in EuroCohort (2019). Since this approach gives equal emphasis on both measures of well-being, it allows researchers to estimate more comprehensively how changes in children's and young people's lives affect their well-being (measured using both subjective and objective indicators) as they grow up.

Paradigm shifts in child well-being research

Research on child well-being, especially in the context of measurement and participatory models, has made significant progress over the last decade. Therefore, the relevance of well-being research for children across the life course needs to be evaluated in the context of scientific advancement in this area of research. This section briefly reviews this development by using the Rees and colleagues (2010b) typology.

Social indicators movement

Influenced by the wider social indicators movement, this approach initially focused on measurement and trends in child well-being primarily using 'survival indicators' (Ben-Arieh, 2008) such as rates of mortality, disease and social problems affecting children (e.gfor example, illiteracy and school failure). Major work informed by this approach includes the Child and Youth Well-being Index (Land et al, 2001) in the USA, the National Set of Child Well-being Indicators (Hanafin and Brooks, 2005) in the Republic of Ireland, the Children and Young People's Well-being Monitor (Welsh Assembly Government, 2008) for Wales, the Local Index of Child Well-being (Bradshaw et al, 2009) published by the Department for Communities and Local Government in England, Kids Count, a national and state-by-state effort to track the well-being of children in the US run by the Annie E. Casey Foundation (2012), OECD research on the comparison of child well-being across its 30 member countries (Chapple and Richardson, 2009) and UNICEF publications (2007, 2010).

These indicator-based measures are useful to understand children and young people's well-being at the macro level. However, as Moore and colleagues (2014) argue, these macro indices predominantly focus on describing children's well-being at the expense of analysing the contexts that may contribute to or undermine their well-being. Using data from the 2007 US National Survey of Children's Health, Moore and colleagues (2014) developed micro-level indices (positive and negative) of child well-being by focusing on the three contextual domains of family, neighbourhood and socio-demographic factors. Their indices significantly contributed to child well-being research as they clearly revealed how the independent variables (environment or context of children) play crucial roles in determining children's development and well-being. While such indicators are important to begin to redress issues of inequalities and social exclusion that negatively affect children's health and well-being, they tend to ignore the potential, attributes and strengths of children. More specifically, this approach can be argued to treat children as passive agents not capable of evaluating their own lives (Goswami et al, 2016).

Self-report surveys

The second approach emphasizes measuring child well-being through self-report surveys. A number of instruments have been developed over the last decade to measure young people's own assessment of their lives. One of the most widely used is Huebner's Multi-Dimensional Student Life Satisfaction Scale (Huebner, 1994), which measures well-being in five domains: family, friends, school, living environment and self. Similarly, Cummins and Lau (2005), in their work with children and young people in Australia, have developed a Personal Well-being Index covering the domains of standard of living, personal health, achievement in life, personal relationships, personal safety, feeling part of the community and future security.

The international Health Behaviour in School-aged Children (HBSC) survey covers a number of key areas of young people's health and well-being. In the UK, several waves of the Tellus survey (Ofsted/ DCSF) have surveyed young people about their well-being and views under the five themes of the Every Child Matters framework – Be

Healthy, Stay Safe, Enjoy and Achieve, Make a Positive Contribution and Achieve Economic Well-being. The survey questionnaire included questions about happiness and relationships with family and friends. In addition, some large social surveys have begun to incorporate self-report instruments for young people. Understanding Society, previously known as the British Household Panel Survey, has a youth questionnaire for young people aged 11 to 15 about their happiness, feeling troubled and self-esteem (Rees et al, 2010b).

More broadly, the Danish Longitudinal Survey of Children, the Youth component of the German Socio-Economic Panel (SOEP), French Longitudinal Survey of Children, Swiss Survey of Children and Youth, the European Social Survey and the European Quality of Life Survey and some cross-sectional surveys (such as Progress in International Reading Literacy Study, Progress for International Student Assessment, Trends in International Mathematics Science Study, the European School Project on Alcohol and Other Drugs) have included questions on well-being and its various domains for young people in various age groups. For a full review of these surveys, see Richardson (2012), Gabos and Kopasz (2013) and Gabos and Toth (2011).

The main advantage of this approach is that it focuses on self-reported well-being. More specifically, the international surveys among children and young people provide precious comparable data on child well-being covering countries in the EU and beyond. For example, the OECD conducted a comparative analysis that provides useful insights on the state of child well-being among 30 OECD countries by focusing on six well-being domains: material well-being; housing and environment; education; health; risk behaviours; and quality of school life (OECD, 2009). Moreover, household panel surveys (for example, Understanding Society) provide new opportunities to explore the effect of changes in young people's lives on their overall well-being. However, the concepts and domains of well-being used in this work were developed primarily from concepts which originated from the study of adult well-being. Fattore and colleagues (2007) argue that these concepts are not directly transferable to the measurement of the well-being of children and young people. Moreover, as Bradshaw (2009) argues, most of these studies include only a limited number of well-being domains and therefore do not provide the full picture on the state of well-being for children and young people. These limitations influence the development of the third approach: child and young people centred studies.

Child-centric approaches

The third approach focuses on developing concepts and frameworks which incorporate children's perspectives. This strand is still at a relatively early stage, but there are a few examples of attempts to develop well-being frameworks from children's perspectives. Consultation exercises with children and young people in the Republic of Ireland (Gabhainn and Sixsmith, 2005, Hanafin et al, 2007) and Australia (Fattore et al, 2007) have identified important differences in children and young people's ideas about well-being which often vary significantly by age (Rees et al, 2010a).

In this regard, the first large-scale project took place in the UK in 2005, undertaken by the Children's Society when it included open-ended questions asking young people about their views on well-being and the factors which promoted and hindered it in its national survey of 11,000 young people aged 14 to 16. The thematic and content-based analyses of these responses identified ten key areas (The Children's Society, 2006). These were, roughly in order of their frequency of occurrence in the responses: (1) family, (2) friends, (3) leisure, (4) school, education and learning, (5) behaviour, (6) the local environment, (7) community, (8) money, (9) attitudes and (10) health. Following this child-centric approach, Rees and colleagues (2010a) developed an index of children's subjective well-being in England. This ten-domain index includes young people's satisfaction on family or carer, friends, health, appearance, time use, future, home, money and possessions, school and amount of choice.

A number of similar initiatives are also observed across Europe. For example, the Danish Youth Survey 2002 (Helweg-Larsen et al, 2004) examined young people's experiences and views on six themes including family, school, leisure and social networks, health and health behaviour, sexual experiences with peers and adults and violence in immediate surroundings. The DJI Youth Survey in Germany explores adolescents' trust in social institutions, their political attitudes, interest in politics, value orientation as well as their willingness regarding political activity (DJI, 2000). Similarly, Mihálik and colleagues (2018) identified four common domains (family, friends, school, material conditions) of well-being in their research with children and young people from four contrasting countries in Europe: Estonia, Slovakia, Greece and Portugal.

This third approach has been taken further by an international group of researchers linked to Children's Worlds (2019). The study aims to collect solid and representative data on children's lives and daily activities, their time use and in particular their own perceptions and evaluations of their well-being in a cross-national context. They gathered data from 33,000 children from 14 countries in wave 1 (2011–2012) and from 60,000 children from 18 countries in wave 2 (2013–2014). The third wave, recently completed, has gathered data from over 120,000 children from 35 countries in Europe, Asia, Africa and North and South America (see www.isciweb.org/; Rees and Dinishman, 2015; Sarriera et al, 2015).

Having the unique position of 'research *with* and *by* children', this third approach reflects a major paradigm shift in child well-being research (Mason and Danby, 2011). Thus, the importance of including children as active agents whose perspectives are heard in matters concerning them, especially in child well-being policies, is gaining momentum. However, child well-being researchers (Richardson, 2012; Bradshaw et al, 2009; Casas, 2011) are increasingly concerned about the shortage of internationally comparable subjective data on children's and adolescents' perceptions, evaluations and aspirations which they consider useful for decision-making and evaluating social change. In this regard, the data from the International Survey on Children's Well-being (ISCWeB) by Children's Worlds (2019) supplies invaluable comparative data on subjective well-being among a number of EU member states and countries beyond Europe. Several waves of data from these countries will also help researchers to examine aggregate change over time for specific cohorts. However, as Howieson and colleagues (2008) argued, such data lack being able to detect change at the individual level. Therefore, they do not enable an understanding of an individual's transition through different activities and statuses that might be linked to their subjective well-being (for example, moving from primary school to high school or changes in family structure for a child living with a divorced mother to a family structure where a step-father joins and then back to living with the single mother after a subsequent divorce and the influence of those changes on children's educational and family well-being). Since childhood is not static but dynamic, a holistic view taking into account changes at different stages of children and young people's development and transitions is required. This explains why there is a growing belief that in order to better understand how these changes and other socioeconomic factors related to these changes affect children's and young people's well-being, a longitudinal survey using a 'children and young people centric approach' is necessary (Pollock et al, 2018; Goswami et al, 2016). The European Cohort Development Project (2018) draws on this child-centric approach in developing a longitudinal framework on well-being research by taking into account the views of children and young people from a diverse sociocultural background across Europe.

Birth cohort surveys

This section describes the way in which birth cohort surveys have become increasingly used as a tool of measuring individual change over time.

The breadth of current birth and child cohort surveys

While the UK was a leader in the development of cohort surveys there now exists a plethora of such survey across the world. Moreover, the advantages of cross-cohort comparisons was also identified and addressed through collecting data from parallel cohorts of different ages in a single study in order to bring forward the analytic potential. This has become known as the 'accelerated' cohort model (Farrington, 1991) and is commonly used to facilitate quicker cross-cohort comparisons that would be possible were single cohorts used. An important example of an accelerated design includes the Young Lives project which covers Ethiopia India, Peru and Vietnam (Briones, 2018). This project was developed to address MDGs and can plausibly demonstrate that policies in each country have been directly influenced as a result of cohort data analysis (see for example Crivello and Morrow, 2019). In Germany, the National Education Panel Survey (NEPS) includes a series of six parallel cohorts, following more than 60,000 participants, making it perhaps the richest educational data source (Blossfeld et al, 2016). An analysis of the existence of surveys across the world, including cohort surveys, shows that there remains a high degree of variability in terms of the country coverage, survey content and research design (Richardson, 2012).

Identification of problems of comparative analysis using post hoc harmonization

The growing range of data sources on babies and children being followed as they grow up give us important representations of similarities and differences across the world. It has been only to be expected that scientists and policy makers became interested in similarities and differences across cultural and national boundaries, especially where welfare arrangements differ and policy interventions have taken place. The trouble is that while many of these surveys have similarities, and in some instances contain identical questions, there are a great many factors which undermine the extent to which valid comparison is possible. Bradbury and colleagues (2011) compared longitudinal birth cohort data from the UK, Canada, the US and Australia with reference to learning inequalities calling for greater international harmonization so as to facilitate comparisons between countries with similar welfare systems and historical trajectories. Their comparisons required a range of assumptions with regard to sampling methodologies, sampling frames, the primary purpose of the survey and question (item) comparability. Where there are methodological differences, it is necessary to work out if there is a way of adjusting one or both data sources to facilitate comparison. This kind of 'post-hoc harmonization' is the current state of the art in comparative birth cohort surveys. Much has been done to facilitate educational comparisons through the International Standard Classification of Education (ISCED) and cross-sectional surveys such as the Programme for International Student Assessment (PISA) and it is the case that educational systems are likely to always require post hoc harmonization. When it comes to subjective and experiential questions to do with, for example, bullying and well-being, there is an opportunity to develop internationally accepted indicators to facilitate comparison. Projects to harmonise international survey data have been around since the 1990s (Freed–Taylor and Schaber, 1995) and have specifically focused upon the harmonization potential of birth cohorts (EUCCONET, 2008). Post hoc harmonization can work and has produced important findings, but where questions are not exactly the same, where data is collected at a different point in time, from participants of unequal age and perhaps also using different data collection techniques, there are acute challenges in the harmonization process and caveats are required so that conclusions are not overreached. There has, therefore, been a growing consensus that, in addition to current cohort surveys, there is a need for an input-harmonized Europe-wide birth cohort which will spread coverage to countries such data is not available at the present time as well as facilitating direct comparisons between a broad range of countries (CHICOS, nd; Pollock et al, 2018). The existence of such data would be able to more effectively contribute towards an increasingly internationalized policy landscape by providing robust comparable evidence in regard to strategies to facilitate child well-being and positive life trajectories (O'Leary and Fox, 2018).

International comparative longitudinal surveys are vital resources for policy making

Longitudinal data has the unique capacity to capture the dynamics of one's development through life and allows the impact of a variety of factors, major life events, and even socio-political changes on future outcomes to be evaluated, making it a particularly valuable source of evidence for policy makers. While insights from surveys have much to offer to policy, it is worth noting that different designs will be associated with answering different research questions and responding to different policy challenges associated with a variety of policy drivers at regional, national and international levels. In Germany, the National Educational Panel Study (NEPS) is one of the largest studies of its kind in Europe. Due to its longitudinal nature it acts as a fundamental source of data for studying the cause–effect relationships between a person's educational paths and multiple dimensions of well-being. By the end of 2018 more than 600 academic publications have used NEPS data (NEPS Bibliography, www.neps-data.de/en-us/datacenter/publications.aspx). The NEPS data is used for educational reporting and monitoring (Federal Ministry of Education and Research, 2017) and is used to inform the decisions of policy makers in Germany. In addition, as a result of cooperation with the German Ministry of Education and Research, the NEPS team has conducted evaluations of federal educational reforms in Thuringia (Rieger et al, 2018) and Baden-Wuerttemberg (Hübner et al, 2017), therefore providing additional information for policy makers on the regional level.

Three important UK cohort studies (Millennium Cohort Study, 1958 National Child Development Study and 1970 British Cohort Study) have provided data for over 4,000 publications that have generated profound and significant insights into how health, education and family backgrounds of children have lasting impacts on outcomes and achievements throughout their lives. One of the key findings of the Millennium Cohort Study (MCS) was that breastfeeding protects against infant hospitalization for diarrhoea and respiratory tract infections and was associated with lower prevalence of overweight at age 3 and higher cognitive scores at ages 3 and 5. These data are used by NICE guidance, the UK Department of Health and Social Care, and documents supporting the Baby Friendly Initiative led by UNICEF and WHO that has been implemented in 134 countries (UCL, 2014), presenting a case of a national survey being used to inform policy on both national and international level.

Although studies such as those raised earlier exist, international comparative surveys are a particularly valuable data source for policy makers, with such data being of use at all levels of policy geography. Comparative aspects can be particularly useful for establishing benchmarks and defining particular goals for policy impact. For example, the data from the European Social Survey (ESS) provided indicators on active citizenship that allowed for international benchmarking, leading Lithuanian policy makers to formulate an action plan aiming to stimulate young people to become more active in civil society. The findings from the ESS 'Trust in the Police and the Criminal Courts' module fed into reorganization of the Swedish police service and has been used in several capacity-building projects in Albania (Technopolis Group, 2016).

The ESRC Longitudinal Studies Strategic Review notes that the 'the proliferation of cohort studies around the world lacks a methodology to make sense of comparative analyses' (Davis-Kean et al, 2017, p 26). It asserts the ongoing need for high-quality longitudinal data, while stressing the importance of the data to be internationally comparable, in order to enable cross-national analysis of phenomena in an increasingly globalized world. Internationally comparable longitudinal data allows for addressing international topics of interests, such as ways in which policy and circumstances affect well-being, health and other outcomes by comparing life-course trajectories and identifying factors that foster successful integration of migrants by comparing experiences in different countries, among many others. Moreover, a vast number of policy questions would profit from larger sample sizes by pooling samples (Davis-Kean et al, 2017).

For instance, findings from the longitudinal comparative Survey of Health, Ageing and Retirement in Europe (SHARE) allow for evidence-based policy making by EU member states, the European Commission and international organizations. In Germany, SHARE data was used to compare people's future pension expectations with the actual projected amount and directly evaluate policy measures incentivizing citizens to prepare for retirement through increased private retirement savings. The Estonian Government Office has used SHARE data to inform the parliament in the ongoing discussion about working opportunities beyond retirement age. The European Commission and the OECD has used SHARE research to analyse the recipients and providers of informal care in Europe and to develop ways of providing support to help the caregivers remain in employment and in good health (the Survey of Health, Aging and Retirement in Europe, now the European Research Infrastructure Consortium [SHARE-ERIC]), 2018).

The examples provided illustrate how valuable longitudinal and comparative data can be to policy makers, allowing for informed decision making and improved policy at national and international levels, which can have tangible benefits for people and societies. By providing deep, insightful, comparative and longitudinal data on the well-being experiences of children and young people across Europe, EuroCohort will allow researchers and governments better understand – and take steps to improve – youth's life chances, outlook, happiness and well-being. By collecting comparable data across member states to provide a comprehensive picture about children's well-being over the next 25 years, EuroCohort will provide evidence not only for implementation of new policies but also benchmark setting and enabling analysts to show the ways in which national policies have made impacts and showing where policy interventions can make significant improvements in different European countries. The international comparative feature of EuroCohort will allow an unprecedented opportunity for member states to recognize and exchange best practices and learn from the wealth of data that the shared EuroCohort infrastructure will provide about child and youth well-being.

The case for EuroCohort, an input-harmonized comparative birth cohort study

Drive from the European Union

In 2012 the European Commission published a call for proposals which recognized that there was a significant gap in European data on children and sought ideas from scientists on how this could be overcome. The call text is an important source document which underpins the origins of EuroCohort as it identifies specific needs and potential solutions while also leaving open the detail of exactly how such data could be collected. That the drive for EuroCohort came originally from the EU is important in emphasizing the policy needs of such data. This is why EuroCohort identifies itself as a policy-driven project. Scientific excellence is, of course, a priority and essential for the data to be regarded as truly representative and of sufficient quality to be able to inform policy, but in being policy-driven, the emphasis is more focused on the practical uses that these data can be put to. It is worth including excerpts from the call text as it demonstrates a high degree of understanding of the shortcomings of the existing landscape of data on child well-being across Europe:

Although it is important that healthy emotional, physical and psychological life-styles should start from an early age, very little European comparative social and educational research is being done in order to ascertain what are the best policies and approaches to effectively promote the well-being of children and young people. Research into the perspective of children and young people with regard to the various aspects of care, education, leisure and well-being seems to be even more overdue – although it involves very significant methodological challenges. Moreover, in order to understand the development of demographic trends in Europe, an investigation of the lower end of the demographic pyramid is required. To do this, we need a robust, representative and comparable dataset on the well-being of children/young people, child/youth related policies, childhood care and access to education, as well as on the environment in which a child grows up, which is primarily the family. Relational, organisational, participation, civic and leisure activities could also be included. To ensure comprehensive coverage of this topic, it might be necessary to conduct a longitudinal survey, which would capture the full picture of the growing-up process from birth to the end of a child's education – possibly including aspects related to the transition to work and parenthood. A multidisciplinary approach is needed in order to grasp the dynamic character of this process. … The conduct of the survey should ensure an ex-ante harmonisation across countries. Ideally, such a survey should be implemented at least in a large, representative sample of the EU countries, in cooperation with Member States. (EC, 2012)

The EU already recognizes the importance of high-quality survey data to inform policy development through its investment in surveys such as SHARE and the European Social Survey. In addition to the requirement that EU member states undertake a Survey of Income and Living Conditions (EU-SILC), the existence of complementary socioeconomic surveys strengthens the evidence base for future policy making. These surveys provide the benchmark, worldwide, for comparative survey methodology and will continue to provide a growing body of data which details the lived, contextual experience of the survey respondents. There is, however, a gap as no prospective data are collected from children or young people across Europe. Existing surveys may contain retrospective life history data collection that allows some analysis of the effects of early life experiences on subsequent outcomes, but there are significant questions as to the reliability of distant memories and events. Only a birth cohort survey can prospectively collect detailed and accurate life history data from children and young people and establish causal explanatory chains that have their origins in the very early years. There is arguably a need for a more connected approach to the collection of longitudinal life-course data where each life phase from birth to death can be analysed throughout Europe using robust comparable survey data (Emery et al, 2019).

Planning for EuroCohort

The EU call for a feasibility study to scope the development of a Europe-wide longitudinal survey with a focus on child well-being was undertaken by the MYWeB project which began in 2013. Working with policy makers and academics, as well as children and young people, the MYWeB project systematically showed that not only was such a survey technically doable (Ozan et al, 2018a), but that there was also a strong desire among policy makers, practitioners and academics for the data that this survey would generate (Ozan et al, 2018b). From the outset MYWeB ensured that children and young people were involved in the research to inform the study about their priorities as well as to give an insight into fieldwork strategies such as response modes, answer structures and question wording (Franc et al, 2018). The challenges of including children and young people in such a large and complex project were explored in order to ensure that they could be used maximally at the highest possible rung on Hart's (1992) ladder of participation (Nico et al, 2018). Having established the feasibility and desirability of a Europe-wide longitudinal child well-being survey, the MYWeB team progressed to undertaking a 'Design Study', again funded by the EU, this time with a view to initiating the preparation of a Europe-wide 'Research Infrastructure'. This new study was known as the European Cohort Development Project (ECDP), or 'EuroCohort'. ECDP completed its work at the end of 2019, by which time the research design, thematic content and draft questionnaires were finalized at the same time as a systematic cost–benefit exercise to show what each country would have to invest to make it happen, as well as what they stand to gain in terms of robust evidence for policy making. At the time of writing (2020) the ECDP team are preparing for further grant applications as well as a submission to be included in the EU's regular refreshment of its research infrastructure roadmap (ESFRI, 2019).

EuroCohort design

EuroCohort is an accelerated birth cohort with data collection for each cohort taking place (mostly) alternately. Figure 7.1 shows how this would work with a birth cohort (C2) starting in 2024 and an age 8 cohort (C1) starting in 2022. Of importance is the collection of age-equivalent data for each cohort; hence from age 8 each cohort is surveyed every three years. There is a common sampling strategy where national criteria are set to ensure that the highest quality available data are used to draw both the birth cohort and child participants. There are minimum target sample sizes for each participating country which are set in conjunction with population and birth rates as well as anticipated attrition rates over the life of the project to ensure that by the age of 24 the samples remain statistically representative and will, therefore, be large enough throughout the whole study to facilitate multivariate analysis using demographic variables. The aim is to facilitate as many EU countries as possible joining EuroCohort; in practice the study has wide coverage with a presence in almost all EU countries (and some beyond the EU). During the preparation phases there will remain the possibility for countries not yet included to join.

The content of the questionnaires is broad and captures familial context for demographic analysis, and a range of themes which contribute to an understanding of how well-being, both objectively and subjectively, changes over the life course. The major themes for the eight-year-old children are: subjective well-being, family and home, friends, school, local area, material conditions, time use, safety, health child rights. The parental questionnaires cover a broad range of demographic issues as well as themes that cross over with those answered by the children.

The survey is child-centric, including children and young people throughout the development of the research design and the content of the questionnaires. It is also child-centric in giving primacy to the voice of the child when it comes to reporting on well-being-related issues. In this regard parental responses are not used as proxy measures for the child. Nonetheless, parents are an important source of data, especially in the earliest year of the study, providing information about the context within which the babies and children are growing up. This is also the case during those years when young children do

Figure 7.1: EuroCohort's accelerated design and an example of a potential timeline

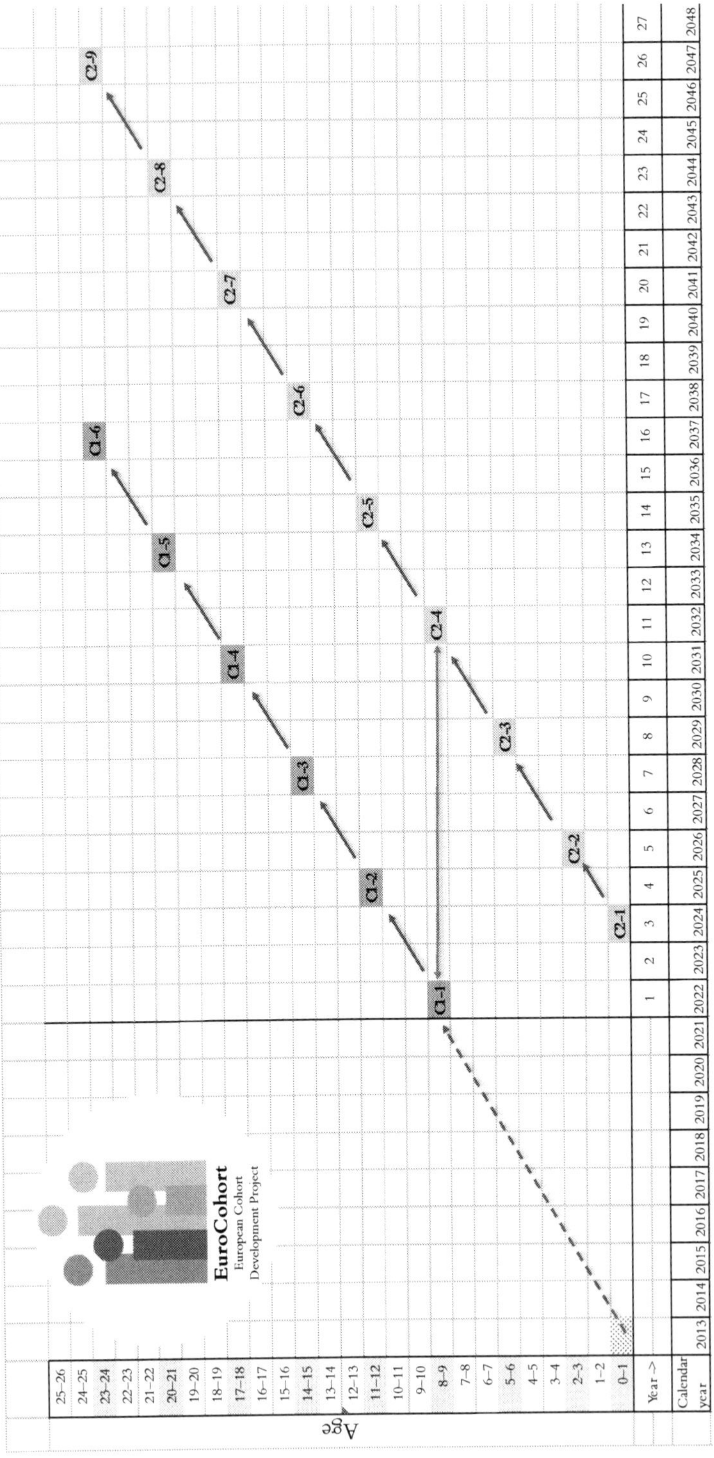

Source: Author's own

not have the cognitive capacity to answer formally put questions for themselves in such a way that can be used scientifically. Children are surveyed from the age of 8 until the age of 24. Parents are surveyed from the birth of the child (at around the age of 9 months) until the children reach the age of 17.

The strategy for the EuroCohort questionnaire content is to prioritize collecting data that will be of use in developing policies to promote child well-being. The survey is not, therefore, a medically driven survey, although there is a health theme which will exist throughout its existence. Socioeconomic conditions, educational experiences, lifestyle, technology and the ways in which these are increasingly subject to volatility and change are included. As well as including the views of children, this strategy looks to the future through an innovative foresight scenario planning exercise involving policy makers and scientists across Europe (EuroCohort, 2019).

Scenario planning is a medium- to long-term analysis and planning technique used to 'develop policies and strategies that are robust, resilient, flexible and innovative' (Rhydderch, 2009, p 5). A number of scenario planning methods exists, each considering different timescales and providing a varying degree of depth of analysis. Scenarios developed for EuroCohort used the 'Two Axes' method. This method is particularly appropriate for investigating medium- to long-term policy directions, by ensuring that it will remain robust in a range of future environments (Rhydderch, 2009). The intention of thinking about the future of Europe was to futureproof the EuroCohort survey to make sure it covers the most pertinent and crucial topics and will allow us to make sense of the lives of the future children and young people in Europe. The purpose of this exercise was to confirm priority policy areas in child and youth well-being in Europe and identify future policy trends by beginning to think about how global and local changes might affect the policy priorities in Europe in ten years' time. It engaged policy makers, practitioners, researchers, academics and young people across Europe and asked them to think about the possible future trends that will impact child and youth well-being in Europe. As with all longitudinal studies, there is a need for a long-term approach to data collection, ensuring comparability over time as well as being responsive to unanticipated contingencies. The findings from the foresight exercise were one of the key content drivers for the EuroCohort questionnaires, allowing the possible needs of evaluating the well-being of the children of the future Europe to be considered and ensuring that the instruments will remain relevant over the 25-year course of the survey.

Conclusions

Central to any initiative seeking to address grand challenges through objectives such as the SDGs are mechanisms whereby progress can be measured. By their very nature, the SDGs are both international and longitudinal: different countries and regions will be at varying stages along the road of achieving them. Cross-sectional measures of poverty, education, gender inequality and so forth are able to show how progress is made at an aggregated level and these measures are important headline figures in being able to understand relative differences and aggregate progress from one country to another. Such data, however, tends to mask individual experiences and is not good at exposing dynamic time-based patterns which are easily hidden in averaged figures. In so doing, cross-sectional data unfairly misrepresents individual life-course experiences and undermines the ability of policy makers to find robust solutions to social problems. As has been argued in this chapter, only through the collection of longitudinal survey data are we able to measure individual experiential changes, such as the varying financial position of a family and then connect this to other spheres of life, such as education, health and lifestyle. Longitudinal analysis has shown us that life circumstances and events are associated with differential outcomes. We are also aware that there are some individuals who appear to be particularly resilient in the face of adverse experiences and mange to overcome multiple disadvantages.

EuroCohort is an important initiative in a number of respects: firstly it prioritizes child well-being above all else and seeks to develop a high-quality evidence base by which it will be possible to monitor comparatively and longitudinally the dynamics of child well-being and find ways of improving it. This imperative is helped by the project being both child-centric and policy focused. Child-centricity is important in order to ensure relevance to the children themselves of the indicators (alongside those survey measures that scientists believe ought to be of importance). Moreover, including children and young people as active participants in as much of the scientific project as is suitable will enhance technical elements such as fieldwork processes. Policy relevance is important as there is a need for public spending to be seen to be cost effective as well as efficient in having the desired impact. Prospective longitudinal data is able to show how policy interventions manifest over time.

Governments across the world spend a vast amount of money on child and family policies, and much of this is devoted to providing basic services such as health and education, with a view to facilitating broadly similar opportunities for all. Given the persistently high and on-going nature of such investments, and within an economic outlook that suggests that there will remain a need to be able to deliver services ever more efficiently, governments need to spend this money wisely and in areas which are most likely to have a positive outcome. Only through investing in high-quality survey data such as EuroCohort will governments truly understand how they are able to effect positive changes to promote child well-being over the next quarter of a century.

Acknowledgments

This chapter is based on research funded under EU FP7 (MYWeB grant agreement no. 613368) and EU H2020 (ECDP grant agreement no. 777449) programmes.

References

Annie E. Casey Foundation (2012) *Kids Count*. Available at www.aecf.org/MajorInitiatives/KIDSCOUNT.aspx

Ben-Arieh, A. (2008) The child indicators movement: past, present and future. *Child Indicators Research* 1: 3–16.

Blanden, J. and Gregg, P. (2004). Family income and educational attainment: a review of approaches and evidence for Britain. *Oxford Review of Economic Policy* 20(2): 245–63.

Blossfeld, H.P., von Maurice, J., Bayer, M. and Skopek, J. (Eds) (2016) *Methodological Issues of Longitudinal Surveys: The Example of the National Educational Panel Survey*. Wiesbaden: Springer.

Bradbury, B., Corak, M., Waldfogel, J. and Washbrook, E. (2011) Inequality during the Early Years: Child Outcomes and Readiness to Learn in Australia, Canada, United Kingdom, and United States. IZA Discussion paper.

Bradshaw, J. (2009) Social inclusion and child poverty. In P. Perrig-Chiello (Ed) *Interdisciplinary Workshop Report on Changing Childhood in a Changing Europe* (pp 29–36). Strasbourg: ESF Social Sciences Unit.

Bradshaw, J., Bloor, K., Huby, M., Rhodes, D., Sinclair, I., Gibbs, I. et al (2009) *Local Index of Child Well-Being: Summary Report*. London: Department for Communities and Local Government.

Briones, K. (2018) A Guide to Young Lives Rounds 1 to 5 constructed files. *Young Lives Technical Note*, 48.

Casas, F. (2011) Subjective social indicators and child and adolescent well-being. *Child Indicators Research* 4: 555–75.

Chapple, S. and Richardson, D. (2009) *Doing Better for Children*. Paris: OECD Publishing.

CHICOS (nd) Strategy for European Birth Cohort Research. Available at http://chicosproject.eu/assets/181/CHICOS_strategic_report_20130712.pdf

Children's Worlds (2019) *International Survey of Children's Well-being*. Available at www.isciweb.org/

Crivello, G. and Morrow, V. (2019) Against the odds: why some children fare well in the face of adversity. *Journal of Development Studies.* https://doi.org/10.1080/00220388.2019.1626837

Cummins, R. and Lau, A. (2005) *Personal Wellbeing Index – School Children*. Melbourne: School of Psychology, Deakin University.

Davis-Kean, P., Chambers, R., Davidson, L., Kleinert, C., Ren, Q. and Tang, S. (2017) *Longitudinal Studies Strategic Review*. London: Economic and Social Research Council.

Diener, E., Lucas, R.E. and Oishi, S. (2002) Subjective well-being: the science of happiness and life satisfaction. In C.R. Snyder and S.J. Lopez (Eds) *Handbook of Positive Psychology* (pp 63–73). Oxford: Oxford University Press.

DJI (2000) DJI-Jugendsurvey 2000, GESIS Datenarchiv, Köln. ZA3609 Datenfile Version 1.0.0. doi: 10.4232/1.3609.

European Commission (2012) Work Programme 2013. Cooperation: Theme 8: Socio-economic Sciences and Humanities. Brussels: European Commission.

Emery, T., Pollock, G. and Scherpenzeel, A. (2019) Securing high-quality data on populations: why we need EuroCohort, GGP and SHARE in Europe. *Population Europe* Policy Brief. Available at https://population-europe.eu/policy-brief/securing-high-quality-data-populations

ESFRI (2019) *Roadmap 2021 Public Guide*. Available at www.esfri.eu/sites/default/files/ESFRI_Roadmap2021_Public_Guide_Public.pdf

EUCCONET (2008) European Child Cohort Network. Available at www.slls.org.uk/eucconet-reports

EuroCohort (2019) Future Trends and Scenarios Shaping the Future of Child and Youth Well-being in Europe. Project briefing. Available at www.eurocohort.eu/files/filemanager/files/ECDP_Future_trends.pdf

European Cohort Development Project (2018) European Cohort Development Project. Available at www.eurocohort.eu/

Farrington, D.P. (1991) Longitudinal research strategies: advantages, problems and prospects. *Journal of American Academic Child and Adolescent Psychiatry* 30(3): 369–74.

Fattore, T., Mason, J. and Watson, E. (2007) Children's conceptualisation(s) of their well-being. *Social Indicators Research* 80(1): 5–29.

Federal Ministry of Education and Research (2017) *Research Report on Vocational Education and Training.* Available at www.bmbf.de/pub/ Berufsbildungsbericht_2017_eng.pdf

Franc, R., Sucic, I., Babarović, T., Brajša-Žganec, A., Kaliterna-Lipovčan, L. and Dević, I. (2018) How to develop well-being survey questions for young children: lessons learned from cross-cultural cognitive interviews. In G. Pollock, J. Ozan, H. Goswami, G. Rees and A. Stasulane (Eds) *Measuring Youth Well-being: How a Pan-European Longitudinal Survey Can Improve Policy* (pp 91–109). Springer International.

Freed-Taylor, M. and Schaber, G. (1995) An integrated longitudinal database for comparative analysis: the panel comparability project. *Innovation: The European Journal of Social Science Research* 8(1): 53–59.

Gabhainn, S. and Sixsmith, J. (2005) *Children's Understandings of Well-Being.* Dublin: National Children's Office.

Gabos, A. and Kopasz, M. (2013) Conception Paper for an Integrated Poverty and Living Condition Indicator System (IPOLIS) Database. Unpublished Paper.

Gabos, A. and Toth, I.G. (2011) *Child Well-Being in the European Union: Better Monitoring Instruments for Better Policies.* Budapest: TARKI Social Research Institute.

Goswami, H., Fox, G. and Pollock, G. (2016) The current evidence base and future needs in improving children's well-being across Europe: is there a case for a comparative longitudinal survey? *Child Indicators Research* 9(2): 371–88.

Guillén-Royo, M. and Velazco, J. (2006) Exploring the relationship between happiness, objective and subjective well-being: evidence from rural Thailand. ESRC Research Group on Well-being in Developing Countries, WeD Working Paper 16. Bath: WeD.

Hanafin, S. and Brooks, A.M. (2005) *Report on the Development of a National Set of Child Well-Being Indicators.* Dublin: National Children's Office/The Stationery Office.

Hanafin, S., Brooks, A.M., Carroll, E., Fitzgerald, E., Gabhainn, S.N. and Sixsmith, J. (2007) Achieving consensus in developing a national set of child well-being indicators. *Social Indicators Research* 80: 79–104.

Hart, R. (1992) *Children's Participation from Tokenism to Citizenship.* Florence: UNICEF Innocenti Research Centre.

Helweg-Larsen, K., Sundaram, V., Curtis, T. and Larsen, H.V. (2004) The Danish Youth Survey 2002: asking young people about sensitive issues. *International Journal of Circumpolar Health* 63(2): 147–52.

Hicks, S. (2011) The Measurement of Subjective Well-Being. Paper for Measuring National Well-Being Technical Advisory Group. Newport: ONS.

Howieson, C., Croxford, L. and Howat, N. (2008) *Meeting the Needs for Longitudinal Data on Youth Transitions in Scotland – An Options Appraisal.* Edinburgh: Scottish Government Social Research.

Hübner, N., Wagner, W., Kramer, J., Nagengast, B. and Trautwein, U. (2017) The G8 reform in Baden-Württemberg: competencies, wellbeing and leisure time before and after the reform. *Zeitschrift für Erziehungswissenschaft* 20(4): 748–71.

Huebner, E.S. (1994) Preliminary development and validation of a multidimensional life satisfaction scale for children. *Psychological Assessment* 6(2): 149–58.

Kroll, C. and Delhey, J. (2013) A happy nation? Opportunities and challenges of using subjective indicators in policymaking. *Social Indicators Research* 114(1): 13–28.

Land, K.C., Lamb, V.L. and Mustillo, S.K. (2001) Child and youth well-being in the United States, 1975–1998: some findings from a new index. *Social Indicators Research* 56(3): 241–320.

Lansdown, G. (2001) *Promoting Children's Participation in Democratic Decision-Making.* Innocenti Insights. Florence: UNICEF Innocenti Research Centre.

Mason, J. and Danby, S. (2011) Children as experts in their lives. *Child Indicators Research* 4(2): 185–90.

McGillivray, M. (2007) Human well-being: issues, concepts and measures. In M. McGillivray (Ed) *Human Well-Being: Concept and Measurement* (pp 3–16). Basingstoke: Palgrave MacMillan.

Mihálik, J., Garaj, M., Sakellariou, A., Koronaiou, A., Alexias, G., Nico, M. et al (2018) Similarity and difference in conceptions of well-being among children and young people in four contrasting European countries. In G. Pollock, J. Ozan, H. Goswami, G. Rees and A. Stasulane (Eds) *Measuring Youth Well-being: How a Pan-European Longitudinal Survey Can Improve Policy* (pp 55–69). Springer International.

Moore, K.A., Murphey, D., Bandy, T. and Lawner, E. (2014) Indices of child well-being and developmental contexts. In A. Ben-Arieh, F. Casas, I. Frones and J.E. Korbin (Eds) *Handbook of Child Well-Being: Theories, Methods and Policies in Global Perspective* (pp 2807–22). New York: Springer.

Nico, M., de Almeida Alves, N., Ferrer-Fons, M., Serracant, P. and Soler, R. (2018) Methodological challenges when involving children and young people in survey research on well-being. In G. Pollock, J. Ozan, H. Goswami, G. Rees and A. Stasulane (Eds) *Measuring Youth Well-being: How a Pan-European Longitudinal Survey Can Improve Policy* (pp 131–36). Springer International.

Noll, H.-H. (2013) Subjective social indicators: benefits and limitations for policy making – an introduction to this special issue. *Social Indicators Research* 114(1): 1–11.

OECD (2009) Doing Better for Children. Available at www.oecd.org/social/family/doingbetterforchildren.htm

O'Leary, C. and Fox, C. (2018) Understanding the potential policy impact of a European longitudinal survey for children and young people. In G. Pollock, J. Ozan, H. Goswami, G. Rees and A. Stasulane (Eds) *Measuring Youth Well-being: How a Pan-European Longitudinal Survey Can Improve Policy* (pp 147–161). Springer International.

Ozan, J., Pollock, G., Goswami, H. and Lynn, P. (2018a) Challenges in conducting a new longitudinal study on children and young people well-being in the European Union. In G. Pollock, J. Ozan, H. Goswami, G. Rees and A. Stasulane (Eds) *Measuring Youth Well-being: How a Pan-European Longitudinal Survey Can Improve Policy* (pp 111–30). Springer International.

Ozan, J., Mierina, I. and Koroleva, I. (2018b) A comparative expert survey on measuring and enhancing children and young people's well-being in Europe. In G. Pollock, J. Ozan, H. Goswami, G. Rees and A. Stasulane (Eds) *Measuring Youth Well-being: How a Pan-European Longitudinal Survey Can Improve Policy*, pp 35–53. Springer International.

Pollard, E.L. and Lee, P.D. (2003) Child well-being: a systematic review of the literature. *Social Indicators Research* 61(1): 59–78.

Pollock, G., Ozan, J., Goswami, H. and Fox, C. (2018) With a view towards the future: working towards an accelerated European cohort survey. In G. Pollock, J. Ozan, H. Goswami, G. Rees and A. Stasulane (Eds) *Measuring Youth Well-being: How a Pan-European Longitudinal Survey Can Improve Policy* (pp 163–78). Springer International.

Rees, G. and Dinisman, T. (2015) Comparing children's experiences and evaluations of their lives in 11 different countries. *Child Indicators Research* 8(1): 5–31.

Rees, G., Goswami, H. and Bradshaw, J. (2010a) *Developing an Index of Children's Subjective Well-being in England.* London: The Children's Society.

Rees, G., Bradshaw, J., Goswami, H. and Keung, H. (2010b) *Understanding Children's Well-Being: A National Survey of Young People's Well-Being.* London: The Children's Society.

Richardson, D. (2012) *An Evaluation of International Surveys of Children.* Social Policy Division. Paris: OECD.

Rieger, S., Hübner, N. and Wagner, W. (2018) NEPS Technical Report for English Reading: Scaling Results for the Additional Study Thuringia (NEPS Survey Paper No. 39). Bamberg, Germany: Leibniz Institute for Educational Trajectories.

Rhydderch, A. (2009). *Scenario Planning.* Foresight Horizon Scanning Centre. Available at https://webarchive.nationalarchives.gov.uk/20140108141323/http://www.bis.gov.uk/assets/foresight/docs/horizon-scanning-centre/foresight_scenario_planning.pdf

Sarriera, J.C., Casas, F., Bedin, L., Abs, D., Strelhow, M.R., Gross-Manos, D. and Giger, J. (2015) Material resources and children's subjective well-being in eight countries. *Child Indicators Research* 8(1): 111–31.

Share-Eric (2018) *Annual Activity Report 2017/18.* Available at www.share-project.org/fileadmin/pdf_documentation/SHARE_AnnualActivityReport_2017-18.pdf

Shaw, C., Brady, L. and Davey, C. (2011) *Guidelines for Research with Children and Young People.* London: National Children's Bureau.

Statham, J. and Chase, E. (2010) *Childhood Wellbeing: A Brief Overview.* Loughborough: Childhood Wellbeing Research Centre.

Stiglitz, J.E., Sen, A. and Fitoussi, J.-P. (2009) *Report by the Commission on the Measurement of Economic Performance and Social Progress.* Paris. Available at http://citeseerx.ist.psu.edu/viewdoc/download?doi=10.1.1.215.58&rep=rep1&type=pdf

Technopolis Group (2016) Comparative Impact Study of the European Social Survey (ESS) ERIC. Available at www.europeansocialsurvey.org/docs/findings/ESS-Impact-study-Final-report.pdf

The Children's Society (2006) *Good Childhood? A Question for Our Times.* London: The Children's Society.

Thomas, W.I. and Thomas, D.S. (1928) *The Child in America: Behaviour Problems and Programmes.* New York: Knopf.

UCL (2014) Millennium Cohort Study: building a picture of a new generation. University College London. Available at www.ucl.ac.uk/impact/case-studies/2014/dec/millennium-cohort-study-building-picture-new-generation

UN (2020) Sustainable Development Goals. Available at www.un.org/sustainabledevelopment/sustainable-development-goals/

UNICEF (2007) *Child Poverty in Perspective: An Overview of Child Well-Being in Rich Countries*. Innocenti Report Card 7. Florence: UNICEF Innocenti Research Centre.

UNICEF (2010) *The Children Left Behind: A League Table of Inequality in Child Well-Being in the World's Richest Countries*. Innocenti Report Card 9. Florence: UNICEF Innocenti Research Centre.

UNICEF (2017) *Is Every Child Counted? Status of Data for Children in the SDGs*. Division of Data, Research and Policy, New York.

Veenhoven, R. (2002) Why social policy needs subjective indicators. *Social Indicators Research* 58(1–3): 33–46.

Welsh Assembly Government (2008) *Children and Young People's Well-being Monitor for Wales*. Available at http://orca.cf.ac.uk/69801/1/110328evidencereviewmonitoren.pdf

8

Mauritian Joint Child Health Project: A Multigenerational Family Study Emerging from a Prospective Birth Cohort Study: Initial Alcohol-related Outcomes in the Offspring Generation

Susan E. Luczak, Shameem Oomur, Kristina Jackson and Tashneem Mahoomed

Introduction

In their 'Key Findings on Families, Family Policy and the Sustainable Development Goals: Synthesis Report', UNICEF (2018, p 5) recognized the family unit as the 'natural and elementary social unit of all modern society' and a key to understanding social progress and development that the UN's Sustainable Development Goals (SDG) seek to address. The family unit, while appreciated, often is not prioritized in development efforts. The UN Secretary General acknowledged that the contribution of families continues to be largely overlooked, and that 'policy focusing on improving the well-being of families is certain to benefit development' (United Nations, 2010). At the global level, there is a need for more research on the family, with the recognition that family policy requires adaptation to the different contexts and countries in which it will be implemented.

This study seeks to contribute to this research literature on family and its role in health behaviour by focusing on alcohol involvement in two generations of the Joint Child Health Project (JCHP), a longitudinal birth cohort study on the East African island nation of Mauritius. This research relates to SDG 3 on improving health and well-being, including via prevention and treatment of substance use (SDG 3.5) and harmful use of alcohol (SDG 3.5.2). The work serves to exemplify how a prospective child health study can be utilized to examine risk relationships within the family unit to better understand each child's risky health behaviour. The unique combination of the JCHP study features, including the multigenerational longitudinal design, cultural setting and inclusion of families that largely remain intact, increases the potential for this study to contribute to our understanding of development of alcohol involvement (and mental health more broadly) within families. The goals are to report initial findings on rates of alcohol use and heavy use in the JCHP offspring (aged 13–24), and to examine how maternal and paternal alcohol-specific factors are linked to offspring alcohol use and heavy use, which may be gender-specific.

To provide appropriate background and context for this study, first the literature on social development models, transmission of alcohol behaviours within families and gender-specific transmission within families is reviewed, noting that most of this research has been conducted in Western societies. An overview of the JCHP is then provided and some of the prospective findings from the original birth cohort are highlighted, ending with JCHP research focused on alcohol outcomes. This background is used to guide predictions for relationships among parental (mother and father) alcohol-specific risk and protective factors and offspring (daughters and sons) alcohol use.

Family and alcohol involvement

A first-degree family history of alcohol problems is a strong and well-established predictor of developing alcohol problems (Cotton, 1979; Merikangas, 1990; Sher, 1991). The underlying mechanisms for family transmission and how these mechanisms are modified by gender and culture, however, remain unclear. Alcohol involvement may be transmitted (1) directly via inherited genetic risk (such as alcohol use disorders, AUDs), (2) directly via alcohol-related environments (such as modelling), and (3) indirectly through environmental effects associated with parental alcohol use (for example, parental monitoring; see D'Onofrio et al, 2007). Behavioural genetics studies indicate that environmental factors are more strongly implicated in early drinking behaviour, whereas genetic factors are more strongly associated with the development of problems including AUDs (Agrawal and Lynskey, 2008; Fowler et al, 2007; Pagan et al, 2006; Prescott and Kendler, 1999). It is recognized that a family study like the JCHP cannot separate genetic and environmental causes of transmission, but it can model risk factors across generations, strength of transmission, and gender as a moderator of this transmission.

The current study is guided by the social development model, which combines key features of social control and social learning theory (see Catalano et al, 1996). This model proposes that children observe various patterns of behaviour and learn normative guidelines for appropriate behaviour from proximal socializing agents, including their families as well as broader groups to which they belong (for example, religious groups). Cialdini and colleagues' (1990) norm-focus theory distinguishes between two types of norms, descriptive and injunctive norms. Descriptive norms are standard behaviour generally guided by what people actually do (Elek et al, 2006). In relation to alcohol, adolescent alcohol behaviours would be triggered by social processes such as modelling and imitation of parental alcohol consumption (see Sieving et al, 2000). Injunctive norms refer to what people 'ought' to do, as imposed by external factors such as parents or the larger society (Elek et al, 2006). Perceived injunctive norms related to alcohol-specific behaviours among adolescents involve the perception of how much parents approve or disapprove of the adolescent's alcohol use.

Research consistently has found perceived parental descriptive alcohol norms are associated with adolescents' alcohol use (for example, Mrug and McCay, 2013; Duncan et al, 2006; Elek et al, 2006), with children who are exposed to parental drinking being more likely to model parental drinking behaviours and to consider it a socially acceptable behaviour, even when parental drinking includes intoxication (Duncan et al, 2006; Rossow and Kuntsche, 2013; Ryan et al, 2010; Chassin et al, 1993, 2016). Perceived parental injunctive norms have also been associated with adolescent alcohol consumption. For example, perceived strict parental rules were associated with lower alcohol consumption in children (Van Den Eijnden et al, 2011). Yu (1998) found that perceived parental attitudes towards alcohol consumption had a greater impact on children deciding to start using alcohol, but once offspring started drinking then parental attitudes were less strongly related to child behaviour. However, in youth aged 11–17, Mrug and McCay (2013) found the relationship between parental disapproval of alcohol use and youth consumption was maintained throughout adolescence, with little decline with age.

How child-perceived and parent-rated disapproval of child drinking, along with parental drinking behaviours, combine to relate to child behaviours warrants continued investigation.

Gender, family and alcohol involvement

Although there are clear gender differences in alcohol involvement, the basis for these differences is not clear. Societal norms for alcohol use often differ by gender, and across cultures rates of alcohol use and problems are consistently lower in women than men, regardless of total overall use (Wilsnack et al, 2009). Poor parental monitoring and inconsistent rules have been shown to be greater predictors of alcohol use for males than females (see Nargiso et al, 2013). For alcohol-specific parenting, however, Mrug and McCay (2013) found daughters perceived greater disapproval of alcohol use from parents than did sons. Additionally, Yu and Perrine (1997) found a gender-specific relationship between fathers' and mothers' alcohol use and drinking behaviour by children, with drinking more likely to occur in the same gender children as the drinking parent. In line with these findings, Burk and colleagues (2011) showed that greater parental alcohol consumption increased adolescents' drinking behaviour for both daughters and sons, but with daughters showing stronger effects. There also is some genetic evidence for specificity of alcohol transmission within genders and for greater risk being transmitted from female- than from male-affected relatives (Prescott et al, 2001). McGue and colleagues (2001) tested associations of early drinking and found only early drinking in mothers, not fathers, was predictive of early use in both daughters and sons. Thus, it is possible that parental risk and protective factors differ across mothers and fathers for their daughters and sons in terms of both absolute levels and strengths of association. Examining familial relationships in a novel cultural setting will provide a unique test of these parent–child risk factors for youth drinking.

The Mauritian Joint Child Health Project (JCHP): a prospective birth cohort family study

Background

The JCHP is conducted on Mauritius, a small upper- to middle-income island nation located in the Indian Ocean. Following an invitation by the World Health Organization(WHO), the JCHP began in the late 1960s as a collaborative effort among American and European researchers Doctors Sarnoff Mednick, Fini Schulsinger and Peter

Venables and the Mauritian Ministry of Health. In 1972, the first data were collected from 1,795 participants who comprised almost the entire population of three-year-olds born in a one-year period (based on immunization records) in two adjacent towns (see Venables, 1978, for details). The ethnic breakdown of the JCHP sample was representative of the island and included 69% Indian, 26% Creole, 2% Chinese and 4% other; 48% of the sample was female. Multiple biological, social and psychological measures have been collected on the birth cohort participants at various data collection phases in childhood and adulthood, including major waves at ages 3, 11, 17, 23, late thirties and mid-forties (see Raine et al, 2010). Data also have been obtained on offspring that matched the timeframes (3–5 years old or 8–13 years old) and assessment domains (behaviour, cognition, psychophysiology) obtained from the original cohort in childhood.

The initial goal of the JCHP was to understand the causes of schizophrenia, but over the years outcomes have been expanded to include additional aspects of mental health including psychopathy, psychosocial well-being and, most recently, substance use. The majority of JCHP publications have focused on malnutrition, temperament, cognitive ability (IQ), behaviour and psychophysiology as childhood risk factors. Here a brief review is given of JCHP findings showing that early childhood malnutrition, a modifiable risk factor, is related to cognitive ability and behavioural problems in childhood, which in turn are risk factors for schizotypy personality, antisocial behaviour and alcohol problems in adulthood. Multiple indicators of malnutrition were obtained on the JCHP birth cohort when they were three years old. A direct path was found between chronic malnutrition (stunting and anaemia) at age 3 and IQ at age 11, and an indirect path was found between acute malnutrition (wasting) to verbal IQ via behavioural inhibition (Venables and Raine, 2015). Clinical indicators of nutrition (protein, riboflavin and iron) deficiency at age 3 also predicted low verbal IQ at age 11 as well as externalizing behaviour (aggression, attention deficit and hyperactivity) at ages 8, 11 and 17 (Liu et al, 2004). The effects of malnutrition on IQ were graded, with even mild malnutrition showing some association with IQ, and were independent of a measure of psychosocial adversity. Low performance IQ at age 11 was associated with features of schizotypal personality by age 23, with the relationship between chronic malnutrition at age 3 and schizotypy at age 23 mediated by performance IQ at age 11 (Venables and Raine, 2012). Low verbal IQ at age 11 was also predictive of alcohol problems by adulthood (mid-thirties) after co-varying for psychosocial adversity and religion, with this relationship being stronger in females than males

(Luczak et al, 2015). Finally, a select sample of 100 of the JCHP birth cohort who were assigned to an enriched pre-school showed reduced schizotypal personality and antisocial behaviour at age 17 compared with controls, with the greatest benefits in those who had signs of malnutrition at age 3 (Raine et al, 2003). These findings highlight how both direct and indirect roles of childhood risk factors, including those that are modifiable, on mental health outcomes in adulthood can be discerned through longitudinal studies.

In addition to shedding light on developmental trajectories for health outcomes, JCHP publications also have examined the nature of psychological constructs in this cultural context (for example, Reynolds et al, 2000; Venables, 1990; Yarnell et al, 2014), including alcohol constructs and their covariates (Luczak et al, 2001, 2014, 2017). Testing the consistency (that is, invariance) of alcohol problem constructs at age 23, consistency was found in how Creole and Hindu males viewed alcohol problems, but differences in Muslim males (Luczak et al, 2001). In adulthood (mid-thirties), we also found variation in lifetime alcohol use and AUDs based on religion and religious commitment that were consistent across gender, despite women in all religious groups having lower rates of alcohol use and AUDs (Luczak et al, 2014). Further, the typology of alcohol problems within male drinkers were examined and four latent classes were found, including a distinct hazardous drinking class that had unique demographic correlates and was thought to represent a cluster of problems more bound by cultural factors, as well as problem classes on a severity continuum from none to moderate to severe problems (Luczak et al, 2017). These studies highlight how examining subgroup and person-level factors in different cultural settings can improve our understanding of the commonality and uniqueness of alcohol problem outcomes and correlates across societies.

Current study

The original birth cohort have now been followed into their mid-forties and concurrent assessment of spouses and children has been added. Thus delineation of familial risk and protective factors for alcohol involvement in the next generation of the JCHP can begin. Several features of the JCHP are beneficial for examining early stages of drinking within the context of the family. First, the original birth cohort was obtained from two adjacent towns, such that many macro-level factors (for example, media, healthcare, primary schools, neighbourhood) have low variability, which affords the opportunity to study young adult behaviour more at the levels of individual- and familial-level factors. Second, the JCHP biological families remain largely intact, with most biological mothers and fathers raising their offspring over the duration of childhood. This makes is possible to examine maternal and paternal direct influences on family environment, in addition to family history, for most of the offspring generation. Third, family remains an important aspect of social control and monitoring into early adulthood in Mauritius, with most offspring living with their parents until they are married (regardless of whether they attend university or enter the work force after secondary school), and then often still living with either their or their spouse's family once married. Finally, national-level surveys show drinking in Mauritian females is on the rise (CDC, 2007; CDC et al, 2013; Ministry of Health and Quality of Life, 2016), which means that examining gender differences in risk factors for Mauritian youth drinking is relevant and timely.

Study hypotheses

The study seeks to extend current knowledge by testing aspects of the social development model in a non-Western setting. It hypothesizes that alcohol consumption in offspring will be predicted by (1) perceived parental descriptive norms (modelling), (2) perceived parental injunctive norms (perceived disapproval), (3) parental attitudes (parent-rated disapproval), and (4) lifetime parental alcohol involvement (family history, regardless of offspring awareness). As in some genetically informative studies, it is possible that (a) mother–daughter and father–son relationships will be strongest, (b) parental injunctive norms will be stronger predictors in sons, and (c) parent alcohol involvement will be stronger predictors for daughters, particularly for binge drinking.

Method

Participants

The study utilizes data collected when the JCHP birth cohort members were in their mid-forties ($M = 43.7$ years, range 41–47, $SD = 1.37$). All available original cohort members ($n = 1,161$, representing 63% of the 1,795 individuals in the original birth cohort in 1972; 48% female), their current or former spouses/co-parents ($n = 876$) and children ($n = 1,911$) were assessed in person on demographic variables and personal and familial alcohol use, norms and problems as part of a larger battery. In the original cohort, this included 72% who were in their first marriage, 8% who were separated or divorced, 2% widowed, 9% remarried or living as married and 9% who were never married (single).

The analytic sample included the 1,147 biological offspring of the original JCHP birth cohort who were aged 13–24 at the time of interview. Sample characteristics are presented in Table 8.1 are stratified by offspring age group and gender. Of these children, 986 (86%) were from intact parenting units where both biological parents were still living together in the same household. Based on their relationship to these offspring, fathers reported on 958 (84%) and mothers reported on 1,083 (94%) of these offspring, including 910 (79%) offspring where both mother and father reported on the child (termed 'Intact' families).

Procedure

All interviews and questionnaires were translated by bilingual JCHP staff into Kreol (the common spoken language of Mauritius), with back translation to provide evidence of semantic and cultural equivalence. Trained research staff conducted structured interviews with each family member separately in private rooms. This research was approved by the University of Southern California Institutional Review Board and received ethical clearance from the Mauritian Ministry of Health and Quality of Life (MOHQL). Written informed consent/assent was obtained for all participants.

Variables

Demographics

Gender, age and religion

All offspring were classified as either male or female, which was termed Gender. Four age groups (13–15, 16–17, 18–20, 21–24 years) were created to disaggregate offspring into age ranges expected to have different prevalence of drinking, with the legal age of drinking being 18 years. Religion was coded into Hindu, Tamil, Muslim, Catholic and other/none, with Tamil kept separate from Hindu due prior findings in the original cohort participants of different associations with alcohol use (Luczak et al, 2014).

Parental predictors

Child-perceived parental injunctive norms

Offspring rated their perception of each parent's approval or disapproval of drinking with (a) family and (b) friends on a five-point scale from 'strongly disapprove' to 'strongly approve'. Each variable was dichotomized into 1 = strongly disapprove, 0 = do not strongly disapprove, with 0 including all response choices other than 'strongly disapprove'.

Child-perceived parental descriptive norms

Using a family tree (Mann et al, 1985), offspring rated each parent as a lifetime 'non-drinker', 'social drinker', 'possible problem drinker' and 'definite problem drinker'. Being a drinker was dichotomized into 0 = non-drinker or 1 = drinker as indicated by all values other than 'non-drinker'. Being a problem drinker was indicated by 1 = 'possible problem drinker' or 'definite problem drinker' versus 0 = 'non-drinker' or 'social drinker'.

Parent-reported attitudes towards child's drinking

Using the same items as rated by each child, parents reported on disapproval of child's drinking with (a) family and (b) friends.

Parent-reported lifetime drinking behaviour

Trained interviewers conducted a structured interview that ascertained lifetime alcohol use and alcohol-related problems using a battery that was adapted for use in multiple countries including developing nations ('Gender, Alcohol, and Culture: An International Study', GENACIS; Wilsnack et al, 2009), plus integrated additional items from other surveys and interviews (Babor et al, 2001; Bucholz et al, 1994; Spitzer et al, 1997). As in prior JCHP waves (Luczak et al, 2014), we defined lifetime drinker as having consumed a full drink, or less than a full drink multiple times. We also created a problem drinker variable based on having one or more self-reported lifetime DSM-V AUD symptoms (APA, 2013; tally sheets rated by first two authors), or informants reporting possible or definite problem drinking with supporting detail (for example, ratings from seven, or 1%, of original birth cohort and spouse interviews were replaced by informant data when self-report was deemed to be of questionable accuracy).

Offspring outcomes

Current drinker

Offspring reported on their frequency of alcohol use over the past 12 months using a nine-point graduated frequency scale (from 'never' to 'daily/almost daily use'). This drinker variable was dichotomized into 1 = current drinker, 0 = current non-drinker, with non-drinker being 'never' in the past year.

Current binge drinker

Offspring reported on their frequency of consuming 4+ drinks for females and 5+ drinks for males in a drinking episode (Wechsler et al, 1997) over the past 12 months using the same nine-point scale. This binge drinker variable was dichotomized into 1 = current binge drinker, 0 = currently not a binge drinker ('never' during the past year).

Analyses

Analyses were conducted in SPSS version 24 (IBM Corp, 2016). Cross-tabulations and likelihood ratio chi-square (LR χ^2) tests of significance were used to examine categorical outcome variables by age group and gender. Logistic regressions were conducted to obtain odd ratios (ORs) with 95% confidence intervals (CIs) and adjusted Nagelkerke pseudo R^2 change (ΔR^2; Homer and Lemeshow, 2000) for the two dichotomous outcome variables.

The datafile was structured as a wide file organized by offspring and including parental variables based on the relation of each parent to the child (mother, father). It was not assumed that parental data were missing at random, and thus missing values were not imputed; analyses were conducted for mother variables and father variables in separate models to examine their unique effects. Demographic variables (religion, age group) were included as covariates in all models and gender differences via interactions were tested for. In addition to running these models co-varying for religion and age group, these models were also run removing Muslims, removing the oldest age group (21–24 years) from the alcohol use analyses and the youngest age group (13–15 years) from the binge drinking analyses, and removing both Muslim and age groups. Results with the restricted samples were largely consistent with the models co-varying for religion and age, so results from the analyses conducted with the full sample are presented.

Two separate series of logistic regression analyses were conducted to examine the two offspring current drinking outcomes: (1) drinker and (2) binge drinker. We began with single block predictor models. In four separate analyses, each of the four sets of mother and father predictor variables (two variables in each block) were entered as a block, followed by gender as a block, and then the interaction terms with gender in a final block (*p*-value set at 0.10 for the interaction step). Based on the results of these analyses, the sample was split by gender and these single-predictor block analyses were repeated.

Parental predictors that were significant in the single-block models were entered into hierarchical multiple block analyses to show relationships among variable blocks for son–mother, daughter–mother, son–father and daughter–father pairs. Child-perceived variables were entered first in a block followed by parent-reported variables in a block to determine if parent-rated variables remained significant predictors (as indicated by the step χ^2 value) after accounting for child-perceived variables.

Results

Descriptive statistics

The top rows of Table 8.1 display offspring demographics for total sample (first column) and stratified by age group and gender. In the two older age groups, participants were more likely to report their religion as other/none and less likely to report as Tamil, which is consistent with Tamil Mauritians often identifying with two religions (that is, 'baptized Tamils'). The middle rows of Table 8.1 display child-perceived parental norms and parent-rated attitudes and behaviours. Perceived descriptive norms were consistent across gender and age groups, indicating that daughters and sons of different ages rated parents similarly. Both mothers and fathers were more likely to strongly disapprove of offspring drinking prior to age 18, with greater differences between son and daughter disapproval for the older age groups. Parents also were more likely to disapprove of offspring drinking with friends than drinking with family.

The bottom rows of Table 8.1 and Figure 8.1 display rates of current drinking and binge drinking in the offspring. Rates of drinking were similar for boys and girls in the younger age groups, but were more divergent in the older age groups where drinking rates for daughters remained close to half, but drinking rates for sons were about two thirds of 18–20-year-olds and three quarters of 21–24-year-olds. In all age groups, approximately twice as many sons as daughters engaged in binge drinking. Rates of binge drinking were low in 13–15-year-olds, but in 16–17-year-olds about one third of male drinkers and one sixth of female drinkers engaged in binge drinking, and once of legal drinking age, binge drinking was common among drinkers, including about 80% of male drinkers and about 40% of female drinkers.

Figure 8.1: Past-year drinking and binge drinking in Joint Child Health Project offspring stratified by gender and age group

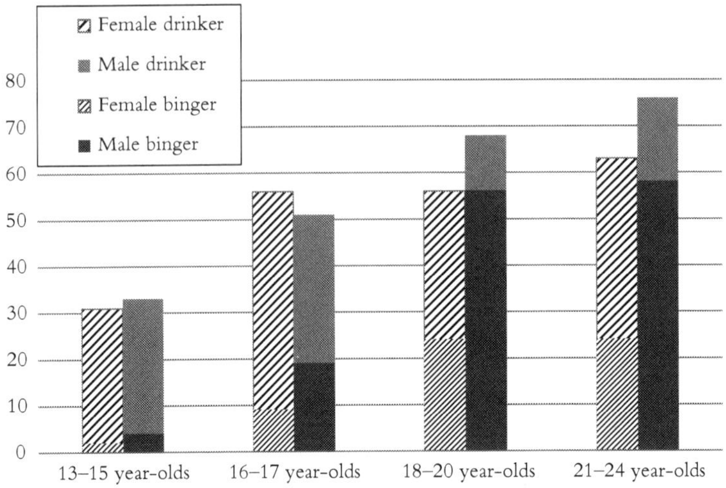

Source: Author's own

Alcohol use

Single predictor block models

Table 8.2 shows the single-block results of each predictor set for offspring current drinking. Interactions with gender were significant for all but three blocks, indicating that most of the parental predictors operated differently for daughters and sons. Thus, the models for the total offspring sample are presented, and split by offspring gender.

For daughters, each of the parental variable blocks were predictive of alcohol use (based on step χ^2 significance), with the sole exception of the intact family block. Within blocks, almost all variables predicted drinking status (based on OR significance). Strong parental disapproval of drinking with family and strong mother disapproval of drinking with friends (both perceived and parent-rated) were associated with a four- to five-fold reduced risk of being a drinker. Three sets of perceived and parent-rated alcohol behaviour variables were also significant: mother being a drinker increased risk by 2.6-fold, father being a drinker increased risk by 4.6–5.6-fold, and father being a problem drinker increased risk by about two-fold (ORs = 1.9–2.1). Mother lifetime alcohol problems had a low prevalence (2% perceived

Table 8.1: Demographic characteristics and alcohol involvement percentages stratified by gender and age of offspring (13–24 years old)

* $p < .05$, ** $p < .01$, *** $p < .001$

	Total	13–15 years old		16–17 years old		18–20 years old		21–24 years old		Significant differences
		Male	Female	Male	Female	Male	Female	Male	Female	
	$n = 1,147$	$n = 184$	$n = 206$	$n = 99$	$n = 99$	$n = 156$	$n = 157$	$n = 111$	$n = 135$	
Demographics										
Religion (4-level, $n = 1,147$)										
Hindu	35	36	37	37	32	35	39	27	34	
Tamil	7	10	8	10	6	3	7	4	5	Age 18 split*
Catholic	26	25	22	19	30	27	24	29	31	
Muslim	24	25	29	25	23	21	22	26	23	
Other/none	8	5	4	3	8	14	8	14	7	Age 18 split*
Current status										
Student ($n = 1,147$)	67	98	99	87	90	41	57	22	25	Age***; gender in 18–20**
Single ($n = 1,144$)	93	100	100	100	99	98	90	87	62	Age***; gender in 18–20*, 21–24***

(continued)

Table 8.1: Demographic characteristics and alcohol involvement percentages stratified by gender and age of offspring (13–24 years old) (continued)

⋆ p< .05, ⋆⋆ p< .01, ⋆⋆⋆ p< .001	Total	13–15 years old	16–17 years old	18–20 years old	21–24 years old	Significant differences
Family						
Living with family of origin (n = 1,147)	90	100	98	90	85	Age⋆⋆⋆; gender in 21–24⋆⋆⋆
Intact (biological parents together; n = 1,144)	86	90	86	86	78	Age in males⋆
Raised by biological (N = 1,146)						
Mother (pre-school: 0–5 years)	98	97	97	99	97	Age in females⋆; gender 13–15⋆, 18–20⋆
Mother (1° school: 6–11 years)	95	97	98	97	92	
Mother (2° school: 12–18 years)	97	95	97	95	92	
Father (pre-school: 0–5 years)	91	95	96	96	94	
Father (1° school: 6–11 years)	95	92	95	93	94	
Father (2° school: 12–18 years)	88	90	92	86	88	Age in females⋆; gender in 18–20⋆

Table 8.1: Demographic characteristics and alcohol involvement percentages stratified by gender and age of offspring (13–24 years old) (continued)

* p< .05, ** p< .01, *** p< .001

	Total	13–15 years old	16–17 years old	18–20 years old	21–24 years old	Significant differences
Offspring-rated parental norms						
Descriptive norms						
Mother lifetime drinker (n = 1,137)	60	58	63	64	66	
Mother lifetime problem drinker (n = 1,137)	2	2	3	3	4	
Father lifetime drinker (n = 1,129)	71	72	71	75	73	
Father lifetime problem drinker (n = 1,129)	18	13	17	19	23	Gender in 16–17*
Perceived injunctive norms						
Mother strongly disagrees with child drinking with family (n = 1,135)	51	71	65	47	37	Age***;gender in 13–15*, 16–17**
Mother strongly disagrees with child drinking with friends (n = 1,136)	76	90	85	73	67	Age***; gender in 18–20*, 21–24*

(continued)

Table 8.1: Demographic characteristics and alcohol involvement percentages stratified by gender and age of offspring (13–24 years old) (continued)

* p< .05, ** p< .01, *** p< .001	Total	13–15 years old	16–17 years old	18–20 years old	21–24 years old	Significant differences
Father strongly disagrees with child drinking with family (n = 1,104)	54	70	63	44	36	Age***
Father strongly disagrees with child drinking with friends (n = 1,104)	79	89	82	58	52	Age***; gender in 18–20***, 21–24***
Parent-reported						
Parental behaviour						
Mother lifetime drinker (n = 1,087)	71	70	69	72	68	
Mother lifetime problem drinker (n = 1,087)	7	4	2	9	12	Age in females*
Father lifetime drinker (n = 956)	84	85	84	86	83	
Father lifetime problem drinker (n = 956)	36	31	28	34	38	Age in males*
Parental attitudes						
Mother strongly disagrees with child drinking with family (n = 1,083)	70	89	78	64	61	Age***; gender in 18–20*, 21–24**

Table 8.1: Demographic characteristics and alcohol involvement percentages stratified by gender and age of offspring (13–24 years old) (continued)

⋆ $p< .05$, ⋆⋆ $p< .01$, ⋆⋆⋆ $p< .001$	Total	13–15 years old		16–17 years old		18–20 years old		21–24 years old		Significant differences
Mother strongly disagrees with child drinking with friends (n = 1,083)	89	97	99	94	95	77	91	71	85	Age⋆⋆⋆; gender in 18–20⋆⋆, 21–24⋆⋆
Father strongly disagrees with child drinking with family (n = 958)	75	86	91	83	84	57	66	51	66	Age⋆⋆⋆; gender in 21–24⋆
Father strongly disagrees with child drinking with friends (n = 958)	90	94	100	94	100	76	89	74	90	Age⋆⋆⋆; gender in 13–15⋆⋆,16–17⋆,18–20⋆⋆, 21–24⋆⋆
Offspring alcohol use (self-report)										
Past year drinker (n = 1,146)	52	33	31	51	56	68	56	76	63	Age⋆⋆⋆; gender in 18–20⋆, 21–24⋆
Past year binge drinker (n = 1,146)	21	4	2	19	9	56	24	58	24	Age⋆⋆⋆; gender in 16–17⋆, 18–20⋆⋆⋆, 21–24⋆⋆⋆

by offspring, 6% lifetime self-report) and although the perceived risk was high (OR = 4.3), it did not reach significance (p = 0.17).

For sons, all variable blocks were predictive of alcohol use except parent-reported lifetime drinking behaviours. Within blocks, all child-perceived parental variables predicted use except mother and father problem drinking; for parent-rated variables, only mother (OR = 0.39) and father (OR = 0.31) strongly disapproving of drinking with family predicted use. Perceived parental strong disapproval of drinking with family and friends, however, was associated with two- to three-fold reduced risk of being a drinker. Mother being a drinker (perceived and self-reported) increased risk by 1.7–1.8-fold, and perceiving father as a drinker increased risk by 3.2-fold. Finally, sons whose parents were not intact were over twice as likely to drink as those from intact families.

Comparing ORs by offspring gender, all parental predictor ORs were higher for daughters compared with sons, except for perceived parental strong disapproval of drinking with friends.

Hierarchical predictor block models

In these models, two blocks were entered stepwise to determine whether parental attitudes and self-reported lifetime behaviours accounted for additional variance beyond that accounted for by child perception of these parental alcohol norms (see Table 8.3). Within daughters in the mother model, both perceived (OR = 0.21) and mother-rated (OR = 0.41) strong disapproval of drinking with family remained significant in the final step, but mother-reported strong disapproval of drinking with friends and lifetime drinking were no longer significant when entered after child-perceived ratings of drinking with friends (OR = 0.39) and perceived mother drinker (OR = 2.0). This pattern was similar in the father model, where both perceived (OR = 0.22) and father-reported (OR = 0.34) disapproval of drinking with family were significant in the final step, along with perceived father lifetime drinker (OR = 2.6).

Among sons in the mother model, perceived strong disapproval of drinking with friends (OR = 0.33) and mother-rated strong disapproval of drinking with family (OR = 0.49) remained significant in the final step. In the father model, both perceived (OR = 0.32) and father-rated (OR = 0.37) strong disapproval of drinking with friends remained significant in the final step.

Table 8.2: Univariate predictors of current (past year) offspring alcohol use in total sample and stratified by gender

Variables in step (block)	n / df	Total sample (n = 1147) OR (95% CI) p	Step χ² (p)	ΔR²	Female (n = 597) OR (95% CI) p	Step χ² (p)	ΔR²	Male (n = 550) OR (95% CI) p	Step χ² (p)	ΔR²	Interaction Gender X step Step χ² (p)
Family not intact	1,143 / 1	1.75 (1.13–2.69) 0.011	6.62 (0.010)	0.006	1.37 (0.76–2.46) 0.30	1.09 (0.30)	0.001	2.23 (1.17–4.24) 0.015	6.26 (0.012)	0.012	ns (0.28)
Child-perceived norms											
Mother SD drink	1,134 / 2	0.33 (0.24–0.47) 0.000	113.04 (0.000)	0.094	0.18 (0.11–0.29) .000	91.83 (0.000)	0.140	0.55 (0.33–0.91) 0.019	33.35 (0.000)	0.059	12.05 (0.002)
with family											
with friends		0.35 (0.23–0.54) 0.000			0.40 (0.22–0.73) 0.003			0.32 (0.17–0.60) 0.000			
Mother drinker	1,136 / 2	2.16 (1.52–3.08) 0.000	18.17 (0.000)	0.015	2.66 (1.64–4.31) 0.000	19.67 (0.000)	0.032	1.77 (1.03–3.03) 0.039	6.44 (0.040)	0.011	11.29 (0.004)
problem drinker		0.90 (0.36–2.30) 0.83			4.34 (0.53–35.65) 0.17			0.34 (0.10–1.18) 0.09			

(continued)

Table 8.2: Univariate predictors of current (past year) offspring alcohol use in total sample and stratified by gender (continued)

		Total sample (n = 1147)		Female (n = 597)		Male (n = 550)		Interaction
Father SD drink with family with friends	1,103 2	104.05 (0.000) 0.32 (0.23–0.45) 0.000 0.40 (0.25–0.64) 0.000	0.089	65.49 (0.000) 0.22 (0.14–0.35) 0.000 0.56 (0.28–1.12) 0.098	0.105	40.15 (0.000) 0.48 (0.29–0.81) 0.006 0.32 (0.16–0.61) .001	0.072	6.81 (0.033)
Father drinker problem drinker	1,128 2	48.72 (.000) 3.77 (2.37–6.00) 0.000 1.76 (1.19–2.60) 0.005	.042	36.65 (0.000) 4.57 (2.35–8.90) 0.000 2.08 (1.253.47) 0.005	0.059	14.95 (0.001) 3.24 (1.65–6.34) 0.001 1.43 (0.77–2.65) 0.26	0.027	5.20 (0.074)
Mother reported								
Mother SD drink with Family with Friends	1,082 2	66.66 (0.000) 0.31 (0.21–0.45) .000 0.41 (0.20–0.83) .013	0.060	46.33 (0.000) 0.25 (0.15–0.42) 0.000 0.23 (0.06–0.86) 0.029	0.078	20.33 (0.000) 0.39 (0.22–0.69) 0.001 0.54 (0.23–1.28) 0.16	0.039	ns (0.19)

Table 8.2: Univariate predictors of current (past year) offspring alcohol use in total sample and stratified by gender (continued)

		Total sample (n = 1147)		Female (n = 597)		Male (n = 550)		Interaction
Mother drinker	1,087	2.05 (1.32–3.17) 0.001	11.27 (0.004)	2.62 (1.40–4.88) 0.003	9.18 (0.010)	1.72 (0.91–3.27) .095	4.73 (0.09) 0.009	5.41 (0.067)
problem drinker	2	1.30 (0.70–2.41) 0.40	0.010	1.02 (0.43–2.43) 0.96	0.016	1.77 (0.72–4.34) 0.22		
Father reported								
Father SD drink	957	0.29 (0.18–0.45) 0.000	41.85 (0.000)	0.27 (0.14–0.50) 0.000	23.19 (0.000)	0.31 (0.16–0.62) 0.001	17.22 (0.000) 0.035	ns (0.31)
with family	2		0.042		0.044			
with friends		0.79 (0.39–1.61) 0.522		0.61 (0.17–2.21) 0.46		0.89 (0.36–2.21) 0.80		
Father drinker	956	1.39 (0.74–2.62) 0.31	12.85 (0.002)	3.57 (1.12–11.39) 0.031	15.07 (0.001)	0.91 (0.38–2.27) 0.84	2.63 (0.27) 0.006	7.66 (0.022)
problem drinker	2	1.72 (1.24–2.40) 0.001	0.013	1.88 (1.19–2.96) .006	0.028	1.50 (0.92–2.44) 0.11		

Note: Results co-varied for religious group and age group

Table 8.3: Parental predictors of current drinking stratified by offspring gender

	Daughters				Sons			
	Mother OR (95% CI)		Father OR (95% CI)		Mother OR (95% CI)		Father OR (95% CI)	
	Step 1	Step 2	Step 1	Step 2	Step 1	Step 2	Step 1	Step 2
Child rated								
Perceived norms								
Mother SD drink with family	0.18*** (0.11–0.29)	0.21*** (0.13–0.35)			0.56* (0.33–0.94)	0.68 (0.39–1.17)		
Mother SD drink with friends	0.34*** (0.18–0.65)	0.39** (0.20–0.75)			0.32*** (0.16–0.62)	0.32** (0.16–0.64)		
Father SD drink with family			0.21*** (0.13–0.34)	0.22*** (0.13–0.37)			0.50* (0.28–0.89)	0.56+ (0.31–1.01)
Father SD drink with friends							0.30*** (0.15–0.61)	0.32** (0.15–0.66)
Descriptive norms								
Mother lifetime drinker	2.22** (1.28–3.4)	2.01* (1.09–3.70)			1.46 (0.83–2.56)	1.34 (0.76–2.37)		
Father lifetime drinker			3.55** (1.63–7.71)	2.58* (1.16–5.77)			1.72 (0.77–3.83)	1.77 (0.78–4.01)
Father problem drinker			1.85+ (1.00–3.43)	1.55 (0.78–3.07)				

+ p < .10, * p < .05, ** p < .01, *** p < .001
Note. SD = strongly disagree

Table 8.3: Parental predictors of current drinking stratified by offspring gender (continued)

	Daughters	Sons
Parent rated		
Attitude		
Mother SD drink with family	0.41** (0.23–0.74)	0.49* (0.28–0.87)
Mother SD drink with friends	0.34 (0.09–1.25)	
Father SD drink with family		0.34** (0.18–0.66)
Father SD drink with friends		0.37** (0.19–0.69)
Behaviour		
Mother lifetime drinker	1.03 (0.47–2.23)	
Father lifetime drinker		2.74 (0.75–10.00)
Father problem drinker		1.58 (0.90–2.77)
Step χ^2	107.50*** · 16.58** · 67.00***	34.84*** · 6.02* · 40.38*** · 9.95**
ΔR^2	0.017 · 0.024 · 0.125	0.066 · 0.011 · 0.084 · 0.019

Binge drinking

Single predictor block models

Table 8.4 shows the single-block results for predictors of offspring current binge drinking for the total sample and split by offspring gender. Interactions with gender in the total sample models were significant at the 0.10 level only for perceived father injunctive norms and father-reported behaviour, and were at 0.20 for the other three perceived parental norms and for intact family. In the total sample, all four parent-rated disapproval variables predicted binge drinking, with mother-rated strong disapproval of drinking with family associated with decreasing likelihood of binge drinking by three-fold (OR = 0.35) and the other three indicators of parental disapproval reducing the likelihood by about two-fold (OR = 0.52–0.57).

Among daughters, all parental variable blocks except mother-reported behaviour were predictive of binge drinking. Daughters who perceived their mothers were drinkers were 2.8 times more likely to binge drink and daughters who perceived their mothers were problem drinkers were 3.4 times more likely to binge drink, although this relationship did not reach significance ($p = 0.07$). Daughters who perceived their fathers as drinkers were over 10 times more likely to binge drink, and in the father-reported model almost all (98%) daughters who binged had a father who reported being a lifetime drinker (note the OR is out of range because it is almost constant, but $LR \chi^2 = 65.73$, $1df$, $p < 0.001$). In addition, perceived and mother-rated strong disapproval of drinking with family and friends were related to a two- to three-fold decrease in binge drinking, and perceived and father-rated strong disagreement with daughters drinking with family (but not friends) was associated with a two-fold reduction of risk for binge drinking. Finally, daughters whose parents were not intact were three times more likely to binge drink.

Among sons, fewer parental variables were significantly associated with binge drinking. Perceived mother (OR = 0.38) and father (OR = 0.28) strong disapproval of drinking with friends were protective against binge drinking, and mother-rated strong disapproval of drinking with family was associated with a two-fold reduction in risk for binge drinking. The only parent alcohol behaviour variable that was predictive of binge drinking in sons was father-reported lifetime problems, which was associated with a 2.2-fold increase in risk.

Comparing the ORs by offspring gender, parental strong disapproval of drinking with family (both perceived and self-reported) was stronger

Table 8.4: Univariate predictors of current (past year) offspring binge use in total sample and stratified by gender

Variables in step (block)	n df	Total sample (n = 1,147)			Female (n = 597)			Male (n = 550)			Interaction
		OR (95% CI) p	Step χ² (p)	ΔR²	OR (95% CI) p	Step χ² (p)	ΔR²	OR (95% CI) p	Step χ² (p)	ΔR²	Gender X Step Step χ² (p)
Family not intact	1,143 1	1.93 (1.25–2.97) 0.003	8.71 (0.003)	0.009	2.99 (1.57–5.72) 0.001	10.68 (0.001)	0.028	1.38 (0.73–2.62) 0.32	0.98 (0.32)	0.002	ns (0.14)
Child-perceived norms											
Mother SD drink with family with friends	1,134 2	0.82 (0.52–1.29) 0.38 0.29 (0.19–0.43) 0.000	54.60 (0.000)	0.057	0.32 (0.13–0.76) 0.010 0.29 (0.16–0.53) 0.000	36.34 (0.000)	0.009	0.91 (0.49–1.68) 0.76 0.38 (0.21–0.68) 0.001	15.56 (0.000)	0.028	ns (0.20)
Mother drinker problem drinker	1,136 2	1.45 (0.93–2.26) 0.10 1.38 (0.56–3.39) 0.48	3.52 (0.17)	0.004	2.84 (1.24–6.46) 0.013 3.40 (0.91–12.68) 0.07	11.25 (0.004)	0.029	0.98 (0.53–1.81) 0.96 0.85 (0.22–3.54) 0.85	0.04 (0.98)	0.000	ns (0.15)
Father SD drink with family with friends	1,103 2	0.76 (0.48–1.19) 0.23 0.36 (0.24–0.54) 0.000	40.09 (0.000)	0.043	0.40 (0.20–0.81) 0.011 0.85 (0.44–1.62) 0.61	9.90 (0.007)	0.025	1.13 (0.59–2.18) 0.71 0.28 (0.15–0.52) 0.000	21.78 (0.000)	0.039	6.05 (0.049)
Father drinker problem drinker	1,128 2	2.32 (1.24–4.35) 0.009 1.43 (0.96–2.13) 0.08	12.78 (0.002)	0.014	10.79 (2.54–45.83) 0.001 1.81 (0.101–3.24) 0.046	22.50 (0.000)	0.057	1.16 (0.51–2.62) 0.72 1.73 (0.92–3.23) 0.09	3.33 (0.19)	0.006	ns (0.14)

(continued)

Table 8.4: Univariate predictors of current (past year) offspring binge use in total sample and stratified by gender (continued)

	Total sample (n = 1,147)	Female (n = 597)	Male (n = 550)	Interaction
Mother reported				
Mother SD drink	1,082 45.48 (0.000) 0.051	24.55 (0.000) 0.070	8.25 (0.016) 0.016	ns (0.38)
with family	2 0.35 (0.23–0.53) 0.000	0.27 (0.14–0.53) 0.000	0.52 (0.28–0.94) 0.031	
with friends	0.57 (0.35–0.93) 0.024	0.53 (0.23–1.23) 0.14	0.76 (0.38–1.50) 0.42	
Mother drinker	1,010 1.53 (0.47) .001	3.22 (0.20) 0.009	1.45 (0.48) 0.002	ns (0.62)
problem drinker	2 1.23 (0.68–2.23) 0.48	2.84 (0.85–9.56) 0.09	0.94 (0.44–2.03) 0.88	
	0.71 (0.38–1.342) 0.29	0.98 (0.38–2.55) 0.97	0.58 (0.24–1.44) 0.24	
Father reported				
Father SD drink	957 22.97 (0.000) 0.029	6.84 (0.033) 0.021	7.63 (0.022) 0.019	ns (0.91)
with family	2 0.52 (0.33–0.80) 0.003	0.46 (0.24–0.89) 0.022	0.59 (0.31–1.13) 0.11	
with friends	0.52 (0.30–0.91) 0.021	0.77 (0.29–2.06) 0.60	0.62 (0.29–1.30) 0.20	
Father drinker	906 5.08 (0.079) 0.007	7.51 (0.023) 0.023	9.37 (0.009) 0.016	6.46 (0.040)
problem drinker	2 1.00 (0.38–2.65) 0.99	# 1.13 (0.62–2.06) 0.68	0.29 (0.07–1.17) 0.082	
	1.56 (1.06–2.31) 0.025		2.21 (1.25–3.90) 0.006	

Note: Results co-varied for religious group and age group. # = Not estimated in range. Almost all female drinkers (98%) have a father who was a lifetime drinker. L–R chi-square 65.73, 1df, p=.000.

in daughters, whereas perceived father strong disapproval of drinking with friends was stronger in sons.

Hierarchical predictor block models

Among daughters in the mother model (see Table 8.5), perceived mother strong disapproval of drinking with friends (OR = 0.29) remained significant in the final step, but perceived mother strong disapproval of drinking with family was no longer significant, with mother-rated strong disapproval of drinking with family (OR = 0.41) included in the model. In the father model, perceived father drinker (OR = 4.8), father-rated strong disapproval of drinking with family (OR = 0.45) and father-reported lifetime drinking (endorsed in 98% of fathers with daughter who binged) remained significant in the final step.

Among sons in the mother model, perceived strong disapproval of drinking with friends (OR = 0.41) remained significant in the final step. In the father model, father-reported lifetime problem drinking (OR = 1.7) did not reach significance ($p = 0.06$) when added to the model in the final step.

Discussion

Rates of alcohol use and heavy use in Mauritian youth

This study found similar drinking rates for male and female JCHP youth under age 18, but higher rates for male compared with female JCHP young adults (aged 18+). Binge drinking was consistently about twice as high in males versus females in all age groups, with almost a quarter of the young adult females and half of the young adult males engaging in binge drinking over the past year. The finding that about a third of 13–15-year-old JCHP offspring were drinking over the past year is higher than the 2011 Global School-Based Health Survey (GSHS) past-month rates for Mauritian schoolchildren (26% of boys, 22% of girls; CDC, 2011). Similarly, the finding that half or more of 16–20-year-olds were drinking, with 80% of these male drinkers and 40% of these female drinkers binging, was also higher than WHO (2018) past-month rates in 15–19-year-old Mauritians, which found that 28% of males drank in the past month and 14% (or 48% of male drinkers) engaged in heavy episodic (binge) drinking, and 11% of females drank in the past month and 2% (or 17% of female drinkers) binged. Drinking behaviour was assessed over an annual cycle because many of the JCHP offspring were interviewed during school holidays,

Table 8.5: Parental predictors of current binge drinking stratified by offspring gender

	Daughters				Sons			
	Mother OR (95% CI)		Father OR (95% CI)		Mother OR (95% CI)		Father OR (95% CI)	
	Step 1	Step 2	Step 1	Step 2	Step 1	Step 2	Step 1	Step 2
Child rated								
Perceived norms								
Mother SD drink with family	0.33* (0.12–0.46)	0.36+ (0.13–1.01)						
Mother SD drink with friends	0.24*** (0.12–0.46)	0.28*** (0.14–0.56)			0.36*** (0.22–0.62)	0.41*** (0.24–0.70)		
Father SD drink with family			0.54 (0.25–1.15)	0.60 (0.27–1.30)				
Father SD drink with friends							0.31*** (0.17–0.53)	0.33*** (0.19–0.58)
Descriptive norms								
Mother lifetime drinker	1.93 (0.74–4.99)	1.50 (0.57–3.97)						
Father lifetime drinker			7.64* (1.62–36.01)	4.83* (1.09–21.46)				

+ p < .10, *p < .05, **p < .01, ***p < .001

Note. SD = strongly disagree

Table 8.5: Parental predictors of current binge drinking stratified by offspring gender (continued)

	Daughters				Sons			
Father problem drinker			1.89+ (0.91–3.90)		1.86+ (0.89–3.90)			
Parent-reported attitudes								
Mother SD drink with family		0.35* (0.18–0.71)						
Mother SD drink with friends						0.60+ (0.34–1.07)		
Father SD drink with family				0.45* (0.23–0.89)				
Father SD drink with friends								
Behaviour								
Mother lifetime drinker								
Father lifetime drinker				#				
Father problem drinker								1.72+ (0.98–3.02)
Step χ²	42.92***	8.75**	18.16***	8.85*	13.96**	2.94+	17.32***	3.49+
ΔR²	0.120	0.024	0.058	0.027	0.027	0.005	0.040	0.008

Note: = Out of range, with 98% of fathers whose daughters binge drink being lifetime drinkers which could bias past-month rates. Thus, the numbers are not directly comparable to these national-level surveys, but trends across gender within each age group are similar to the broader population of youth on Mauritius in these national surveys that show increasing rates in recent years (for example, in the 2006 GSHS rates were only 19% for boys and 17% for girls; CDC, 2007). It is also possible that the lifelong participation of the JCHP families, the established relationships and rapport with JCHP staff, and the detailed assessment battery in this JCHP wave may have yielded higher reported levels of use than in national surveys. These numbers indicate that drinking among Mauritian youth is common and should be considered a potential public health concern, particularly binge drinking, which is often linked to negative consequences in adolescence and young adulthood (for example, Wechsler et al, 1997, 1998).

Parental risk and protective factors

The findings within families show consistency in how children view their parents' drinking behaviours across offspring age groups and gender. It is common for Mauritians to socialize with their families, and the findings show that children are able to perceive parental consumption and problems in ways that are consistent across age groups and gender. It is also shown, however, that offspring have received different messaging regarding the appropriate use of alcohol based on their age and gender. Most Mauritian parents are providing clear messages of disapproval to their children regarding the use of alcohol, and these perceived injunctive norms are associated with their children's drinking behaviours. By parsing parental injunctive norms by context (drinking with family versus drinking with friends), it can be seen that parents may be guiding their children to consume alcohol under their supervision and thus drink with family in situations that do not include heavy drinking. Norms that relate to binge drinking were more focused on drinking with friends, which likely is a context in which more extreme consumption occurs. It is also possible, however, that parental influence is working in reverse, with those children who are drinking heavily doing so with friends, which parents then strongly oppose. The findings also highlight that not only what parents say, but also what parents do makes a difference in offspring drinking behaviour – parental drinking behaviour modelled to offspring played an important role in offspring early drinking behaviour, and to some extent to offspring early heavy drinking. Continuing to follow the JCHP offspring over their early drinking years and assessing drinking behaviours at multiple time points will enable the progression of offspring drinking to be observed and the directional influence of familial factors on early drinking trajectories to be determined.

Gender-specific parental risk and protective factors

Daughters

It was predicted that daughter alcohol use would be influenced by maternal alcohol norms and attitudes and this was the case, but it was also true that paternal alcohol use behaviours were strong predictors of daughter alcohol use. Thus, it was not that gender-specific modelling was the critical factor for daughter drinking and heavy drinking, but rather that daughters were broadly influenced by parental alcohol-specific risk and protective factors. Alcohol use in females is now more common in this younger generation of Mauritians than it was for females in the older generation, so it is possible that daughters are taking their drinking cues from their fathers more than their mothers. Understanding what constitutes acceptable behaviour now for females in this changing society warrants further attention. In addition, better knowledge of how binge drinking is linked to negative consequences in Mauritius, and if these relationships are consistent with youth from other societies (for example, Brown et al, 2008; Wechsler et al, 1997, 1998), will be important for understanding its impact on health in this society.

Sons

Among sons, there was indication of modelling of drinking behaviour, with perceiving parents to be drinkers linked to increased likelihood of being a drinker, regardless of actual lifetime parent self-reported drinking. For parental monitoring, the role of mothers operated via expressed disapproval of drinking, and a protective role of paternal disapproval of sons drinking with friends (but not family) as also found. Questions about parental alcohol-specific attitudes were split to distinguish between drinking with family, which is common among non-Muslim Mauritians, who often socialize within family units (including across generations), and drinking with friends, which is more common among Mauritian youth than Mauritian adults and may be influenced by factors specific to developmental stage (see Maggs et al, 2008).

That only a few parental drinking variables were predictive of a son's binge drinking was not expected (even though stronger relationships were hypothesized for daughters than for sons), but suggests this common behaviour among young Mauritian males may be more influenced by non-familial factors such as peers or availability, or perhaps by more nuanced familial factors than were captured in this study. The only father alcohol behaviour that significantly predicted a son's binge drinking was father-reported lifetime problem drinking, indicating that the risk from father's drinking history is contained within variance not captured by what the son observes of the father; this is suggestive of a stronger genetic influence than environmental influence, although no definitive conclusions can be drawn regarding genetic versus environmental contributions in this family study of primarily intact families. Among sons, being from a parental unit that was not intact also doubled the risk for binge drinking, however, indicating that reduced parental presence may also indirectly play a role in binge drinking (for example, perhaps father drinking contributed to the parental unit split and indirectly to son binge drinking). Additional examination of parental alcohol use and problems while raising children during different child developmental periods (pre-school, primary school, secondary school) may yield further insight into how fathers' lifecourse alcohol involvement predicts the future alcohol consumption trajectories of their sons.

Summary

Taken together, the findings show important mother–daughter and father–son relationships, supporting the hypothesis that modelling within genders is critical for use, but also indicate that daughters may utilize descriptive norms from fathers as well as mothers to guide their alcohol use and heavy use. Based on prior behaviour genetics studies, it was explored whether these descriptive relationships would be stronger in daughters than in sons, which was supported in relation to drinking and partially supported in relation to binge drinking, where for son's binge drinking evidence was only found of self-reported father lifetime problems being a significant parental behaviour predictor. Regarding injunctive norms, parent-rated disapproval adds protection for drinking and binge drinking beyond child-perceived parental injunctive norms, indicating that parental disapproval of drinking may be indicative of more than just what the child perceives as disapproval and perhaps represents a broader range of parental controls that operate both directly and indirectly on offspring behaviour. Injunctive norms were expected to be stronger in sons than daughters, but what consistent relationships were found across parents that varied by offspring gender (that is, strong parental disapproval of drinking with family related to daughter alcohol involvement, strong parental disapproval of drinking with friends related to son alcohol involvement). Finally, we see context-specific variations in injunctive norms that are consistently reported across generations but differentially related to alcohol use versus heavy use. This variation in norms–behaviour associations is similar to the earlier findings in the original birth cohort that religious abstinence norms were protective against being a drinker, but did not afford additional protection for AUDs (Luczak et al, 2014), supporting the specificity of the impact of norms on different alcohol behaviours.

Study strengths and limitations

Findings from a birth cohort study like the JCHP have the advantage of not being a biased sample due to selection criteria, and thus results found with these Mauritian families may generalize to broader populations. It is possible these findings would be relevant to other middle-income nations where relative financial security provides for youth spending on alcohol, or in nations where alcohol use among females is growing in similar ways as in Mauritius. It is also possible, however, that the results are not applicable within nations where rates of intact families are much lower than in Mauritius. Interpreting research findings within the contextual constraints of the sample and society will help lead to a more complete picture of unique and common risk factors for youth drinking across nations as well as within dynamic cultures where the norms for drinking may be changing to support more female drinking and heavier drinking in youth overall.

It is also recognized that reporting biases in alcohol research differ by assessment format, rater, demographic groups and contexts. Having multiple assessment waves on the original cohort and multiple informants within the family, however, made it possible to remove several self-reports that were deemed inconsistent, highlighting an important benefit of conducting research over time within families. In this example of work conducted with the JCHP sample, the first wave of data collection on offspring drinking is presented, and thus it is recognized that these initial finding do not highlight all benefits of a longitudinal study. The best way to look at family influences is through multiple-rater studies that track behaviour over time, and at key developmental periods. Over the last several decades, the JCHP has made contributions to understanding how early childhood health affects mental health outcomes into early and mid-adulthood within the original birth cohort. The JCHP is now in the process of expanding into a multigenerational family study, including collecting many of the same constructs on the offspring as were obtained on the original cohort. The study presented here represents initial efforts to understand how gender and parental alcohol risk and protective factors relate to drinking and heavy drinking in Mauritian youth. The findings point to the notion that parental lifetime alcohol behaviours relate to current offspring drinking in multiple ways through modelling, monitoring, family constellation and family history, and provides avenues to investigate next in multi-informant prospective designs. Gathering additional waves of data on the offspring will make it possible to examine how risk and protective factors obtained from multiple generations affect early drinking trajectories in this next generation, thus, building upon the longitudinal findings, the JCHP can contribute to understanding the lifecourse development of mental health.

Acknowledgments

This research was supported by US National Institutes of Health grants K08AA14265 and R01AA18179 and the Mauritian Ministry of Health and Quality of Life. We gratefully acknowledge the contributions of founding investigators of the JCHP Sarnoff A. Mednick, Peter H. Venables, Fini Schulsinger, Abdul C. Raman, Cyril Dalais, current Co-International Director of the JCHP Adrian Raine and researchers who have published JCHP findings over the decades, Joint Child Health Project staff including Naajiyah Seesurun, Luczak USC Laboratory staff including Emily B. Saldich, and the JCHP birth cohort and their families for their lifelong participation in this study.

References

Agrawal, A. and Lynskey, M. (2008) Are there genetic influences on addiction: evidence from family, adoption and twin studies. *Addiction* 103(7): 1069–78.

American Psychological Association (APA) (2013) *Diagnostic and Statistical Manual of Mental Disorders* (5th edn). Arlington, VA: American Psychiatric Association.

Babor, T.F., Higgins-Biddle, J.C., Saunders, J.B. and Monteiro, M.G. (2001) *The Alcohol Use Disorders Identification Test* (2nd edn). Geneva: World Health Organization.

Brown, S.A., McGue, M., Maggs, J., Schulenberg, J., Hingson, R., Swartzwelder, S. et al (2008) Developmental perspective on alcohol and youths 16 to 20 years of age. *Pediatrics* 121: 290–310.

Bucholz, K.K., Cadoret, R., Cloninger, C.R., Dinwiddie, S.H., Hesselbrock, V.M., Nurnberger, J.I. et al (1994) A new semistructured psychiatric interview for use in genetic linkage studies: a report on the reliability of the SSAGA. *Journal of Studies on Alcohol* 55: 149–58.

Burk, L.R., Armstrong, J.M., Goldsmith, H.H., Klein, M.H., Strauman, T.J., Costanzo, P. and Essex, M.J. (2011) Sex, temperament and family context: how the interaction of early factors differentially predict adolescent alcohol use and are mediated by proximal adolescent factors. *Psychology of Addictive Behaviors* 25(1): 1–15.

Catalano, R.F., Kosterman, R., Hawkins, J.D., Newcomb, M.D. and Abbott, R.D. (1996) Modeling the etiology of adolescent substance use: a test of the social developmental model. *Journal of Drug Issues* 26(2): 429–55.

Centers for Disease Control and Prevention (CDC) (2007) Global school-based student health survey. Available at www.who.int/chp/gshs/Mauritius_2007_fact_sheet.pdf

CDC (2011) Global school-based student health survey. Available at https://www.who.int/teams/noncommunicable-diseases/surveillance/systems-tools/global-school-based-student-health-survey

CDC, Ministry of Health and Quality of Life, Mauritius, and World Health Organization (2013) Global school-based student health survey 2011. Country report: Republic of Mauritius. Available at www.who.int/chp/gshs/mauritius/en/

Chassin, L., Pillow, D.R., Curran, P.J., Molina, B.S.G. and Barrera Jr, M. (1993) Relation of parental alcoholism to early adolescent substance use: a test of three mediating mechanisms. *Journal of Abnormal Psychology* 102(1): 3–19.

Chassin, L., Haller, M., Lee, M.R., Handley, E., Bountress, K. and Beltran, I. (2016) Familial factors influencing offspring substance use and dependence. In K.J. Sher (Ed), *Oxford Library of Psychology: The Oxford Handbook of Substance Use and Substance Use Disorders* (pp 449–82). Oxford: Oxford University Press.

Cialdini, R.B., Reno, R.R. and Kallgren, C.A. (1990) A focus theory of normative conduct: recycling the concept of norms to reduce littering in public places. *Journal of Personality and Social Psychology* 58(6): 1015–26.

Cotton, N. (1979) The familial incidence of alcoholism: a review. *Journal of Studies on Alcohol* 40: 89–116.

D'Onofrio, B.M., Van Hulle, C.A., Waldman, I.D., Rodgers, J.L., Rathouz, P.J. and Lahey, B.B. (2007) Causal inferences regarding prenatal alcohol exposure and childhood externalizing problems. *Archives of General Psychiatry* 11: 1296–304.

Duncan, S.C., Duncan, T.E. and Strycker, L.A. (2006) Alcohol use from ages 9 to 16: a cohort-sequential latent growth model. *Drug and Alcohol Dependence* 81: 71–81.

Elek, E., Miller-Day, M. and Hecht, M. (2006) Influences of personal, injunctive, and descriptive norms on early adolescent substance use. *Journal of Drug Issues* 36: 147–72.

Fowler, T., Lifford, K., Shelton, K., Rice, F., Thapar, A., Neale, M.C., McBride, A. and Van Den Bree, M. (2007) Exploring the relationship between genetic and environmental influences on initiation and progression of substance use. *Addiction* 102: 413–22.

Homer, D. and Lemeshow, S. (2000) Applied Logistic Regression, 2000. *Journal of Biomechanics* 29: 723–733.

IBM Corp (2016) IBM SPSS Statistics for Windows, Version 24.0. Armonk, NY: IBM Corp.

Liu, J., Raine, A., Venables, P.H. and Mednick, S.A. (2004) Malnutrition at age 3 years and externalizing behavior problems at ages 8, 11, and 17 years. *American Journal of Psychiatry* 161: 2005–13.

Luczak, S.E., Prescott, C.A., Dalais, C., Raine, A., Venables, P.H. and Mednick, S.A. (2014) Religious factors associated with alcohol involvement: results from the Mauritian Joint Child Health Project. *Drug and Alcohol Dependence* 135: 37–44.

Luczak, S.E., Prescott, C.A. and Venables, P.H. (2017) Latent classes of alcohol problems in Mauritian men: results from the Joint Child Health Project. *Drug and Alcohol Review* 36(6): 805–12.

Luczak, S.E., Raine, A. and Venables, P.H. (2001) Invariance in the MAST across religious groups. *Journal of Studies on Alcohol* 62: 834–7.

Luczak, S.E., Yarnell, L.M., Prescott, C.A., Raine, A., Venables, P.H. and Mednick, S.A. (2015) Childhood cognitive measures as predictors of alcohol use and problems by mid-adulthood in a non-Western cohort. *Psychology of Addictive Behaviors* 29: 365–70.

Maggs, J.L., Patrick, M.E. and Feinstein, L. (2008) Childhood and adolescent predictors of alcohol use and problems in adolescence and adulthood in the National Child Development Study. *Addiction* 103: 7–22.

Mann, R.E., Sobell, L.C., Sobell, M.B. and Pavan, D. (1985) Reliability of a family tree questionnaire for assessing family history of alcohol problems. *Drug and Alcohol Dependence* 15: 61–7.

McGue, M., Iacono, W.G., Legrand, L.N., Malone, S. and Elkins, I. (2001) Origins and consequences of age at first drink: II. Familial risk and heritability. *Alcoholism: Clinical and Experimental Research* 8: 1166–73.

Merikangas, K.R. (1990) The genetic epidemiology of alcoholism. *Psychological Medicine* 20: 11–22.

Ministry of Health and Quality of Life (2016) Mauritius non-communicable diseases survey. Available at https://health.govmu.org/Pages/Statistics/NCD-Survey-Reports.aspx

Mrug, S. and McCay, R. (2013) Parental and peer disapproval of alcohol use and its relationship to adolescent drinking: age, gender, and racial differences. *Psychology of Addictive Behaviors* 27(3): 604–14.

Nargiso, J.E., Friend, K. and Florin, P. (2013) An examination of peer, family, and community context risk factors for alcohol use and alcohol use intentions in early adolescents. *Journal of Early Adolescence* 33: 973–93.

Pagan, J.L., Rose, R.J., Viken, R.J., Pulkkinen, L., Kaprio, J. and Dick, D.M. (2006) Genetic and environmental influences on stages of alcohol use across adolescence and into young adulthood. *Behavioral Genetics* 36: 483–97.

Prescott, C.A. and Kendler, K.S. (1999) Genetic and environmental contributions to alcohol abuse and dependence in a population-based sample of male twins. *American Journal of Psychiatry* 156: 34–40.

Prescott, C.A., Aggen, S.H. and Kendler, K.S. (1999) Sex differences in the courses of genetic liability to alcohol abuse and dependence in a population-based sample of U.S. twins. *Alcoholism: Clinical and Experimental Research* 23: 1136–44.

Prescott, C.A. and Kendler, K.S. (2001) Associations between marital status and alcohol consumption in a longitudinal study of female twins. *Journal of Studies on Alcohol* 62(5): 589–604.

Raine, A., Mellingen, K., Liu, J., Venables, P.H. and Mednick, S.A. (2003) Effects of environmental enrichment at age 3–5 years on schizotypcal personality and antisocial behavior at ages 17 and 23 years. *American Journal of Psychiatry* 160: 1627–35.

Raine, A., Liu, J., Venables, P.H., Mednick, S.A. and Dalais, C. (2010) Cohort profile: the Mauritius child health project. *International Journal of Epidemiology* 39(6): 1441–51.

Reynolds, C.A., Raine, A., Mellingen, K., Venables, P.H. and Mednick, S.A. (2000) Three-factor model of schizotypal personality: invariance across culture, gender, religious affiliation, family adversity, and psychopathology. *Schizophrenia Bulletin* 26: 603–18.

Rossow, I. and Kuntsche, E. (2013) Early onset of drinking and risk of heavy drinking in young adulthood – a 13-year prospective study. *Alcoholism: Clinical and Experimental Research* 37 (Suppl 1): E297–304.

Ryan, S.M., Jorm, A.F. and Lubman, D.I. (2010) Parenting factors associated with reduced adolescent alcohol use: A systematic review of longitudinal studies. *Australian and New Zealand Journal of Psychiatry* 44(9): 774–83.

Sher, K.J. (1991) *Children of Alcoholics: A Critical Appraisal of Theory and Research.* Chicago: University of Chicago Press.

Sieving, R.E., Maruyama, G., Williams, C.L. and Perry, C.L. (2000) Pathways to adolescent alcohol use: potential mechanisms of parental influence. *Journal on Research on Adolescence* 10(4): 489–514.

Spitzer, M.B., Gibbon, M. and Williams, J. (1997) Structured clinical interview for DSM-IV Axis I Disorders. New York, NY: Biometrics Research Department, New York State Psychiatric Institute.

United Nations General Assembly Economic and Social Council (2010) Report of the Secretary-General on the follow-up to the tenth anniversary of the International Year of the Family and beyond. A/66/62-E/2011/4. Available at https://undocs.org/A/66/62

UNICEF (2018) *Key Findings on Families, Family Policy and the Sustainable Development Goals: Synthesis Report.* Office of Research Innocenti, Florence, Italy.

Van Den Eijnden, R., Van De Mheen, D. and Vet, R. (2011) Alcohol-specific parenting and adolescents' alcohol-related problems: the interacting role of alcohol availability at home and parental rules. *Journal of Studies of Alcohol and Drugs* 72: 408–17.

Venables, P.H. (1978) Psychophysiology and psychometrics. *Psychophysiology* 15: 302–15.

Venables, P.H. (1990) The measurement of schizotypy in Mauritius. *Personality and Individual Differences* 11: 965–71.

Venables, P.H. and Raine, A. (2012) Poor nutrition at age 3 and schizotypal personality at age 23: the mediating role of age 11 cognitive functioning. *American Journal of Psychiatry* 169(8): 822–30.

Venables, P.H. and Raine, A. (2015) Poor nutrition at 3 and schizotypal personality at age 23: the mediating role of age 11 cognitive functioning. *The American Journal of Psychiatry* 169: 822–30.

Wechsler, H., Fulop, M., Padilla, A., Lee, H. and Patrick, K. (1997) Binge drinking among college students: a comparison of California with other states. *Journal of American College Health* 45: 273–7.

Wechsler, H., Dowdall, G.W., Maenner, G., Gledhill-Hoyt, J. and Lee, H. (1998) Changes in binge drinking and related problems among American college students between 1993 and 1997. *Journal of American College Health* 47: 57–68.

Wilsnack, R.W., Wilsnack, S.C., Kristjanson, A.F., Vogeltanz-Holm, N.D. and Gmel, G. (2009) Gender and alcohol consumption: patterns from the multinational GENACIS project. *Addiction* 104: 1487–500.

World Health Organization (WHO) (2018) *Global Status Report on Alcohol and Health 2018*. Geneva: WHO. Available at www.who.int/substance_abuse/publications/global_status_report_2004_overview.pdf

Yarnell, L.M., Sargeant, M.N., Prescott, C.A., Tilley, J.L., Farver, J.A.M., Mednick, S.A. et al (2013) Measurement invariance of internalizing and externalizing behavioral syndrome factors in a non-Western sample. *Assessment* 20: 642–55.

Yu, J. and Perrine, M.W. (1997) The transmission of parent/adult–child drinking patterns: testing a gender-specific structural model. *American Journal of Drug Abuse* 23: 143–65.

Yu, J. (1998) Perceived parental/peer attitudes and alcohol-related behaviors: an analysis of the impact of the drinking age law. *Substance Use & Misuse* 33(14): 2687–702.

Conclusion: The Future of Longitudinal Research

Prerna Banati

The landscape of longitudinal research today

This volume has presented examples of world class longitudinal research with policy and programme relevance. They join a growing number of researchers working with longitudinal data. In the last ten years, the number of publications citing use of longitudinal data has grown by 75%, shown in Figure 9.1. This growth presents an important resource for policy makers and practitioners towards meeting their sustainable development targets.

Despite the innovations presented, the potential relevance and impact, it is no doubt that longitudinal researchers today have experienced challenges in their dedication to this type of work.

To further unpack the landscape of longitudinal research, a systematic analysis of 122 longitudinal studies was conducted (Banati, 2019). A comprehensive search of the published literature was undertaken in Google Scholar, Pubmed and Scopus using the following search terms: birth cohort, longitudinal, child, life course and life stage. The study also drew from the largest open source database of longitudinal studies available – the Low and Middle Income Longitudinal Population Study Directory developed by the Institute for Fiscal Studies (2018). Inclusion criteria were (1) a minimum of two rounds of data collection; (2) first round conducted after 1970; (3) capturing information and responding to questions relevant for children. The studies are located in high-, middle- and low-income countries. Without a doubt, this was not an exhaustive process and may not have captured all available studies. Despite this, to our knowledge, we have identified and analysed the largest collection of longitudinal studies among children to date.

Figure 9.1: Growth of longitudinal research in peer-reviewed journal articles

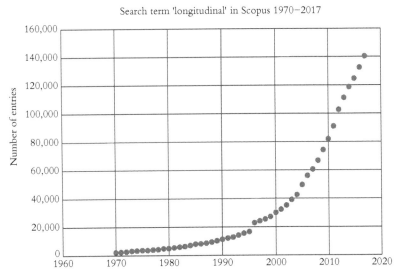

Search term 'longitudinal' in Scopus 1970–2017

Source: Author's own

In addition, an online survey was created and shared with UNICEF's GLORI network members and additional investigators identified from the systematic analysis. GLORI – the Global Longitudinal Research Initiative – is a research network of longitudinal researchers working on topics relevant for children. It has 31 members working in 41 countries. The membership list can be found on the GLORI website (UNICEF, 2020). These were largely observational studies (61%). Most studies (63%) had more than five years of data collected, the average attrition rate was 19.8%.

Challenges experienced by longitudinal research today

The results of our examination of studies indicate that good longitudinal research is costly, and funding tends to be secured by wave and through multiple donors, with differing priorities. Only 13% of studies were identified as funded by national (governmental) entities, raising questions of sustainability. Of the respondents, 36% noted funding considerations as a key challenge. Long gaps can be experienced until funding is identified, creating challenges for sample tracking, particularly in areas of high movement. The value of the longitudinal design is often seen only after subsequent rounds, and it can take years for longitudinal studies to produce results. Ethical considerations may present additional complexities. In order to secure follow-ups with participants, data requires identifiers, meaning that identity protection becomes a greater concern. Of critical importance, many survey respondents noted the need for a better bridge between research and practice; and better ways to document these impacts when they do exist. A recent (2017) Economic and Social Research Council review of the UK's investments in longitudinal research agreed. They panel noted:

> Although numerous studies have been published from ESRC-funded longitudinal studies, the review panel has found it difficult to trace specific evidence of the 'instrumental' or 'direct' policy impacts from these investments ... If left unchecked, a lack of evidence is likely to undermine the case for future investments. (Economic and Social Research Council, 2017, p 6)

The next section focuses on this last challenge, identified as an absolute necessity to ensure the wealth of longitudinal evidence is more fully brought to bear on programme design, implementation and evaluation.

Bringing longitudinal research into the policy-practice space

Ensuring the relevance, timeliness and quality should be the top priorities of any new longitudinal research undertaking. However, research uptake strategies for such research are rarely considered beyond inclusion in the donor proposal, and infrequently translated into action plans. As demands to demonstrate 'value for money' increase, researchers are seeking ways to intensify the impact of their studies, and ways to measure it. In reflecting on their longitudinal research, Jones and Villar (2008, p 1) identify five dimensions of policy impact: 'framing debates and policy agenda formulation; securing discursive commitments from key policy actors; bringing about procedural changes; policy reform; and behavioural change'. Their analysis highlights the roles of culture, politics and values in research uptake, and the challenges inherent in partnership models of knowledge translation. Acknowledging trust, co-creation and inclusion in the research process have been identified as key factors in the success of longitudinal impact evaluations such as the Transfer Project (2020, p 2). The authors note that '[e]ngaging government ministries in large-scale, highly public impact evaluations can also bring about an "evidence culture" with profound effects on all aspects of their decision-making, strengthening their standing within government, and leading to better policy overall'. The authors convincingly detail an engagement process which places a priority on the role of policy makers in the research process, with an emphasis on engagement through every wave of data collection and every stage of research, ensuring that from the beginning, the research 'asks the right questions'. This results in a 'virtuous evidence cycle' with the ultimate benefit of credibility and trust in evidence. Longitudinal evidence has the significant benefit of a long-term time horizon to grow and engender trust and credibility among public policy makers and practitioners.

A policy evaluation framework for longitudinal studies

Figure 9.1 proposes a research uptake framework for longitudinal research that rests on three elements of the 'research dynamo'. The cornerstone of successful impact is quality research results that demonstrate strong internal validity and generate accurate policy and programme recommendations. Noting that over 80% of longitudinal studies surveyed used tablets for data collection, longitudinal research can exploit this use of technology to generate more real-time quality data sets, even extending to cell phone and GPS technology.

A wide and transparent partnership model is central to the dynamo. The majority of longitudinal research in developing contexts are anchored in northern academic institutions. Over one third of the studies surveyed received funding for their longitudinal study through an academic grant. A successful example of a wide partnership model is that utilized by the GAGE research programme, which has an active and expansive research consortium with members from leading research institutions from Africa, the Middle East and North Africa (MENA), South Asia, the UK and the US, and also globally renowned non-governmental organizations working on adolescence and gender.

Finally, the third piece of the dynamo brings continuous dialogue and participation to the research process. Dialogue at the governmental and agency level is perhaps most commonly seen among policy-engaged longitudinal studies. Participatory research models – involving the participation of communities and individuals – have been in existence a long time. The influential work of Robert Chambers using community-based participatory action research has raised the bar for researchers (Chambers, 1994). Engagement with communities and individuals in longitudinal research processes has not been systematically done, with only 23% of the studies surveyed embracing participatory approaches. Robust participation is a core component of the EuroCohort study, presented in this volume. Arguing for participatory approaches also for children, the authors describe the use of parallel child advisory panels composed of children from different age groups that could create room for evolving the framework to guide participation across age groups.

Recognizing that direct policy impact is uncommon, four proposed avenues of influence are described in Figure 9.2. Academic impact is identified as the contribution that research makes in 'shifting understanding and advancing scientific, method, theory and application across and within disciplines'. It may also include methodological innovation. Instrumental impact describes the altering of programme or policy behaviours, including policy development, practice or service provision or directly shaping legislation. Conceptual impact is achieved through reframing debates, changing the understanding of the situation; or it might provide new or different ways of thinking about the policy problem or context being considered. Finally, capacity-building impact is achieved through technical and personal skill development, both among researchers and research users (Economic Social Research Council, 2020).

These avenues exploit a set of tools and instruments in support of reaching SDG impact, including programme adaptation and scale-up, policy agenda formulation or procedural change. An important part of policy process analysis that longitudinal studies could benefit from is a rigorous assessment of amplifier platforms at community, national, regional and global levels. These include governmental or intergovernmental events, media venues or traditional leaders' groups.

Donor perspectives of longitudinal research

In recent years, several large donors – the Economic Science Research Council (ESRC), Wellcome Trust and the Medical Research Council (MRC) – have undertaken reviews of their longitudinal investments. An independent process – undertaken by ESRC for example – can give rise to clarity in how funding should be prioritized going forward. A description of donor strategies for a selection of funders is described in Table 9.1. While not an exhaustive review, the table illustrates that donors seem to have a number of common elements of agenda or strategy in defining and sustaining their longitudinal investments.

Figure 9.2: The research dynamo for sustainable development impact

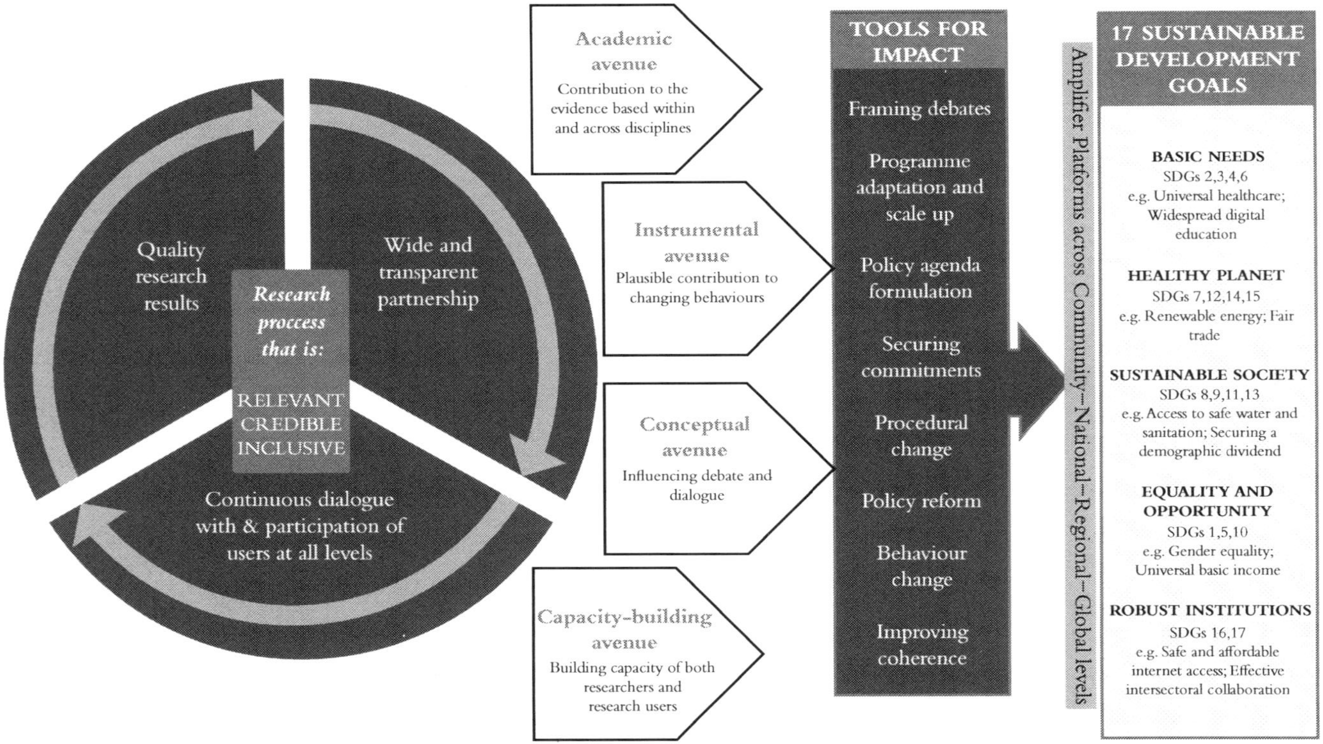

Source: DfiD research uptake guidance (2016); ESRC impact statement (2020); UNICEF Innocenti research uptake strategy (unpublished); Jones and Villar (2008); and Robercosam (2019)

Table 9.1: Summary of selected foundations and agencies financing longitudinal research

Donor	Financial investment	Strategic focus
Wellcome Trust	Over the past ten years, more than £120 million has been invested in longitudinal population studies in the UK and low- and middle-income countries (Wellcome Trust, 2017).	Data linkage, data sharing and discoverability; Co-ordination, networking between studies, standardization; Emerging technologies, cost efficiency; Capacity strengthening and research translation; Encourage data that is useful both locally and more widely; that answers several questions; that endures for currently unforeseen future uses (Wellcome Trust, 2017).
Gates Foundation	Approximately $76 million over the last 15 years.	Global Development, Global Health and Global Growth and Opportunity Divisions and US Programs Division all exploit longitudinal data and research. Many investments focus on integrated data, or creation of data exchange platforms. There is also support for development of innovative methodologies for longitudinal science. However, an explicit data strategy is not readily available.
U.K. Economic Social Research Council (ESRC)	Over £20 million annually (Economic Social Research Council, 2020).	2017 review identified the following priorities: Creation of an administrative data spine from which to sample a new cohort or refresh existing samples; A new birth cohort with accelerated longitudinal design; Continuation of understanding society and an additional 'transition to adulthood' sweep of the Millennium Cohort Study; Competitive bids to an innovation fund, including an option for the other cohorts to develop innovative bids for this resource; Continuation and further development of a longitudinal resource centre (currently CLOSER).
US National Institutes of Health	Over the last five years, over $500 million has been spent on longitudinal studies (NIH, 2020).	NIH strategy for 2016–20 explicitly mentions longitudinal research. The strategy describes the Precision Medical Initiative, a cohort at the forefront, that takes advantage of emerging biomedical tools and technologies, such as availability of electronic health records, DNA sequencing, and exposure monitoring.

(continued)

Table 9.1: Summary of selected foundations and agencies financing longitudinal research (continued)

Donor	Financial investment	Strategic focus
UK Medical Research Council (MRC)	£9.6m per year on 19 cohort studies (Medical Research Council 2014).	2014 review identified the following priorities: Use standardized or validated sample collection, storage, tools and platforms for evolving technologies; Promote collaborations with centres of excellence such as the Farr Institute; Expand data linkage to the increasing number of routine health records and administrative data sets available in the UK; Increase discoverability and accessibility of studies (though data sharing and access to samples if possible); Adopt core common data standards, sharing knowledge and improving meta-data quality; Cost-effective methods such as digital technologies should be adopted; Effective models of two-way engagement between cohort study teams and policy makers.

Improving the effectiveness of longitudinal studies

Given their significant potential to shape development policies and programmes, maximizing the returns to these studies is a worthwhile aim. Drawn from analysis of our survey of studies, as well as existing reviews (Economic Social Research Council, 2017, for example), four recommendations are made for improving the effectiveness of longitudinal studies.

- *Ensure data are open access:* Democratizing data to enable the wider research and policy community to access and use it and facilitating better access to data will boost knowledge and is a public good in and of itself. In our analysis, only 37% of the 122 studies identified were available in the public domain. Access to data will allow timelier analysis and increase publication of the data. It will encourage triangulation of findings, and support improvements in quality. Very few longitudinal data resources are publicly available. Herbst (2002, p 43) notes that this challenge relates to the balance of priorities of data collectors, data subjects and data users. Employing his analysis, we see that while data collectors and analysts are interested primarily in ensuring quality, generating useful findings and project sustainability, data subjects' interests relate to protecting their own confidentiality, being informed of the use of the data and seeing the benefits of research. And finally, data users are interested mostly in setting research-based policies and informing programmes, as well as gaining credibility through their affiliation with the evidence.

Young Lives provides a good example of data transparency, as all data sets are available in the public domain. To improve discoverability, an online portal repository that hosts all longitudinal studies can be developed, making an effort to capture those in low- and middle-income settings. Such an online portal can share technical lessons as well as examples of policy impact.

- *Foster data linkage:* Linking data across sites or studies increases the value by increasing the number of variables, the size of the sample or the geographic scope of the analysis. Data sets that are linked can shed light in new areas, answering novel questions by expanding the potential of a singular data set. Linkage can overcome data-quality issues by allowing triangulation of outcomes, increasing completeness and improving ascertainment. Linkage of data sets can allow the evaluation of rare events. The use of data linkage in research studies has increased almost six-fold within the last two decades (Bohensky et al, 2010). Efforts to create interoperability with longitudinal data and other data sets (terms 'longitudinal linkage') is also becoming more common, with 63% of the studies in the analysis undertaking some form of linkage or harmonization activity. This was the most frequently mentioned methodological issue of UK-based longitudinal studies (Economic Social Research Council, 2017). The most common type of longitudinal linkage between data sets occurs between household data and facility-level data, such as patient health outcomes. The UK Administrative Data taskforce notes that linked data – longitudinal and administrative for example – could facilitate policy-relevant research, by expanding the number of data sets (and thereby variables) from which researchers can draw for analysis (UK Administrative Data Taskforce, 2012).

The Brazilian 100 million cohort provides a good example. The 100 million cohort project was set up in 2013 aiming to build a population-based cohort to be used to assess the effects of Brazil's social programmes on health and other outcomes. A probabilistic linkage pipeline was used to link the cohort with different health databases (Pinto et al, 2016). Unique identifiers (NIS) are available for all individuals who are recorded in the CadastroUnico (CADU), a central register for all social programmes kept by the

Brazilian government. The cohort comprises all individuals who have received payments from Bolsa Familia (a conditional cash transfer programme) between 2007 and 2015, resulting in a total of 114 million records. Pita and colleagues (2017) report efforts to link this cohort to the Unified Health System (SUS), including hospitalizations (SIH), notifiable diseases (SINAN), mortality (SIM) and live births (SINAC) registers. The authors show 95% linkage is possible between CADU and Brazil's Unified Health System (SUS) database using a combination of increasing sizes and manual review. The researchers note the importance of developing techniques in the absence of a 'gold standard'. In the report by Pinto and colleagues (2016) estimating accuracy of linkage efforts, the conclusions note that, given the size of the cohort and number of records, manual reviews to improve accuracy are limited, and machine learning techniques are under exploration.

- *Build interventions into the design of longitudinal data:* Experimentalists are typically at odds with the observationists, yet many of the challenges and opportunities of longitudinal research are shared by both. The demand for rigorous determination of 'what works' drives donors and policy makers alike and has created an industry of longitudinal intervention research. Longitudinal intervention studies are repeated surveys that include an experimental intervention. Over the last decade, we have seen the rise of the Randomized Control Trial (RCT) – a type of longitudinal data collection effort – which in many ways is considered a gold standard for evaluating the effect of a given intervention (Rothman and Greenland, 1998). The main advantage of these surveys is that it is possible to study both the natural history of development and the impact of interventions in the same research project. At the same time, strictly defined RCTs are not flexible enough to embrace serendipity, and hence cannot take advantage of one of the key benefits of longitudinal research – capturing unintended or unplanned events and picking up problems not envisaged before the studies were planned. There are both advantages to and problems with longitudinal observational studies, randomized control trials and longitudinal-experimental designs (quasi-experiments) – and each brings its own value (Banati, 2017).

For example, the GAGE study has embedded a set of experimental and quasi-experimental impact evaluations within the panel data collection activities. This allows investigators to complement the observational study with causal questions on programme impact. Some questions regarding the 'dynamism and diversity' of adolescent transitions and trajectories, particularly those relating to gender norms, are best understood through observational means. The presence of the embedded impact evaluations enables the study team to effectively disentangle the mediating roles that particular programme interventions play in gender socialization at different stages of adolescence. Noting that girls' experiences differ during early and later adolescence, while most interventions group adolescent girls aged 10–19 together, GAGE uses the longitudinal design to answer the question: When is the best time to intervene in adolescence, using what types of change strategies, and in what contexts? Relatedly, their research addresses questions such as: Are current interventions too short and/or lack intensity? And which programmes must be delivered in early adolescence in order to see significant returns on investment?

- *Creating cross-comparative (harmonized) studies:* Some of the most powerful longitudinal studies exist as cross-comparative national studies, coordinated through large networks. Notably, the INDEPTH network and the Living Standards Measurement Surveys (LSMS) are examples of multi-country comparative initiatives that utilize similar tools to compare conditions and situations over time and across country contexts. INDEPTH, founded in 1998, is a network of longitudinal community field sites based on health and demographic surveillance systems to capitalize on the research and policy-informing capabilities organized by researchers from various field sites. Standardized data sets enable cross-site and cross-national research, increasing the power of each individual study. Increasingly, with global goals pushing the development community to scale up programmes, longitudinal research is also keenly interested to explore external validity, the validity of applying research findings across contexts. Here the questions that can be answered include: How generalizable are findings from a single research study to other contexts? And under what general conditions are the results confirmed?

Other benefits to cross-comparative studies include the establishment of benchmarks, the engagement of transboundary and increasingly global issues (such as internet use or migration). Common frameworks, survey instruments and methodologies also facilitate pooling, allowing studies to profit from larger sample sizes. The European Cohort Development Project (Chapter 7) describes an input-harmonized birth cohort survey that exploits many of the advantages described earlier. It comprises a common questionnaire, sampling and fieldwork procedures across EU member states which allow a direct comparison of the well-being of children as they grow up across Europe in different national contexts.

The future of longitudinal research

A content analysis of SDG domains was undertaken in the 122 longitudinal studies we reviewed. Most studies were focused in the areas of health, poverty and inequality and education (SDGs 1, 3 and 4). Fewer studies focused on other SDGs such as clean energy; water, sanitation and hygiene; climate change and environment; or peaceful and inclusive societies (SDG 7, 8, 9, 12, 14, 15, 16). Among the survey respondents, when asked 'what topical areas do you consider high priority for longitudinal research on children in the next 3–5 years?' most researchers mentioned the terms 'health' and 'development'.

The analysis raises the question of how new waves and new studies could align more firmly with key policy challenges articulated in Agenda 2030, particularly in sectors that are understudied (such as environment, water and sanitation, migration or climate change), or could inform interlinkages across policy areas. As noted in a report by the Sustainable Development Solutions Network (SDSN, 2015), 'many important issues, such as gender equality, health, sustainable consumption and production, or nutrition cut across different goals and targets. Similarly, the goals and targets are interdependent and must be pursued together since progress in one area often depends on progress in other areas'.

Extending current longitudinal research towards understanding and exploring the links between different development domains can serve as a useful basis for arguing for greater integration of service sectors (such as early childhood education; and water, sanitation and hygiene).

Two areas where longitudinal research could be launched in the future include:

- *Migration:* The dynamism of migration makes longitudinal data a relevant tool for this topic. As migration steadily increases (UNICEF, 2016), an adequate evidence base on the drivers and possible determinants of migration has yet to be established. While most researchers might be concerned with attrition, adopting innovations that allow us to follow individuals over time, even when they move from one place to another, and interviewing them about the changes in their life, can help better describe the changes individuals experience when they migrate.

- *Climate and the environment:* Environmental and sustainable aspects and their impacts on human well-being has not been the topic of many longitudinal studies. The interconnections between energy, food and water, as well as water and sanitation links to environmental health, human well-being and the quality of the economy make the longitudinal design worth exploring. Such a study evaluating the impacts of interventions that mitigate climate change on human well-being and natural systems is one example (UNRISD, 2015).

Conclusions

In what has been termed 'the decade of action', the United Nations Sustainable Development Agenda has much progress to make in order to realize its ambition. With less than 10% of developmental science research from regions accounting for over 90% of world's population (Bornstein et al, 2012), the need to bridge research to solutions in low- and middle-income settings is even more acute. Longitudinal research has an influential role to play in delivering for those not yet counted within the current measurement framework. For policy and practice, new concepts and analyses are needed that place the individual within a life course of exposure, realities and opportunities. Current and conventional analysis both undervalues human futures and, in maintaining silos, undermines the fullness of human life. This volume has tried to open up and explore concepts and relationships between trajectories of human development and the sustainability agenda. It has exemplified these through a selection of high-impact longitudinal studies. Collectively, the studies have demonstrated the value of life-course examination – through analyses of transitions, trajectories and turning points – in answering questions of human development. In addition, the exploration of intergenerational transmission, inequalities, coherence, participation and sequencing, have enriched our understanding while simultaneously pointing to gaps in our current measurement efforts.

References

Banati, P. (2017) In God we trust, all others must bring data: is better longitudinal research the best response to the new 'post-truth' order? UNICEF Connect Blog, 10 March. Available at https://blogs.unicef.org/evidence-for-action/is-longitudinal-research-the-best-response-to-the-post-truth-order/

Banati, P. and Oyugi, J. (2019) Longitudinal research for sustainable development: towards a policy driven agenda – research spotlight. *Zeitschrift für Psychologie* 227(2): 149–53.

Bohensky, M.A., Jolley, D., Sundararajan, V., Evans, S., Pilcher, D.V., Scott, I. and Brand, C.A. (2010) Data linkage: a powerful research tool with potential problems. *BMC Health Services Research* 10(1): 1–7.

Bornstein, M., Britto, P., Nonoyama-Tarumi, Y., Ota, Y., Petrovic, O. and Putnick, D. (2012) Child development in developing countries: introduction and methods. *Child Development* 83(1): 16–31.

Chambers, R. (1994) The origins and practice of participatory rural appraisal. *World Development* 22(7): 954–69.

Economic and Social Research Council (2017) Longitudinal studies strategic review. Available at https://esrc.ukri.org/files/news-events-and-publications/publications/longitudinal-studies-strategic-review-2017/

Economic and Social Research Council (2020) UK's ESRC impact statement. Available at https://esrc.ukri.org/about-us/50-years-of-esrc/50-achievements/longitudinal-studies/

Herbst, K. (2002) Wider accessibility to longitudinal data sets: a framework for discussing the issues. Paper presented at Workshop on Leveraging Longitudinal Data in Developing Countries hosted by the National Research Council.

Institute for Fiscal Studies (2018) Low- and middle-income longitudinal population study directory. Available at www.ifs.org.uk/tools_and_resources/

Jones, N. and Villar, E. (2008) Situating children in international development policy: challenges involved in successful evidence-informed policy influencing. *Evidence and Policy: A Journal of Research, Debate and Practice* 21: 31–51.

Medical Research Council (MRC) (2014) Maximising the value of UK population cohorts: MRC strategic review of the largest UK population cohort studies.

National Institutes of Health (NIH) (2020) National Institutes of Health Research Portfolio Online Reporting Tools (RePORT). Available at https://report.nih.gov/

Pinto, C., Dantas, R., Sena, S., Reis, S., Fiaccone, R., Amorim, L. et al (2016) Accuracy of probabilistic linkage: the Brazilian 100 million cohort. Available at www.atyimolab.ufba.br/BHI2017_Accuracy_vFinal.pdf

Pita, R., Mendonça, E., Reis, S., Barreto, M. and Denaxas, S. (2017) A machine learning trainable model to assess the accuracy of probabilistic record linkage. In L. Bellatreche and S. Chakravarthy, *International Conference on Big Data Analytics and Knowledge Discovery* (pp 214–27). Regensburg, Germany: Springer.

RobecoSAM (2019) SDG Impact Framework. Available at www.robecosam.com/en/insights/2019/robecosam-impact-framework-bridging-impact-investing-to-mainstream-investors.html

Rothman, K.J. and Greenland, S. (1998) *Modern Epidemiology.* Philadelphia, PA: Lippincott-Raven.

SDSN (2015) Sustainable development solutions network: indicators and monitoring framework for the SDGs. Available at https://sustainabledevelopment.un.org/content/documents/2013150612-FINAL-SDSN-Indicator-Report1.pdf

Transfer Project (2020) Beyond internal validity: towards a broader understanding of credibility in development policy research. *World Development* 127: 104802.

UK Administrative Data Taskforce (2012) The UK administrative data research network: improving access for research and policy. Available at https://esrc.ukri.org/files/news-events-and-publications/publications/themed-publications/improving-access-for-research-and-policy/

UNICEF (2014) UNICEF's Office of Research – Innocenti 2014 Results Report. Available at www.unicef-irc.org/publications/774-2014-results-report.html

UNICEF (2016) Uprooted: the growing crisis for refugee and migrant children. Available at www.unicef.org/publications/index_92710.html

UNICEF (2017) UNICEF Innocenti Research Uptake Strategy (unpublished).

UNICEF (2020) Global Longitudinal Research Initiative (GLORI). Available at www.unicef-irc.org/research/longitudinal-and-lifecourse-research-for-children/

UNRISD (2015) 100 key questions for the post-2015 development agenda. Available at www.unrisd.org/80256B3C005BCCF9/(httpAuxPages)/AC45AB8A6F43AFA2C1257E0E006A9993/$file/100%20questions.pdf

Wellcome Trust (2017) Longitudinal population studies strategy. Available at https://wellcome.org/sites/default/files/longitudinal-population-studies-strategy_0.pdf

Index